THE LOST KHRUSHCHEV

A JOURNEY INTO THE GULAG OF THE RUSSIAN MIND

THE LOST KHRUSHCHEV

A JOURNEY INTO THE GULAG OF THE RUSSIAN MIND

NINA L. KHRUSHCHEVA

TATE PUBLISHING
AND ENTERPRISES, LLC

Published by Tate Publishing & Enterprises, LLC
127 E. Trade Center Terrace | Mustang, Oklahoma 73064 USA
1.888.361.9473 | www.tatepublishing.com

Tate Publishing is committed to excellence in the publishing industry. The company reflects the philosophy established by the founders, based on Psalm 68:11,
"The Lord gave the word and great was the company of those who published it."

Book design copyright © 2014 by Tate Publishing, LLC. All rights reserved.
Cover design by Junriel Boquecosa
Interior design by Mary Jean Archival
All photographs used in the book are from the family archive of Yulia Khrushcheva.

Published in the United States of America

ISBN: 978-1-62994-544-6
1. History / Europe / Russia & the Former Soviet Union
2. Political Science / Political Ideologies / Communism, Post-Communism
14.02.24

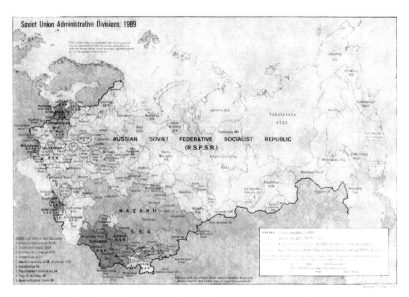

Map of the USSR in 1989. Circled are geographical locations that had witnessed the unfolding drama of *The Lost Khrushchev*: Kaluga, Karaganda, Kiev, Kuibyshev, Kustanai, Mordovia and Moscow.

DEDICATION

To my mother

ACKNOWLEDGMENTS

This book is written with editorial assistance from R. M. "Ross" Schneiderman, who helped to shape, phrase, and refine its final, publishable version. To his steadfast contribution, I owe more than I can say.

My genuine gratitude goes to my mother, Yulia Khrushcheva, to whom this book is dedicated. Also very special thanks are to my New School colleague, Mark Johnson, whose edits have helped tremendously in turning a large and convoluted story of Soviet history and family politics into a clearer, more reader-friendly narrative. A great deal of gratitude goes to Helen Atlas for her assistance in editing the manuscript in its earlier stages and Barbara Paca for her patient listening and thoughtful suggestions. I would like to thank Michael Cohen, director of the New School's Graduate Program International Affairs, where I teach, for being the first to read the original version of *The Lost Khrushchev* (all lengthy four hundred pages of it) and appreciating my story even in its rough draft. I am grateful to Eri Hotta for her kind encouragement during the arduous process of writing and to Philip Akre for holding my hand when I was ready to quit the whole endeavor altogether. I am enormously indebted to my sister, Ksenia Khrushcheva, who shared in part my investigation into family history and to our aunt Rada Adzhubei-Khrushcheva for keeping the family memories alive. I also want to thank Andrzej Rapaczynski for his assistance and support. And last, but not least, I am grateful to the following people (in alphabetical order) who were kind enough to share with me their views of Soviet history, Nazi Germany, Russian politics, and American perceptions: Rebecca Berlow, Gertraud Borea d'Olmo, Ian Buruma, Fiona Hill, Steven Lee Myers, Kenneth Murphy, Susanne Scholl and Miriam Ticktin.

CONTENTS

PRELUDE: ALL IN THE NAME

"This is Nina, Yulia's oldest daughter," my cousin said. It was the spring of 1981—the late Brezhnev era in the Soviet Union—and I was standing in the shadow of two giant pine trees as my cousin Nikita introduced me to an old, balding man with glasses. The man greeted me with silence, holding his gaze.

"Leonid's granddaughter?" he said. "The KGB recently uncovered a *versiya* [account] saying your grandfather was a Nazi traitor."

I cringed. *A Nazi traitor?* At the time, I knew little of Leonid Khrushchev, but what I did know—that Iosif Stalin had honored him with two medals for his bravery in battle—implied heroism, not treachery.

All at once, I realized who this man was: Vyacheslav Molotov, Stalin's all-powerful foreign minister, a man once considered almost as ruthless and terrible as Stalin, the Generalissimus himself. Perhaps because Molotov's name had inspired the infamous cocktail, that makeshift bomb, I had always imagined his voice would be gruff, sinister. Instead, it was surprisingly subdued, though beneath it, I detected something sharp and ominous, like the gleaming point of a dull blade.

"Don't worry," Molotov added. "It's *erunda* (rubbish). Everyone knows Leonid died in a plane crash in 1943."

If it was such erunda, I thought, *why mention it at all?* Growing up in the USSR, I didn't have to read George Orwell to know all about double speak.

As fate would have it, Molotov was living just half a mile away from my grandmother Nina Petrovna Kukharchuk, the widow of his rival and Stalin's successor, former Soviet Premier Nikita Sergeevich Khrushchev. Technically, Nina and Nikita are my great-grandparents. But after the death of their son, Leonid, the Khrushchevs adopted his daughter, Yulia—my mother—and raised her as their own, so I have always thought of them as my real grandparents.[1]

Molotov and my grandmother were neighbors in a retirement community for party apparatchiks in Zhukovka, an upscale housing development located some twenty miles west of Moscow. Grandmother called the neighborhood Widows Village because most of its residents were the wives of the *nomenklatura*, women who had outlived their once prominent husbands. Though a distinguished Soviet retiree, Molotov had lost his job and his grandeur some thirty years prior when Khrushchev booted him out of office following Stalin's death in 1953. A widower himself, Molotov was living out the remainder of his years beside other men's wives.

By Soviet standards, Zhukovka was quaint. A gray fence surrounded the fifty or so homes in the complex. They were built close together, but the pine trees and birches growing around the gray cottages afforded each some degree of privacy. Uniformity, as one might expect, was the rule in the USSR, and every two-story wooden structure featured identical layouts with a kitchen, a living room, three bedrooms, and a picnic table outside—all of it shared by two former Kremlin families. Zhukovka also had its own grocery, a dining hall, and a movie theater. Taken together, the compound resembled a strange Soviet iteration of Westchester or some idyllic American gated community.

My grandmother occupied one of these gray half-homes. Another nearby belonged to Molotov, a man whose decision to sign an armistice with the Nazis in 1939 in effect permitted the Third Reich to take over Europe. Yet by the 1980s, this former Soviet emissary was a sweet, shriveled pensioner with a knack for free-form woodcarvings; his giant bowls and formless stools could be found all over Zhukovka.

Molotov shared his passion for woodcarving with my cousin, Nikita, Grandfather's namesake. The younger Nikita, then a Moscow University student, was an unusual person: his wandering mind had an unlimited capacity for sociability and the uncanny ability to turn our family's political enemies into close friends. I lacked that skill. I wasn't fooled by Molotov's modest, unassuming appearance—the halo of white, thinning hair around his bald head and his old gray flannel suit, made perhaps at the special Kremlin atelier for one of his 1940s diplomatic excursion. I couldn't help but see the former minister as he was—my grandfather's nemesis—and felt uncomfortable, disturbed even, by his presence.

As Molotov's words sunk in, I glanced at my cousin, who no longer seemed to be listening. True to form, Nikita was deeply engrossed in polishing a pine table. This was long before the invention of the cordless phone, so the moment that Molotov returned to his sculpting, I sprinted across the asphalt, my feet splashing through the spring puddles as I made my way to Grandmother's house to call my mother.

I arrived out of breath and dragged the large, black rotary phone from the hallway into a spare bedroom behind the staircase, unsuccessfully trying to tuck the thick cord under the door so I could shut it. I wanted to tell my mother what that horrible man had said, to find out if there was any truth to his allegations. I was so shaken that I kept dialing the wrong number or dropping the receiver. When my mother finally picked up, she quickly dismissed what had happened but without any further explanation.

"Why are you listening to Molotov?" she said. "It's a shame your cousin spends time with him, and you certainly shouldn't."

Then she hung up.

I was afraid to tell my grandmother of the exchange. At that time, I didn't discuss it with my cousin Nikita either, although as I later learnt he took note of the conversation and did provide me with his insight when I was finally ready to listen. But then, in my adolescent liberal idealism, my mother's irritation sealed my impression of Molotov, and I deliberately avoided him when visiting Zhukovka. His words struck me as little more than crude Stalinist slander against my grandfather and his son. But I wasn't sure. I felt like I had to react, to respond in some way.

I was sixteen years old and full of rebellion. All Soviet citizens were required to apply for passports at that age, but for me, this rite of passage was also an opportunity to change my last name from my father's "Petrov" to my mother's "Khrushcheva."

Before I was born, my father, Lev Petrov, had been an international affairs correspondent in Washington, DC, and New York City. Like many Soviets who had permission to live or travel abroad, he was also an unofficial spy and thus required to inform on the inner workings of the American government, the Soviet Union's Cold War enemy. Along with filing regular articles, my father also submitted in-depth, classified reports to security officials in his news organization, APN, a Soviet version of the Associated Press. My father passed away when I was just seven years old, and it was a tremendous loss. But as I thought about what Molotov had said, about what it meant, I realized that I was willing to part with my birth name. My father's memory wasn't at stake, my grandfather's was.[2]

Of course, I always knew that Khrushchev's legacy was a mixed matter, not a straightforward story of democratic good overcoming totalitarian evil. Stalin's loyal lieutenant for more than twenty years, some still considered my grandfather a despot.[3] But for many, he earned his reputation as a reformer due to his secret speech, a four-hour address to the twentieth party congress in 1956. Khrushchev delivered the speech at night to a limited one-hundred-person audience to prevent Kremlin hardliners from staging a pro-Stalin coup. He became the first leader to publicly attack the dictator's legacy of terror and totalitarianism, which—from industrialization, famine, war, detentions and executions—killed nearly thirty million people, and some accounts list it as twice that.[4]

These revelations left many across the country stunned. Some cried, others fainted. Those unable to bear the horrible shock—Alexander Fadeev, chair of the Soviet Writers Union is perhaps the most prominent example—committed suicide. In the USSR, Stalin was God, "the father of the nation," someone to whom many felt closer than their own family members. Khrushchev not only showed the Soviet people that their God didn't exist; he unmasked him as the devil.

After the speech, Soviet authorities released millions of Stalin's victims or posthumously rehabilitated their reputations,[5] even though many groups of political "enemies"—the peasant middle class (the *kulaks*), Nikolai Bukharin, Lev Trotsky, and their supporters—remained unmentionable for decades to come. Khrushchev also ordered to close the gulag, the agency that ran the Kremlin's prison system, although some individual camps continued to function.[6] Taken together, my grandfather's reforms spearheaded the Thaw, an era during which the government relaxed its censors, allowing for greater political, personal, and artistic freedom. By 1961, the process seemed almost irreversible, so much so that eight years after Stalin's death, his body was taken out of Vladimir Lenin's tomb in Moscow's Red Square and reburied a few yards away next to the Kremlin wall, where it remains to this day. As one Soviet writer from the Thaw generation put it, "The premier is the only guarantee against the possible restoration of the Stalin order."[7]

The view of my grandfather in the United States, however, was far different. In the 1960s, American schoolchildren ducked and covered under their desks in case menacing Khrushchev, or Hurricane Nikita as he was called, carried out a nuclear missile attack. Stories of him banging his shoe on the desk at the United Nations in 1960 or sending rockets to Cuba in 1962 were central to the American public's narrative. They also captured the imagination of Hollywood—Don Siegel with his 1956 *Invasion of the Body Snatchers* or Stanley Kubrick in the 1964 film *Dr. Strangelove*, featuring Khrushchev's replica, the erratic Premier Dmitri Kissoff.

And in the USSR, the premier soon became menacing too. As quickly as he had denounced Stalin, acolytes of the fallen communist God denounced my grandfather in turn, voting him out of office. On October 14, 1964, Leonid Brezhnev took over the Soviet Union. As Molotov, my brief childhood acquaintance and a die-hard Stalinist to his last breath, once put it: "With Stalin we followed the directions of a strong hand; when the hand got weaker, each started to sing his own song...Nikita let out a beast that brings horrible harm to our society. It's called democracy, humanitarianism, but it's simply a bourgeois influence."[8] The liberal intellectuals were right: Khrushchev was the "only guarantee" against Stalinism, and with Brezhnev at the helm, the premier's name was immediately deleted from the history books and any official public record.

At the primary school that I attended with other children of elite party members on the communist-chic Kutuzovsky Avenue, my teachers never once mentioned his rule. Anything that happened in the annals of government between Stalin and Brezhnev, they merely described as the work of the communist party. It was as if Khrushchev didn't exist, that he never had. He had become a ghost, spending his retirement years in virtual isolation with the

KGB closely monitoring his visitors and the infrequent trips he took outside his country home west of Moscow.

———⟪∿⟫———

Close to twenty years after Grandfather's ouster, my encounter with Molotov taught me the power a name can hold. A name, after all, is more than mere identification—it shapes identity itself.[9] My amiable cousin, Nikita, struggled all his life to fill the large shoes of our famous grandfather. "Playing a double to Nikita Sergeevich Khrushchev could be quite burdensome," he once admitted. I understood what he meant. Named after my grandmother, the former Soviet first lady, I have never escaped that kind of pressure either; I am always expected to comport myself exactly as she did. But at sixteen, I was idealistic. Formally adopting the Khrushchev name was my way of proclaiming how much my grandfather mattered—even if his history had been erased.

My mother was impressed with my decision, but my aunt Rada, Nina's and Nikita's eldest daughter, vehemently objected. "I am afraid of the extra fuss around our name," she wrote in a letter to my mother. "If Nina takes it, the result will be far from beneficial—in practical terms she will have many difficulties." Yet Mother was unyielding; Khrushchev deserved all the support he could get. "Your choice has inspired my own," she told me. She decided to return to her maiden name, Khrushcheva, although she later admitted that Rada might have been right.

Like most people in the USSR, my mother was a kitchen dissident, someone who opposed the government but didn't do so publicly for obvious reasons—namely the gulag. She worried that my brash, youthful revolt would fail, that the system would eventually swallow me whole, consuming my dreams just as it had hers. In 1969, *Time* magazine got a hold of my grandfather's memoir and the following year announced it would publish excerpts in the West. Khrushchev was so upset by the leak; he suffered a heart attack and died a year later. In the memoir, my grandfather contradicted the party line by expressing his candid, often critical views of Soviet politics, including his own. When the book's abridged version came out in 1970, many—my grandmother Nina included—blamed my father for the leak. My mother knew her husband was innocent: he had helped Khrushchev conceive of the book, but hadn't been involved with it for years. In 1968 he began to suffer from kidney failure; by the time the memoirs were published, he had died and was unable to defend himself. The KGB searched our house for evidence, and although they found nothing, Mother remained terrified for years. She worried that speaking out and defending her late husband would only make things worse. Silence, she thought, was her only recourse. Eventually, the Brezhnev state would forget. Life would go on.

Life did go on, but things changed. The memoir cast a cloud of suspicion on our family. Not long after the excerpts came out, my mother, then a journalist, wrote a short piece about a theater school graduation in Moscow. It was supposed to run in *Pravda* (Truth) under her married name, Petrova. But the paper shelved the article. An editor later confided in her that the KGB feared readers would make a connection between her, my father and the former Soviet premier. She never wrote a word of journalism again.

A decade later, however, taking her maiden name back and giving it to me too became my mother's way of showing that she never completely caved. The youngest in her family—she was only thirteen when Stalin died—she still had a pit of rebellion that despotism couldn't touch. My mother was a voracious reader like the majority of Soviets and often circulated anti-Stalinist literature among her friends, the Moscow intellectuals. For decades, she hid these volumes in a drawer under her collection of colorful silk scarves. She even encouraged Grandfather to read underground books such as Eugenia Ginzburg's *Journey Into the Whirlwind* (1967) and Alexander Solzhenitsyn's *First Circle* (1968), which she received in secret from the dissident historian Roy Medvedev.

For almost twenty years, Medvedev, the author of the monumental exposé of Stalinism *Let History Judge* (1972), delivered those self or foreign-published tomes—*samizdat*—to our home, and his frequent visits always reminded me of something out of a Cold War spy thriller. A middle-aged tall man with gray hair and a distinguished professorial look, Medvedev wandered endlessly around Moscow in order to lose his tail and never turned up on the same day or at the same time so he could avoid any extra attention from boys from Lubyanka, the infamous KGB headquarters just a few blocks from the Kremlin.

Upon arrival, Medvedev would always settle in the armchair that sat in my father's former study, which became my bedroom after his death. It was left just the way Father had it: walls covered with books, a dark-blue divan, and a glass bar in which I kept my childhood mementos, diaries, scrapbooks, and an occasional box of chewing gum—the most coveted capitalist luxury. During Medvedev's visits, my mother would sit on the blue divan, and I would sit at a desk. Sipping strong black tea with honey, the historian would stay for hours discussing the future of Russia, the dissident movement, human rights, and Stalinism. These conversations were fascinating—even the uncomfortable wooden chair couldn't break my attention. At times, I wanted to ask him about Molotov, about the KGB *versiya* and Leonid's fate, but my mother's presence stood in the way of my curiosity. I didn't want to upset her or alter the dynamic of these meetings; they were about serious Soviet politics, not some minor family story, as I then understood it.

For my mother, these sessions with Medvedev represented a form of protest but never a drastic change. Instead, she saw her efforts as a way of reforming the system. I always admired her bravery, yet for me, talking to Medvedev was something else entirely: a formative education, which sparked my growing conviction that the Soviet system was fundamentally rotten. Steeped on its horrors, I never believed in the USSR. I never experienced the hope and enthusiasm of Grandfather's reforms, and unlike my mother, I wasn't afraid to openly mock our country, which is perhaps why I remained determined to keep the Khrushchev name alive.

In fact, it was only after 1985, when Mikhail Gorbachev came to power, that I considered dropping my adopted surname and going back to my birth one. At the time, Moscow was abuzz with speculation. Unlike his predecessors, Gorbachev was young, only fifty-four, the Thaw generation age, and with a law degree from Moscow University. Yet the new communist party secretary's allegiances weren't immediately clear.

During one of his secret trips to our home, Medvedev insisted that with the KGB watching his every move, Gorbachev simply couldn't rule as a liberal right away. "Like Nikita Sergeevich," Medvedev explained. "With such powerful figures as Molotov or secret police chief Lavrenty Beria at the Stalin side, Khrushchev was the most improbable Kremlin successor and certainly was the least likely to denounce Stalin. Gorbachev is just that type." Yet Mother thought it was too good to be true; after twenty years, the thought that Khrushchev might take his proper place in the history books seemed an unattainable dream.

I was optimistic. The night after Medvedev left, I had that dream. I saw the whole family gathered in our dining room around an antique mahogany table. In my dream, my grandmother Nina, who had passed away a year earlier, sat on our recently restored pre-Bolshevik walnut wood sofa, holding Grandfather's head in her lap, the rest of his body lay stretched out beside her. I remember wondering why his corpse was lying on our "aristocratic couch," as he would have disdainfully called it. Then he sat up abruptly, looked around, and sneezed. That sneeze woke me up.

Our live-in nanny, Maria "Masha" Vertikova, like most women from the Russian provinces, was an expert in deciphering dreams, an indispensable skill in a country that is often cruel and irrational. When I told Masha about my dream, her response was encouraging: "Sneezing is a good sign. Nikita Sergeevich is back." In a despotic society, everyone is always looking for glimmers of hope so that very morning my typically rational mother began excitedly calling around Moscow, announcing that the system was about to change for the better.

A few months later, the unimaginable happened. In a September 1985 interview with *Time* magazine, Gorbachev broke the twenty-one-year silence surrounding my grandfather's name: "I recall still further back in 1961 the meeting between Khrushchev and President Kennedy in Vienna," he said. "There was the Caribbean Crisis [Cuban Missile Crisis], yet in 1963 we saw the partial test-ban treaty. Even though that was again a time of crisis, the two sides and their leaders had enough wisdom and the boldness to take some very important decisions."[10]

Gorbachev's reference to the "wisdom" of my grandfather caused many to reconsider his legacy and see it in a more positive light. And though two major Soviet papers, *Pravda* and *Izvestiya* (Information), first reprinted this interview with Khrushchev's name cut out of the text because of KGB pressure, Gorbachev's outlook proved influential—he clearly considered himself the former premier's disciple.[11]

Gorbachev's policies of *glasnost* (open speech) and *perestroika* (restructuring) marked the first honest debate about government performance and economic reform—all of it unscripted and broadcast on television. Suddenly, my grandfather no longer needed defending. His place in our nation's history had been restored, and continuing as Nina Khrushcheva became more of a luxury than a necessity. But at that time, I was too busy thinking about what to do with my newly acquired freedoms than which surname I should sign under my travel documents—it became suddenly possible when the government permitted international travel. With ideas of seeing the larger world, I left the Soviet Union and moved to the United States in August of 1991 to get my PhD in literature from Princeton University, even while my conversation with Molotov still haunted me a little.

It was from America that I watched the hardliners try and fail to take power away from Gorbachev, that I watched the people pour into the streets, as Boris Yeltsin, then president of the Russian Republic, led the way, that I watched the Soviet Union fall and Russians welcome a free market economy, that I watched the dream that Yeltsin-inspired curdle to anarchy as this former Soviet apparatchik came to see himself as an infallible czar. And it was from the United States that I watched the rise of the oligarchs, well-connected individuals who received sweetheart deals on the country's newly privatized natural resources, while my family and others saw their life-savings disappear.

On New Year's Eve, 1999, I found myself back in Moscow with my mother on the same day that Yeltsin—by then feeble and universally despised—resigned. It was a cold and snowy winter day when I walked into our Moscow apartment.[12] My mother was tuning into Vladimir Putin's speech on television as the new president vowed to battle the Kremlin oligarchy, praised the supremacy of the law, and promised not to stay in office a day past his two constitutionally allowed four-year terms.

"Doesn't he sound really smart and decent?" my mother said.

"He used to be a KGB colonel," I replied. "Once an agent always an agent."

"No, he is from St. Petersburg, our window into Europe. He is young, only forty-eight, and anybody is better than Yeltsin." Mother was channeling the traditional Russian belief that the next czar will always be better than the previous one.

I shook my head.

"Yeltsin was corrupt, horribly, I am sure.[13] He was drunk and shameful most of his presidency, but there were free elections, free speech. You'll see: Putin will be another Brezhnev, if not Stalin, his absolute power will corrupt absolutely." I didn't say it at the time, but I also had a hunch that Putin's years in power would not be good for our family, for Grandfather's legacy.

My predictions were quickly confirmed. The incoming president's promise to restore Russian self-respect after the anarchy of the Yeltsin era seemed to be an alarming reminder of our despotic past—from his top to bottom approach to governance, to his control of the media and the electoral process. What's more, having lived through an impossible transition, two-thirds of the country at the time believed that the postcommunist reforms had done Russia more harm than good.[14] Having been taught that the state's interests are greater than the people's, half of the public was yearning for a return to Stalinesque tough leadership and mourned their lost "status of a great respected world power."[15] It was as if they were saying, "Yes, we were killed and imprisoned by the millions, but how grandiose were our victories and military parades!" They voluntarily surrendered to Putin's guarantee of "stability and order," which, even then, I perceived as a new type of gulag—a place with no barbed wire or guards carrying Kalashnikovs but the gulag of the Russian mind, an invisible prison within us all.

Worried about our democratic future, I began writing a syndicated column pointing to various similarities between Putin's style of leadership and that of Brezhnev and Stalin. One of my articles appeared in the Moscow liberal daily *Kommersant's* section titled, "No Comment."

I was flattered by the recognition, but my mother was not. She called from Moscow to complain: "Horrible translation," she said. "And it's on the last page. Now when there is the increasing public praise for Stalinist rule everyone hates Khrushchev."

"The paper is not to blame," I replied. "You are too sensitive. Translators are always in a rush. 'No Comment' happens to be on the last page. And I don't even mention Khrushchev."

"Of course, he is mentioned," Mother exclaimed. "His name is on it!"

She meant my byline. But after twenty years, it wasn't just his name; it was mine as well. Before I started this book, I rarely wrote about Grandfather. Yet most of the readers treated my writing as if Khrushchev was speaking from the grave anyway, and this time, they saw my criticism of Stalin as some sort of secret speech *déjà-vu*.

But the public's pro-Stalin reaction to my articles paled in comparison to what was in store for the Khrushchev legacy. In 2000, former Soviet Defense Minister Marshal Dmitry Yazov— one of the leaders of the 1991 hardliner coup—released a best-selling memoir called *Blows of Fate*. The minister, whose reputation had been fully refurbished under Putin, conveyed "an unattractive story of the 20th Party Congress main speaker's son."[16] "It is well known," Yazov wrote, "[that] Leonid Khrushchev actively worked with the fascists."

As the Putin era progressed, Leonid became the Benedict Arnold of contemporary Russia when a number of stories about his alleged treason emerged in films, publications, and news reports. Some claimed that Stalin had learned of Leonid's betrayal and ordered his execution and that Khrushchev had allegedly begged on his knees for his son's life but to no avail. Most went even further, suggesting that my grandfather only denounced his dictatorial predecessor's "pernicious cult of personality and its consequences" because Stalin had killed Leonid, and by extension, there was nothing virtuous in Nikita's effort—however imperfect—to steer Soviet society toward greater openness and less repression. As a nation, we had come full circle, reverting back to the Stalinist state of mind. As the accusations continued, I realized that I could no longer write only about Putin's politics and pretend my name has no bearing on my views. The public thought otherwise, and I was finally ready to openly say it: Khrushchev's legacy matters, as does honoring the memory of his son. Without someone to defend them, they would become distorted, tarnished, ripped from the roots of reality in the Putin state, which was steering our country back toward autocracy.

Three decades have past since I met Molotov in 1981. Today, I regret that I didn't talk to him more when I had that chance. In writing this book, I have set out to answer the questions that our conversation raised: What did *exactly* happen to Leonid "Leonya," the lost Khrushchev, only twenty-five at the time of his death? Is it possible that he really was a Nazi traitor? Or was he—as I always thought—a hero, a pilot who, like millions of others, perished during the war?

Over the past decade, I have learned much truth about Leonid's fate. I have discovered that there was an overwhelming extent of uneasiness that characterized the young man's relationship with other family members, that the older Khrushchev was almost always disappointed in his son. A rebel *within* the communist cause, Leonid took pride in constantly defying his politically important father, and through that defiance, poked a finger at all figures of Soviet authority. And it was this spirit of rebellion that led many to wonder: had he betrayed not only his father, but also his country?

Though primarily a family portrait, *The Lost Khrushchev* also speaks to my grandfather's legacy—the consequences of his position in the Stalin entourage in the 1940s as well as of his decision to denounce his former boss while ruling the USSR from 1953 to 1964. Along the way, I delved into letters, diaries, notes, and photographs from our family's archive. I also draw on almost thirty years of conversations with relatives, friends, as well as Khrushchev's political opponents and intellectual supporters.

In many ways, this story is more my mother's than my own. It was she, after all, who had to live without Leonid, her biological father. And it was she who was raised by the Khrushchevs during and after the war. Given my mother's intimacy with Nikita and Nina, at times I've been disappointed, even angry, that she has chosen not to tell our family's story. I realize now that, merely because of circumstance, my mother felt she could not do it. She had become too jaded with Russia's pendulum swings—dictatorship to democracy and back again. Like most Russians she wondered, *What could it change, anyway? There's nothing I can do.*

Her feelings of powerlessness are as much the products of our Soviet past as they are of our Russian present. In the mid-2000s, as Putin's power grew, Mother tried to fight the system through law: she filed a number of grievances against several individuals who made allegations about Leonid's treason and Nikita's revenge in books and films. But the Russian courts disregarded every motion she made—all twenty-five of them—ruling that writers and broadcasters have a right to air accounts of historical figures. Having given up on justice in Russia, my mother now has taken her complaints to the European Court of Human Rights in Strasbourg, where her case *Khrushcheva v. Russia* is still waiting to be heard. She has been so discouraged by the process that I simply *had to* step in to write about our family's saga of Stalinism and slander.

But in more consequential ways, this is not my mother's story at all; rather, it is part of the larger narrative of our country, of modern Russia, of a people still too easily swayed by the siren's song of strongmen, whether it be Stalin or Putin, his ideological successor. As former German Foreign Minister Joschka Fischer once explained to me casually: "I am a child of the Cold War. Never could I have imagined to live through the Berlin Wall's collapse in 1989. It has been more than twenty years, and it still feels unreal."

What has been equally unreal, and infinitely more disheartening, is how Russia has regressed, how it has begun discarding any and all links to democracy, a free press, human rights and modernity in favor of its Stalinist past: authoritarianism and isolation, repression and propaganda. And so *The Lost Khrushchev* is also an attempt to understand my country, a nation where the gulag is as much a state of mind as it is a physical reality.

THE SOVIET SUPERMAN AND HIS MAID

I n the summer of 1943, my mother, Yulia Khrushcheva, then a pudgy toddler in tiny slippers, remembers being surrounded by too many people. They towered over her, forcing her to crane her neck upward and stare. She didn't really understand who these people were; all she knew is that they were part of something called a family, and within that family, two people stood out, two people whom she knew were more important than the others: Grandma and Grandpa.

My mother didn't like the commotion in Grandma and Grandpa's house. She wanted to be back in her own home, with its familiar sights and sounds: the loud kettle in the morning and the sunshine streaming through the curtains in her private bedroom. Her aunts and uncle—soon to become her sisters and brother—later told her she had longing in her eyes, the longing of a child who seemed to be dreaming of sitting on her father's lap or draping her arms around her mother.

The previous year, her father had disappeared. She and her mother left their apartment in Moscow and went far away to live with the rest of the family,[17] but then her mother suddenly vanished too. All little Yulia knew was that there was something called a war and that her mama and papa had left because of it.

She was taken care of well in her new home. Her grandmother Nina gave her milk every morning, put her to bed at night, and insisted on tying her blonde hair into pigtails. But the girl protested too much, and Grandma shaved her head as a result; Grandma was very strict. She didn't smell like flowers as Mama did but instead carried the clean, matronly aroma of fresh linens. It seemed impossible to get Grandma's full attention. She was constantly busy with others, her own children—serious Rada, silent Lena, and disagreeable Sergei, who was always sick.[18] My mother envied them all.

Every night, she tossed and turned in her small bed, her miniature arms crossed, her eyes opened wide, stubbornly trying to fight back sleep in the room she shared with Lena. She hoped her parents would come home soon. What if they came at night? She didn't want to miss them. Despite her best efforts, her eyelids would eventually grow heavy and close. Sleep would come. In the morning, she would wake to the sound of the front door opening. She would grow excited, expect to see her mother, her father. Instead, it was usually Sergei's nurse.

One day, however, she learned that Grandpa was coming home from the war. War—that word was on everyone's lips, echoing off the white walls of their tidy apartment. All day long, little Yulia would wander around her new home, tottering over the wooden floors and through the endless tall corridors. She didn't remember her Grandpa too well, but he seemed important. If anyone could bring back her parents, it was he. She wanted to get to him first, before the others would overwhelm him, vie for his attention, just as they did with Grandma. Every day she would wait by the window, fidgeting with her mottled summer dress, watching the sky grow dark.

One night, a black car pulled up to their home, a car she thought must be Grandpa's. She staked out a place next to the coat hanger on the wall by the front door where he'd have to pass by her. But all the other children were waiting for him too. They had heard the car stopping in the courtyard and had come running from their rooms. With all this excitement, my mother was pushed aside, losing her place near the entrance as the other children crowded around the heavy door. Outmaneuvered, she backed up and stood next to her room.

Grandpa entered, dressed in his military uniform, donning the same shiny, black leather boots that her Papa wore in the photo she kept next to her bed. He was not as handsome as Papa, she felt. Too old and bald. Her papa was taller; he smiled wider.

Grandpa hugged Grandma and the other kids, but his little granddaughter stubbornly refused to participate in the family greeting. But then she heard Grandpa's voice from down the hallway rising over the excited chatter: "And you, what are you standing there for? Come here." It took her a second to realize he was talking to her. She stumbled toward her grandpa and hugged his leg. He picked her up, and her throat tightened. In that instant, my mother knew her parents were gone, that they were not coming back. She held back her tears—Grandma didn't approve of crying—and buried her face in Grandpa's shoulder, smelling the leather that reminded her so much of her father. Would she ever see him again?

—⊸⊸⊸—

My mother (who from that pudgy three-year-old grew into a tall good-looking blonde) first told me this story not long after I had started investigating what happened to her biological father, Leonid, whose plane was shot down in 1943 during World War II, or the Great Patriotic War, as the fight with fascism is known in Russia. What had happened to her biological mother, Lyubov Sizykh, Leonid's thought-to-be wife, seemed to be no mystery at the time; in that same year, the NKVD [People's Commissariat of Internal Affairs, precursor to the KGB] arrested Lyubov on the then-common charge of "contact with foreigners" and sent her to a gulag labor camp in Mordovia. My mother was too young to remember everything about the day she realized her parents weren't coming home. What she couldn't recall, I managed to learn from Aunt Rada. I spoke to each of them by phone from my apartment in New York and also during my visits to Moscow over the course of several years.

As I delved into my family's history, it quickly became clear that to learn the truth about Leonid, I would have to merge the gaps between my private memories of my grandparents and their very public, Soviet lives. As I began interviewing other family members and friends, I also began reading, devouring the history of my country as I once devoured the dissident poetry that my mother hid in her drawers.

Of course, the official image of the Soviet premier—a powerful man who, depending on your worldview, was either set to put an end to Russian despotism or irredeemably damage the power of the Stalinist Soviet Union—is not how I remember my grandfather. By the time I was born in the mid-1960s, he had been banished to Petrovo Dalnee, a secluded ten-acre, government-issued property located about an hour drive from the Kremlin. By Russian standards, Khrushchev's ousting wasn't tragic—de-Stalinization had paid off. The czars and their Soviet heirs usually saw their rule come to an end in one of three ways: murder, imprisonment, or natural death. But Grandfather was the first leader to actually retire from power, something he proudly announced to his Kremlin rivals on his last day on the job: "My greatest achievement is that today I am dismissed by mere voting."

Yet the downside of staying alive and (relatively) free was that Khrushchev was able to contemplate his legacy and the lapses in his rule. Living in comfort, with a generous state pension and excellent healthcare, he was nothing more but a political corpse. His downfall, though not fatal, harmed our whole family:

my mother could no longer see her writing published even under her husband's name. Rada's husband, Aleksei Adzhubei, Khrushchev's son-in-law, the editor of the leading Soviet daily *Izvestiya* was demoted and forced to write photo captions. And there was, of course, Leonid. By then dead for more than twenty years, he would suffer the most from Grandfather's ouster.

To dim the thoughts of failure, Khrushchev, a reformer even in retirement, didn't let himself stay idle for a minute. He immediately transformed the Petrovo Dalnee estate into a country farm, replete with tomato gardens, beehives, and pumpkin patches. Mother remembers how Grandfather, now with considerable time on his hands, was eager to develop a new tomato-growing technique. In 1968, he did grow the best tomatoes anyone had seen in the area. They were huge—"The size of a giant's fist," he bragged—and their skin was a deep shade of red. Every morning, he would run outside to admire his work. The fruit was so beautiful that for days he couldn't bring himself to harvest the crop. That year there was an early September frost. One morning the former premier awoke to find his prized tomatoes black and ruined on the vine. My mother says he was devastated, even more devastated than he appeared on the day he was forced to step down.

"This is a bad year all around—in weather as in politics," he told his children, referring to Soviet tanks rolling into Czechoslovakia a month before. The Prague Spring, an anti-communist rebellion, was no longer in bloom; Brezhnev had squashed it just as Khrushchev had squashed a revolution in Hungary more than a decade prior. Now a pensioner, Khrushchev came to regret that decision. "In twelve years, we still haven't learnt of a better way," he said as he trampled over the damaged tomato patch on his way home. At the time, I couldn't fully comprehend the connection between tomatoes and tanks, but on some level, I was already aware that what happened in our private lives was somehow inseparable from politics.

In the short run though, the challenges of farming were far easier to overcome than his political regrets, and so Khrushchev was fond of his *dacha*.[19] State mandated or not, it was a special place for him—and others—a way to escape the government's all-seeing eye. The three-bedroom house—large by the standards of the Soviet Union in the 1960s—was located in a woody area with a tall fence running around it. Normally, having a fence was an indication of privilege. In Grandfather's case, it was also an indication of exile.

For years, Petrovo Dalnee was my family's weekly Sunday destination. During our visits, there was an unspoken rule that we had to temper Grandfather's solitude, to provide him with support. That pressure is what I recall most about the *dacha*, along with the sense of tragedy that hung around Grandpa Nikita like a dark cloud.

I also remember how even a simple stroll could turn into a state affair. Once in the late summer of 1970, my cousin Nikita and I walked around Petrovo Dalnee with Grandfather, who was adamant that we should cross its bounds to check on a large field of wheat. "It is high time for it to get harvested. It's so pregnant," he said as we tried to find a *kolkhoz* (farming cooperative) worker and ask him why this wheat was still untouched. When we finally found one, the farmer—who was jaded by years of Soviet collectivism—laughed at Khrushchev's demand that he care for the *narodny khleb* (people's bread). "You are not the boss of us any more," he said. "Go to hell with your instructions!"

Soon the guards from Petrovo Dalnee were rushing toward us, eager to take their "prisoner" and his grandkids back to their assigned territory. With the KGB a few steps behind us, we walked back in complete silence. Grandfather kept taking off his new hat, a fancy gift (hats were his favorite presents), and wiping sweat from his brow. It was a chilly day in August, and I wondered why he seemed so feverish. Looking back on it now, he must have been humiliated. He had spent decades serving the

USSR and must have felt the affront acutely, perhaps even more than his removal from power. And yet his dedication to the Soviet Union was unshaken. When we arrived for dinner, all he talked about was calling the chairman of this *kolkhoz* in the morning to remind him that this wheat was not his private property.

I never learnt if he had ever made the call. But today, I still feel uneasy when surrounded by trees and greenery. I'm reminded of these sad emotions, and I panic. I even dislike melons—they were often stacked high on the porch next to the front door—with their sweet, pungent scent, which I will forever associate with a sense of doom and decay.

Yet Grandfather never entirely succumbed to misery. At times, there was a delightful impetuousness about him, a wonderful sense of spontaneity. Even if the adults were determined to keep children behaving like perfect little Soviets at his *dacha*, Grandfather would always allow us to have kid time.

I think back to one time when I was hiding in the Petrovo Dalnee library with my younger sister Ksenia, trying to avoid gardening chores. Even as small children, we were, in Grandfather's words, "to be educated by labor" and had to regularly gather strawberries or tomatoes. But it was dirty and tedious work and not how I wanted to spend my weekend. At five or six years old, the library—with its solid, imposing desk and wall-to-wall barrister-style shelves—felt grand to me, almost holy. The shelves were filled with books of all colors and sizes, along with Kremlin-era memorabilia—small personal gifts from heads of states and organizations my grandfather used to deal with. Nearby was a brocade marigold couch, and you could almost feel the springs underneath. Always a troublemaker, I encouraged Ksenia to test their bounciness. We were jumping up and down, screaming with delight, when my mother walked in and gasped in horror. How dare we act so irresponsibly in this house!

Mother's scolding was so loud that Grandfather, attracted by the noise, walked into the room, a stout man wearing his customary white shirt and baggy gray pants. He had a distinct walk, quick and smooth with a wide gait that made him appear to sweep across the floor. He stood in the doorway and surveyed the scene, my sister and I gazing at him sheepishly as Mother's face curled with contempt. Grandfather burst into hearty laughter and said to my mother: "Please, they are children, of course they want to test the springs. I want to test the springs too, but they'll collapse if I jump. So they are doing this for me." We giggled, triumphant.

Grandfather's joyful sense of levity wasn't restricted to this one incident. Another time, I remember how we all gathered for a lunch at the long table in the expansive dining room, a formal open space with government-issued, dark wood panels. The lunch, like many others, bored me to tears. The children were expected to be silent throughout the *very* adult ordeal, but to pass the time, I slurped my noodle soup. My mother saw—and heard—what I was doing, and her face turned white. Once again, I was embarrassing her. A Khrushchev, her face seemed to be saying, should have better manners. She ordered me to stop, but I was feeling snotty and shot back that I would only stop if I were able to leave the table. My mother insisted I finish my soup. And suddenly we were in the middle of a public standoff.

Everyone stopped talking and turned toward us. I kept eating my soup, the sound of my defiant slurping echoing off the walls. I wanted to stop, but somehow I couldn't—all eyes were on me. Finally, Grandfather punctured our silence: "Well, Nina, you think you are good at this, but I can slurp louder. Let's make a bet. If I slurp louder, you'll stop. If you are the loudest, we will all cheer, and you can continue." I agreed. He bent over his soup and expertly sucked a noodle from his spoon, making an incomparably loud sound. I had lost graciously, and everyone broke into laughter. And that's what I loved about my grandpa— he was not embarrassed to act silly in front of guests; he was willing to embrace irreverence to help his grandchildren out of awkward situations. This sympathy was indicative of his nature, and as I later learned, explained a lot about his politics, his absolute devotion to the communist cause but also his human approach to people, which wasn't the usual Soviet, top-down directive that everyone was expected to follow blindly. But as I have also discovered, this kind of understanding and tolerance was *never* extended to his oldest son.

At the time, however, I knew nothing of Leonid and simply remember how later that day, Grandmother took me to the orangery, which was filled with strawberries, flowers, and honeydew, all thriving year-round in the warm, moist air. Steps away from the main house, this hothouse was Grandfather's pride—he built it himself out of plastic sheeting and wood planks—but I hated going in there because it was difficult to breathe. Grandmother insisted that she needed my help with the summer squash. In truth, she wanted to express her concerns in private. She told me if I continued to act up, my mother would no longer bring me to the *dacha*.

"I don't mind staying home," I replied with relief, hoping to finally escape the pressure of perfection. But Grandmother was ready with a rebuttal.

"Grandpa will be disappointed if he doesn't see you next Sunday. And so will I," she said, her sense of calm pacifying me, wearing me down.

This was classic Nina: composed, strict and fair, invariably insisting on people's best. Even her husband's political downfall had not shattered her Bolshevik convictions. We were all expected to uphold a set of faultless standards. "It always matters what we do," she would often tell us. My mother says that must have been her way of warding off the chaos, which she feared would ensue if everyone were as impetuous as my grandfather, who, despite his career as a Soviet apparatchik, never subscribed to its dour style. Not only did Grandmother firmly believe in Karl Marx's scientific teachings of dialectic materialism—that the material, that is physical, world is reflected by the human mind—she applied it to everyday life.

For years, I thought that these early memories were nothing more than just part of my childhood. I viewed my grandmother as serious and my grandfather as whimsical, but most of all, I saw them as loving and caring. And though my mother often told me they were strict, it wasn't until I began digging into their past that I really considered that they might have treated their own children differently, that decades of political change—from Bolshevism to Brezhnev—had changed them too and made them both less demanding of perfection. The Khrushchev I knew was humbled by his downfall and on the other side of his career. "I am now a pensioner," he often repeated with a mixture of surrender and disbelief. But as I learned more of my grandparents' lives— where they were raised and how they met—I realized the extent to which the rigid revolutionary spirit of the nascent Soviet era defined the rearing of their oldest son, Leonid.

Originally from a peasant family in the village of Kalinovka located in the Kursk region along Russia's border with Ukraine, my grandfather herded sheep as a child. His father, Sergei Khrushchev, a czarist army soldier, was always good with his hands. Hoping to escape poverty and wanting to put his dexterity to use, Sergei left his Russian village for the Ukrainian mines in 1908. Nikita, then age fourteen, was also handy and joined him in an attempt to rise above his lowly status as a local shepherd. The two settled in Yuzovka of the Donbas region and immediately began to learn their new trades. As a young man, Nikita spent much of his free time outside the factory as a makeshift mechanic. He once found broken parts in a scrap yard and built a primitive but working *velocipede* (motor bike) entirely on his own, then rode around on it proudly through the streets of Yuzovka, its loud roars drawing attention wherever he went.

Working at the factory allowed the twenty-year-old Nikita to escape conscription by the Russian army during World War I. He was therefore free to court his first wife, Efrosinia Pisareva, whom he met one evening at a youth social. Two years Nikita's junior, Frosya—as her friends called her—was a striking redhead with gentle features, pale skin, and a slender, hourglass figure. Her family was well educated, and Efrosinia and her four younger sisters, whom she helped raise, all attended a local gymnasium, a finishing institution for young ladies. Nikita, a respectable worker with fair wages, was a good catch and the couple married quickly in 1914. A year later, Frosya gave birth to their first child, my grandaunt (henceforth aunt) Yulia, and, in 1917, to Leonid.

During high school, I stumbled across family photos from this period, which my mother—who found the past painful—kept in haphazard piles in empty shoeboxes beneath her bed. The pictures, circa 1916, show a dashing couple, posing for the camera in their best Sunday outfits: a lace white blouse on Efrosinia and a dark jacket and bow tie on Nikita, who was thin and fit but shorter than his wife and already balding. I loved these photos, loved being able to look back on my grandfather's life, if only through captured moments. I was taken by the appearance of the pre-Bolshevik Khrushchevs—middle class, almost bourgeois, a far cry from disheveled workers or miserable czar-era serfs usually depicted in every Soviet textbook I'd ever seen.

But as the communist movement gained strength, my grandfather, the son of a peasant turned coal miner, had "nothing to lose but [his] chains," just in line with Karl Marx's *Communist Manifesto*. Khrushchev became active in the proletarian struggle shortly before the 1917 Revolution. In 1918, during the fights between Reds and Whites for control of Ukraine, he formally joined the Russian Bolsheviks.[20] By 1919, at the age of twenty-five, he was quickly ascending the ranks of the Red Army, rising from a simple soldier to the position of junior political commissar. At the end of the Russian Civil War in 1921, he returned home to Yuzovka, only to learn that his wife and the mother of his children—the beautiful Frosya—had died of typhus during a famine, a common fate in rural Russia during the postrevolutionary upheaval. Her death was particularly devastating for Grandfather; the revolution was supposed to be a force of pure good—something that would improve humanity and enrich each person's life.

Despite the tragic loss, the young Bolshevik carried on, trying to make it to the top of the communist pantheon. His lack of education—he had received just a few years of Bible study in his village—was an advantage in the Soviet state. After all the Russian monarchy abolished its centuries-long practice of backward serfdom only in 1861, barely fifty years before the country embraced communism. By the early twentieth century, it was populated by a rural peasant majority and a small minority of aristocrats; therefore the democratizing influence of the new order, the "dictatorship of the proletariat" (admittedly brutal and bloody, with an estimated nine million deaths from the war, famine, and disease—not counting the two million people who had emigrated)[21] provided a host of opportunities for those at the bottom.

For some at least, the tectonic shift of communism was just as the revolutionary anthem, "The Internationale," promised: "We are nothing, let us be all. Will be the human race." This new race that officially declared itself a "state of workers and peasants" (peasant as a rural social class of state farmers) initially gave an equal chance to everybody. People were expected to get the education necessary to assure, as Trotsky put it, "an *earthly paradise* [that] was the raison d'être of the Communist movement."[22] And Khrushchev was ready to follow Trotsky's call "to extend the wires of [a Soviet man's] will into hidden recesses, and thereby to raise himself to a new plane, to create a higher social biologic type...a superman."[23]

Literacy became one of the main ways the new Kremlin leaders hoped to enlighten an uneducated nation. Creating a socially conscious industrial collective of self-realized proletarians—Soviet Supermen—would lead to the greater glorification of communist ideals. Or so the thinking went.

For my grandfather, that line of thinking worked. He couldn't wait to engage in self-realization through learning. More than just a communist soldier, he was also responding to Lenin's revolutionary call "to teach every *kukharka* (maid, cook) how to rule the state."[24] And as that determined "maid," he attended a new Soviet workers' school in Yuzovka in 1921, where aspiring proletarians studied math, literature, science, and ideology. He soon became a student political leader and was appointed school secretary of the communist party committee. As a prominent student body figure, he quickly attracted the attention of his political history teacher Nina Kukharchuk, who was as enamored with her new man as she was with Bolshevism. And very soon she became more than his teacher.

—⁓⁓—

I first learned these details of my grandparents' lives in the summer of 1981, shortly after I had changed my last name. At the time, I was preparing for my entrance exams to attend Moscow University, but I wasn't doing much studying. I was proud of my independence and wanted to spend more time with boys and friends. Truth be told, I was madly in love and ready to get married.

At a loss of what to do with me—her rebellious, willful child—my mother reached out to her own mother for help, and the two decided I should spend a few months in Zhukovka. After all, Grandmother used to be a professional educator in a strict Soviet mold, and my mother still remembered her own uneasy years in high school. "Once," she told me, "my whole class skipped chemistry, but only I got caught. The teacher called Nina to tell her what had happened, and I got an earful. 'As a Khrushchev you should set an example, not join the delinquents,' Nina said.

From there on out, she had weekly conferences with teachers who updated her on *everything*."

Mother later admitted that, given the history, sending me to Grandmother's was a tough decision. Our own upbringing was more normal than hers had been. With my father dead and my mother busy with work—she was the literary director at the Vakhtangov Theater in Moscow—it was left to our nanny, Masha, to discipline my little sister and I. All well-to-do households had hired help in the USSR, and in our case, Masha was a full-fledged family member. There could be no more caring, firm, and reliable a person. Masha, from a poor farming village in the Orel region, southwest of Moscow, was deeply superstitious, believing that a full moon could cure a sty or that traveling on Monday was bad luck. Even if our nanny's humanizing presence was crucial for our otherwise overly intellectual upbringing, her standards of excellence were not nearly as absolute as my grandmother's. My mother felt that this time I needed more cerebral tutelage; although she was mindful that I might consider a rigid timetable an imposition on my freedom and see the Widows Village as my own personal gulag.

Grandmother worried about me even more. According to Masha, she told my mother that she thought I might end up like Leonid. Masha didn't know what that meant—except that if I had born a boy, I would have been named after him. I didn't know what that meant either and trained not to ask any unnecessary questions about our family's history, I simply surrendered, held captive by a sinking feeling that autumn would never come.

Despite my initial rebellion, it turned out to be one of the best summers of my life. I proudly figured out how to circumvent Grandmother's rules. Around midnight, I would often make a sleeping dummy in my bed and climb out of the window and take a thirty-minute train ride to Moscow to see my soon-to-be (and now ex) husband, Dmitry Margolis. Dmitry was an eighteen-year-old college student, a good-looking soccer player with a dark mustache—"like a young Alain Delon,"[25] my girlfriends used to say with envy. I was still in high school, obviously flattered by his attention and eager to keep his interest. When he came to Zhukovka, I would drop everything to see him. My excuse to Grandmother: that I needed to study Russian history alone under the pine trees on the other side of the village or that I urgently had to pick up a jar of milk from the food store five minutes away—a simple task which often took me at least two hours.

Later Grandmother told me my sneaking around didn't escape her, but she never breathed a word to Mother. She could have caught me many times but chose to pretend that everything was normal, trusting me to figure out love and life for myself. Recently, when my mother and I finally got to discuss our family's history, she said that Nina seemed like a different person with me. "I would never—and more so Leonid, no doubt   have been able to get away with the disobedience that you were allowed," she marveled. It's surely true what they say—tough with their own children, parents turn into mush with grandkids.

In my case, her leniency also reflected a unique trajectory—our family had maintained a high social status, but we had become political outcasts. Grandmother must have felt she had to balance her drive for perfection with the demands of regular life, in which personal interactions were more important than communist purity. Still, she kept me on a very firm schedule: breakfast, then world literature, followed by lunch, modern history, and English. Because of her determination to keep me on track, I was easily accepted into the Moscow University literature program.

Most afternoons, after I took a break from my studies and my grandmother finished reading a variety of Soviet literary journals, we would sit down for tea and conversation in her small living room, which was decorated with a wooden dining table, a console radio, an old record player, a television, a couch, and a few simple chairs. These items were the center of her secluded existence. Piles of newspapers and magazines lay stacked on the table with tabs of paper sticking out from their pages, waiting to be "worked on." Sometimes I thought: *This is what the great Soviet power came down to.* I was dying to ask about Molotov's KGB *versiya*; I wanted to know more about Leonid. Why was it wrong for me to turn out like her stepson? But as usual, I said nothing. I just watched Grandmother in her simple cotton dress with an old dark wool cardigan thrown over her shoulders for warmth expertly operate her scissors. While telling me her life story, she would cut out inspiring articles and edifying passages and send them to her family and friends. My mother still keeps these pages and notes.

———◆———

Nina was born in 1900 to the peasant family of Peotr and Ekaterina Kukharchuk in Vasiliev, a small village near the city of Kholm (now Chelm) in Lublin province of Western Ukraine, which today is part of Poland.[26] The Kukharchuks had a house, a small plot of land and even a horse. "We were doing better than the Khrushchevs in Russia," she used to say, with an air of comic superiority. She was also proud that she had been a perfect student—a didactic nod in my direction—so good that a local pastor convinced her father, once a military man who believed in learning, that she should receive further education on scholarship. Nina's studies brought her to Odessa, the Black Sea port and the fourth largest city in the Russian Empire, widely known as the Rio de Janeiro of the East due to its warm climate and beautiful architecture. After successfully completing courses in the elite Maryinsky Women's Gymnasium, Nina stayed on in Odessa teaching and tutoring younger girls.

I was reading Charlotte Bronte for my English exam at the time Grandmother told me her story, and I marveled at the resemblance of her fate to that of Jane Eyre. "My favorite book—the best example of perseverance," Nina explained. "When your mother was little, I read it to her at bedtime." Of course, Grandmother, who was always ready to tout the merits of communism over capitalism, made a distinction: the Victorians allowed only a limited possibility of marrying up for women in the British bourgeois society. She proudly told me how she responded to the revolutionary call by joining Odessa's underground Bolsheviks. I thought, the Gods of rebellion had a sense of humor: my grandmother's last name, Kukharchuk, means cook in Ukrainian and Russian. But I didn't make the joke, because she was in the middle of earnestly describing how she began to cultivate the perfect image of the progressive Leninist "maid-cook."

During the Civil War, Nina was sent to the Western Front because of her knowledge of Polish, in addition to her native Ukrainian and Russian. She became the leader of the local communist women, entrusted with explaining to the peasants in the surrounding villages the advantages of Soviet egalitarian power. Then after a year of an advanced propagandist training in Moscow, my grandmother received a new revolutionary command to teach history of the communist party and Marxist thought at district party schools in the Donbas mining region. She assumed this position in Yuzovka in 1922.

That same year, she met my ambitious, young grandfather. Although they shared a simple background, she was worldier than he was—and better educated too, which perhaps made up for the fact that she was not as conventionally beautiful as Nikita's late wife. Nina was rather plain looking with a button nose and wheat-colored hair. She was of average height and built like a bit of a dumpling. Her feet were so large that she and Grandfather wore the same size shoes.

Despite her average appearance, she was quite a catch for a coal miner from Yuzovka. Their courtship was truly an extreme case in which a teacher changes her student for the rest of his life. And in addition to her wholesome character, she was from Ukraine, an area that Nikita had a soft spot for because of his background as a miner. Grandmother told me that every time her husband insisted on speaking his "fair but foreign Ukrainian as if he were a native—and he insisted all the time," she was so embarrassed she could "fall through the floor."

My grandparents were never formally married. As devoted Leninists, they fully subscribed to the leadership's position on marriage as the "bourgeois institution"[27] intended to keep women in domestic chains. A 1918 Soviet Code on Marriage and Family, dubbed the "most progressive family legislation the world had ever seen,"[28] did away with centuries of patriarchal power and established a new "civil union" doctrine of the equality of sexes during the first postrevolutionary decade. "The fetters of husband and wife" were now considered "obsolete," family was to be replaced by radical social relations. As a couple fully devoted to each other for fifty years, beginning in 1922 and lasting till Grandfather's death in 1971, my grandparents' free union was a case in point.

The couple's lack of a formal marriage certificate notwithstanding, Nikita's mother, Ksenia Khudyakova, was pleased that her son had found someone new. Khrushchev was busy with advancing communism and needed a woman to look after his children—Yulia, then seven, and Leonid, five. Ksenia and Sergei, her husband, were getting old. When Nina appeared on the scene first as Khrushchev's teacher and then his companion the family was complete from the traditional Russian point of view. The problem was that Nina, a first-rate Soviet propagandist, also worked and relied on schools, kindergartens, and the old woman for help, a fact that Ksenia always resented, insisting that a village mother needs no other job than to care for the kids.

And so decades before my grandmother tried to tame me—then the most unruly child of the family—she had tried to tame her stepchildren, Big Yulia (as opposed to my mother, Little Yulia, as they were called at home) and Leonid.

As I would soon learn, the children, especially the boy, didn't take well to Nina's ideological rigor.

COMMUNISM'S PRODIGAL SON

In October 1961 Anastas Mikoyan, the deputy soviet premier, was enjoying a morning stroll through the park near the grand, white Livadian Palace on Russia's Black Sea Coast, when he ran into my grandfather, then the premier. Once property of the czar, the opulent palace was now a people's sanatorium. Palms and magnolias bloomed year-round in the warm southern climate, and white wisteria vines climbed up pavilions and along large stone fences. Every year the Soviet *nomenklatura* came to this part of the Crimean Peninsula (now part of Ukraine), staying in nearby Mukholatka at a Politburo guesthouse on the hill with a gorgeous view of the water. As it was with the royals, the Bolsheviks imitated the vacation habits of their leaders. First Stalin and now Khrushchev held court, day and night, during the summer and autumn months in a quiescent villa in Oreanda, a mile down the shore from the guesthouse.

Grandfather loved to take long walks after an early breakfast, often dragging along the whole family for his morning stroll. But Khrushchev was alone on that sunny day in October when Mikoyan ran into him and said hello. A close political ally and fellow anti-Stalinist, Mikoyan was out walking with his oldest son, Stepan, a test pilot who had stopped by for a short visit. The three men exchanged some brief pleasantries, and then Stepan addressed the premier.

"Your son Leonid and I were friends during the war," he said. "All these years, I never got a chance to tell you how sorry I am that he died."

After a long pause, the old man looked at the pilot.

"Ah," said Khrushchev, shaking his head, "*neputeovy byl* (he was a screwup)." He turned around and marched home alone, leaving the Mikoyans behind.

Stepan had clearly touched a nerve.

—◆◆◆—

I first met Stepan Mikoyan in 2005 when my mother brought me to talk to him about what Leonid was like. We settled into the living room at his moderate home near Paveletsky—one of the stops on the subway's main Circle Ring encompassing central Moscow—where I eagerly waited for him to tell me the story of Leonid's youth. At eighty-three years old, Stepan was small in stature, but thin and fit, with a shock of white wavy hair and a valiant mustache. He looked like he could have once been a successful jockey, riding feral horses instead of flying test and fighter planes. During his decades as a pilot, he earned numerous medals including the USSR's highest honor, Hero of the Soviet Union, which he mentioned to me with a flirtatious smile as if he was forty years younger. Speaking of Leonid, he was warm and amiable—"Leonya was a wonderful, dear friend"—and though he exuded a survivor's sense of superiority in the way he spoke about his deceased friend, Stepan said he was taken aback by Nikita's openly negative assessment of his son.

The elder Khrushchev made Leonid sound like a felon, not a human being. That was the first time I wondered: *Did Grandfather's overly harsh judgment contribute to the mythology surrounding his son's fate?* I too had been raised a Khrushchev in the USSR and knew all too well of my family's expectations of perfection. Still, I was stunned by Stepan's story. What could Leonid have done that his father remained so unforgiving two decades after the young man's death?

———

Growing up in Ukraine in the 1920s, Leonid was always surrounded by friends. He was the center of attention, the leader of a group of blue-collar sons of workers and craftsmen. I imagine him as Mark Twain's Tom Sawyer, a natural showoff with unchallenged authority, a host of fanciful ideas burning brightly in his adolescent mind. Just like Tom, Leonid was always getting into trouble. His older sister, my aunt Yulia, thought he was too carefree. She was constantly scolding him for his misadventures.

Once, when Leonid was ten and Yulia was twelve, they went fishing together by themselves in Kiev on the rustic left bank of the Dnieper River. Leonid wanted to spend the night on the boat, waiting for dawn to arrive when the fish were more likely to bite. He planned to run home, sneak into their house, put pillows under the blankets to make it look like they were asleep in their beds, and then sneak back out to the boat and resume his post. He was so excited by this idea, by its danger and defiance; he knew that if their stepmother Nina caught them, she would ground them for at least a week. But his sister didn't let him stay on the Dnieper in someone else's boat no less. She insisted that they return.

That evening, as the sky darkened and they left for home, Leonid carried the day's meager catch in a small bucket, which he decided to give to a few friends. Yulia was angry—they had been out there all day—but Leonid said that "only dawn counts," that anything else wasn't a real feat. When his older sister continued to protest, the other boys made fun of her, calling her stingy.

That only made Yulia angrier. She hardly remembered their mother. Their father was often working, and growing up, it had been her job to carry out the adult responsibilities, to act as Leonid's "mother" together with their grandmother Ksenia. Leonid, in turn, resented his sister's authority, and when Nina joined the family in 1923, Leonid, a mere six-year-old boy, had already decided he would never allow any woman to run his life.

To prove his independence, Leonid insisted on unconditional freedom, a demand that lay at the root of most of his troubles with the women of the house. They watched him like a hawk; one of them always seemed to be around, ready to lecture or punish him whenever he tried to steal apples and watermelons from a neighbor's garden and when he impulsively gave away all his clothes or skipped school to play with his friends in the street.

No formal transcripts remain of his early years as a student. But everyone in my family says that Leonid had few academic achievements—unlike Big Yulia, who was always an A student and an obedient if not overly enthusiastic young Pioneer (the Soviet version of the Girl Scouts). Today he would be the poster child for the sort of hyperactive and impetuous behavior that once was so easily cast aside without concern; boys will be boys, as they used to say. At the age of eight, Leonid broke windows playing football; at ten, he biked down the school's front staircase, crashing his bike and denting the school's front door. He was always planning some great adventure, some grand scheme—anything to escape the monotony and boredom of his home and his school.

When Leonid turned twelve, he refused to live with his stepmother any longer. Stealing his father's rifle, he decided to go to Africa for a hunting trip, a safari like the ones he read about in class. Leonid wanted to see the jungle firsthand, to take aim at lions and tigers and elephants. Big Yulia, always on the lookout for her brother's latest scheme, somehow found out about his plans and immediately told their stepmother. Nina proceeded to lock Leonid in his room, taking away his trousers and hiding her husband's rifle.[29] When Nina punished Leonid, he felt little remorse. Instead, he reproached *her*: "I wish you'd take my pants when it's time to go to school."

Despite his frequent clashes with female authority, there was one woman with whom Leonid always got along: his grandmother. In the eyes of Ksenia, Leonid was a little prince, someone who could do no wrong. She adored him so much, my family often jokes that, after having chicken for dinner, Ksenia—a peasant at heart who couldn't waste even a small piece of meat—chewed on her grandson's discarded chicken bones. Keeping with patriarchal Russian culture, she felt that her granddaughter Yulia was Nina's responsibility but that Leonid would suffer from the lack of male influence in his life and thus needed more attention.

Yet for most of Leonid's life, Nikita was not around save for an occasional lecture to his young children on the perfect Soviet man—the Trotsky Superman. Khrushchev was out fighting the White Army and building the nascent Bolshevik state. In 1925 he became the communist secretary of one of Yuzovka's districts, distinguishing himself by his knowledge of mining and industry. He was soon invited to become a nonvoting delegate to the Fourteenth Party Congress in Moscow, an immense honor for a man from the provinces. For the next four years, in Yuzovka, Kharkov, and Kiev, Khrushchev worked tirelessly as a party organizer in Ukraine and in 1929 received permission to study metallurgy at the Stalin Industrial Academy in the Soviet capital. In 1932, however, he had to interrupt his studies to assume a full-time job as the second in command of Moscow's communist party. Nikita's importance awarded him an apartment in the fancy Zamoskvoretsky area (translated as "the other side of the Moscow River") with a view of the bright red stars on the famous Kremlin towers. The family now had five spacious rooms on the fifth floor of *Dom na Naberezhnoi*—the House on the Embankment, as it was known in Soviet folklore—a daunting, gray, eleven-story building that housed the city's political elite.

In Moscow, Nikita was even more focused on the state and had less time to discipline his wayward son. Meanwhile, Leonid's grandfather, Sergei, his lungs ridden with tuberculosis contracted in the Ukrainian mines, was too sick to be an example for the children. Smaller in stature and meeker in character than his wife, he was always under her thumb. Ksenia called him *moi durak* (my fool) and said on occasion that ambitious Nikita may not have been his.[30]

In Russia, especially during Soviet times, men were mythical figures, super heroes of the state, hell-bent on forging a utopian society from the ashes of serfdom. At home, however, it was the women who ruled while the men were absent; the women who held the family together and put food on the table while the men were unavailable, seemingly not even human to their own flesh and blood.

To make up for the meekness of her husband and the absence of her son, Ksenia encouraged her grandson's rebelliousness, spoiling him rotten. She felt it was not only acceptable for Leonid to give away food, clothes, and toys but also, now that the family was no longer poor and struggling, it was his obligation to do so. Nina objected to this wastefulness and tried to appeal to Leonid's common sense. "I refuse to sew a new shirt for you every few months because you give your old ones away," she protested. She hated how Leonid and his friends were always running amok in their apartment, shouting, screaming, and eating everything in sight. "They are like locusts," my grandmother used to complain. Yet Ksenia wanted to stick it her daughter-in-law by encouraging Leonid to follow his heart's desire. And so decades before his father became known as Hurricane Nikita around New York's United Nations headquarters, Leonid already had this nickname at his Moscow's home.

The tug of war between Nina and Ksenia over disciplining Leonid only made him more incorrigible. And the boy eventually took his grandmother's advice to heart. Barely out of high school in 1935, he was madly in love and ready to marry—so ready, in fact, that he became a father at age seventeen.

Tall and lean with his mother's good looks and a dashing personality to boot, Leonid met Esfir Ettinger, a technician about five years his senior, through mutual friends. After the birth of their son, Yury, the young woman thought Leonid would settle down. Esfir's father also insisted on marriage. Leonid was keen on tying the knot, even though he was a year shy of the legal age to marry in Russia. But the elder Khrushchev was adamant that his son was too young to have a family. Nikita, of course, would give the newborn the family's surname and help him out financially, but fostering formal ties was out of the question. The two never married; facing pressure from his father, Leonid broke off the relationship.[31]

—⁓⁓⁓—

By the time Leonid's son Yury was born in 1935 (and not long before the birth of the Khrushchevs's own son, Sergei), Nikita was promoted to become the head of the Regional and City Moscow Communist Party Committee, a position similar to that of the region's governor. His new importance made him even more concerned about Leonid's reckless behavior.

Wanting to please his father, the young Khrushchev applied to one of Moscow's Factory Training Professional Schools (FZU). In receiving a technical education at FZU, which was the equivalent to a trade school, Leonid was following in his father's proletarian footsteps. Though he had shown little interest in becoming an ideal communist, it was atypical for the son of someone as high in the party as Khrushchev to attend such a nonelite school. Nikita, ever the proud proletarian, was thrilled. Leonid didn't pursue a job mending tractors or mining equipment as his father had, but at least the younger Khrushchev was ready to service airplanes. He needed this skill to fulfill his dream of becoming a pilot, a cult profession in the 1930s, when the call for heroes of *vozdukhoplavanie*—translated literally as air swimming—swept across the Soviet Union.

Flying was brave, novel, and sexy, a way to prove that communism was extraordinary, destined to dominate the world. At the time, Europe and America were in the throes of a great race to rule the skies, and the Soviets seemed to be falling behind, in part due to the recent civil war. Stalin had to play catch up and set up an air force as quickly as possible. As part of the country's recruitment efforts, billboards that read, "Youth, Take to the Skies" and "From Models to Gliders and from Gliders to Aircrafts" covered the streets from Leningrad to Vladivostok. The Soviet Union was a young country, and its youth were tasked with building a society for the world to envy. These slogans echoed through the opulent halls of the newly erected Soviet Palaces of Culture—Stalin, after all, was creating a nascent communist empire in which the people's palaces were intended to upstage those of the czars.[32] And so at youth group gatherings across the country, Komsomol (Young Communist League) leaders were calling for the development of new Soviet heroes, Supermen and Superwomen, for establishing amateur flying clubs alongside professional aviation schools.

After the FZU graduation in 1936, Leonid enrolled in the Third Joint School of Civilian Pilots and Aviation Mechanics in Balashov in the Voronezh region, a province located 630 miles southeast of Moscow. The school, however, was too far from the parties he longed to attend in Moscow, and studying the emerging science of Soviet aviation was not what he expected: instead of freely soaring the skies, as he imagined a Soviet Superman should, there were too many courses devoted to communist ideals. In the span of a year, the young cadet was on the verge of expulsion three times.[33] According to his school transcript, he received quite a few Ds and Fs. The Russian curriculum was based on a 5-grade system—5 being the highest—and Leonid's most common mark was a 3. But beyond subpar grades, the school's instructors were furious about his complete lack of interest in politics and the theoretical disciplines, such as the history of the communist party and revolutionary thought.

One instructor, Comrade Alekseev, filed a slew of complaints to the school administration. The head of Leonid's pilot crew, Sergeant Morozov, along with the commander of his flight division, Lieutenant Gundarev, and other officers insisted that, "Any unit, large or small, Leonid was assigned to he immediately found ways to act selfishly and refuse to respect any command figure in a position of authority." The other complaints ranged from his "drinking and partying" to a "ragged haircut" to "being involved with the Trotskyites from 1935 to 1937."

The young Khrushchev's instructors supervised him constantly, documenting even the tiniest transgression. But oddly, their biggest objection was not his Trotskyism, arguably the worst accusation of the era because Trotsky challenged the absolute power of Stalinism.[34] In Leonid's case it was his habit of "repeatedly mixing up the uniform" that angered school authorities most. Sailors were known as the greatest of Soviet dandies, and Leonid, a dandy in his own right, wore a striped sailor shirt under his pilot jacket, an unacceptable *faux pas* for a bona fide airman. He never wore his peaked cap straight, an offense that actually led to most of his detentions, although occasionally his superiors tossed him into a guardhouse cell for unconventional behavior not fit for a communist. This charge referred to his habit of booing speakers off the stage at political meetings. He was undisciplined at such gatherings; his loud comments were seen as disrespectful of the communist party and disruptive of the political discussions of the day.

In the USSR, these actions immediately branded the younger Khrushchev a bad Soviet. "Mixing the uniform today, betraying the motherland tomorrow," Sergeant Morozov wrote in June 1937. There was no future for this "budding Trotskyite, the worst student at the School" who should be expelled since his crass behavior not only pulled the school's statistics down, but he also "had badly influenced and demoralized the rest of the student mass."

The complete "Reference of Cadet Leonid Nikitovich Khrushchev, Group 12, Regiment One" reads:

> Khrushchev L.N., of workers origins, not a member of the communist party, not a member of trade unions. While at the School proved himself an undisciplined cadet. In 1935–1937 had a connection—friendship— with instructors Ovchinnikov and Melikesov, who were tried as Trotskyites. Often partied with them; during unauthorized leaves spent nights at their apartments. In 1936 Ovchinnikov was sent on a business trip. He arranged for Khrushchev to accompany him. Khrushchev didn't go, but didn't return to the dormitory for the next ten days, for which was arrested for ten days. Altogether has many unauthorized leaves, drinking incidents, missed classes; doesn't follow orders. For mixing up the uniform was arrested for three days. For unauthorized leaves and mixing up the uniform another five days of arrest. He has numerous reprimands and removals from flights. Expelled from the Komsomol and trade unions for lack of discipline. Very weak political development; no participation in political-societal life. Despite assigned extracurricular activities does nothing. Likes to go into town, likes women. Knows many people in town; once even rented an apartment together with Ovchinnikov's brother. Doesn't have good comradely relations; mean to comrades. At the meetings is out of control. Often shouts and remarks from his seat. No interest in theoretical and military subjects; has bad grades in these disciplines. Likes to have younger cadets under his influence. According to rumors Khrushchev was frivolous while on vacation.
>
> Instructor Alekseev. / With instructor Alekseev's reference fully agree, crew leader, Morozov. / With instructor Alekseev's reference agree, Commander of First Division, Gundarev. / With reference agree. Recommend expulsion, Commander of First Regiment, Irza. 22/VII-37.

In 1955, a year before the secret speech, my fifteen-year-old mother first saw this horrid evaluation. She had opened the elder Khrushchev's top desk drawer looking for her own school transcript and found Leonid's aviation service file in a dark-blue laminated cardboard folder with a gold hammer and sickle insignia on it. She opened the folder, read a random page, and as her eyes registered the word Trotskyism, she almost fainted. Terrified, she put away the documents and never asked about them again. Aunt Rada later confided in her that Grandmother had wanted to burn Leonid's transcript. "All Khrushchev children have been honor students, and Leonya was a worrisome exception," Nina lamented.

Aunt Rada talked Grandmother out of destroying the damning file, and in the 1990s, after the Soviet Union had dissolved, Rada gave the folder to my mother. Not wanting to reckon with the past, Mother put it under her bed along with other family memorabilia. "When I even touch this, my hands shake," she told me when she gave me the file roughly ten years ago.

She wanted me to better understand who Leonid was, yet I know that both she and Aunt Rada must be upset that I've included it in this book. Given the Kremlin's secretive history, which they were once part of, they can't help but see this as airing our family's dirty laundry. They still cringe when the truth is not flattering to Grandfather, to our clan.

Leonid, a far cry from a model of perfection, defied his commanders even when they gave him a chance to improve. Initially, he seemed to comply, getting involved in extracurricular activities—a skilled accordion player, he joined a patriotic choir—but soon grew bored, tired of the mandatory responsibility and returned to his unpredictable ways.

Spoiled brats surely exist in all cultures, yet some complaints against cadet Khrushchev should be understood in the context of the Bolshevik behavioral formula. The USSR celebrated the unity of the proletariat, but Leonid didn't see himself as a faceless member of Soviet society. As one of the school evaluations described him, he was an "individualist, with disregard for the communist cause and no interests for the group in his heart... thus the worst threat to the Soviet collective." Then individualism was a sin and disinterest in Leninism-Stalinism was in and of itself a crime. In the 1930s, people went to the gulag for much less than poor political development.

"Loving women" was another repeated accusation in his evaluations, but the school authorities didn't know the worst of it. Those weekends he failed to return to the barracks in Balashov, he wasn't spending in the nearby Borisoglebsk or even in Saratov, a much larger regional center hundred and eighty miles away. He traveled six hundred miles all the way to the Bolshoi in Moscow to party with actresses. According to his friend Mikoyan, Leonid had always been enamored with actresses and ballerinas.

In 1937, Leonid momentarily married Rosa Trevis, an unknown but attractive actress a few years his senior. Nikita didn't know what he should be more upset about: his son's poor grades, his disregard for communism, or his incessant womanizing. Per the family rumors (no one openly discussed Leonid's multiple love interests), when the younger Khrushchev tried to introduce Rosa to the family in September 1937, his father grabbed the marriage certificate out of his hands, tore it up in front of everyone, and made his son annul the relationship the next day.[35] Irina Sergeevna—Arisha—Nikita's younger sister, remembered that it was the angriest she had ever seen the elder Khrushchev.

After that family row, Leonid finally had a talk with his father, which Aunt Rada remembered as "tense and somber." In one of our many conversations, my aunt explained why she thought Grandfather was so worked up about Leonid's misbehavior.[36] His oldest son, she said, "More than any of us, inherited Father's effortless charm." I knew what she meant; it was that impetuousness and levity that I loved as the little girl. But the problem laid in their existential disagreement about how to use it. In Grandfather's view all personal qualities, including love for women, should have political relevance. Rada reminded me of the 1959 Soviet state visit to America to promote the new Thaw policy—communism with the human face—Khrushchev cheerfully practiced his dance steps with young Shirley MacLaine and flirtatiously enjoyed Marilyn Monroe's company. But twenty years earlier, for Leonid, a Soviet nonconformist, "communism" and "human" did not belong in the same vocabulary.

It was 1937, the year of the Great Purges, when people accused of the unspeakable crimes against the state had disappeared left and right. And so Leonid and his father also talked about something far more serious than womanizing: the gulag, which the elder Khrushchev assured his son would be his new home if he continued to act irresponsibly. Nikita certainly knew what to fear. As he wrote in his memoir:

> [S]everal people were simply charlatans who took up the profession of exposing enemies of the people. They terrorized everyone. They would unceremoniously look a person right in the eye: "Here this one, he's an enemy of the people." Such an accusation would stick to a person, it would attract attention, and the NKVD would start to investigate. The investigation of course was conducted secretly; agents were assigned to follow the person, and later they testified that indeed this was an enemy of the people.[37]

With his father's encouragement, on September 19, 1937, Leonid sent a request for an extended leave from school "to arrange his personal affairs" in Moscow, to take care of his *delo* (case) at the Komsomol Central Committee (months earlier he was barred from this youth organization for insubordination). That same day, he wrote an explanatory note pleading for another chance to change his ways. His promise to become a better Soviet seemed to have convinced his superiors into letting him finally graduate.

Did Leonid, fearing possible arrest, really straighten up? How did he avoid the Trotskyism charge? It's unlikely that Nikita directly influenced his son's graduation; in our family, it was a matter of principle to vehemently disprove of *blat* (favors). In another conversation, Aunt Rada insisted: "It was against parents rules to pull children up, to arrange privileges for them. Father thought we should be proud of any labor, and for example, Leonya's FZU experience was welcome. Also, he went to a pilot school in the provinces, not to a prestigious military academy that children of other political dignitaries attended."

And yet Russian culture is so mired in favoritism that sometimes you simply can't avoid it. The elder Khrushchev may not have deliberately spoken for his son, but the Soviet system was excellent at recognizing how to help important officials and their families. I was told that after the war Uncle Sergei, always an honor student, joined Kiev's Boy School number 24, and upon receiving his first excellent grade, he rushed to tell his parents. Nina immediately asked whether the grade was well-deserved, and Sergei honestly replied, "Not so much." The next day his mother went to the principal and asked to grade her children only according to their real achievements. Similarly, the authorities in charge of the aviation education must have instructed Leonid's school to give him a diploma since they didn't want to upset his influential father.

Leonid's close friendship with known Trotskyites at school was a different matter entirely, and it is remarkable that he didn't get arrested. The Khrushchev name could not have helped deflate these accusations; Nikita certainly knew better than to get involved with the gray suits from Lubyanka. Even those very close to Stalin—Cavalry marshal Semeon Budenny, Lazar Kaganovich, Moscow's party chairman before Khrushchev, or even Molotov—didn't and couldn't speak on behalf of their family members.[38] Stalin's own sister-in-law, Anna Alliluyeva-Redens, was accused of espionage and spent six years in the gulag.

In his memoirs, Khrushchev details his challenging experience with the sudden arrest of his assistants in Moscow and Kiev in 1938:

> That was the kind of situation that took shape then…
> People disappeared without a trace, as though the ocean
> had swallowed them up. When they began to arrest leaders
> of the party and of the trade unions, military comrades,
> and factory directors, two of my personal assistants were
> arrested…exceptionally honorable and decent people…
> But "factual material" was concocted…and I had no
> possibility of refuting it. All I did then was curse myself
> for letting myself be fooled. Here were these men who had
> been closely associated with me, and they had turned out
> to be enemies of the people![39]

There is no hidden sarcasm in Grandfather's reaction. The gap between what he was told to be true and what he knew to be true was shared by most Soviets at the time and often still is today. Such is the mythology of our great nation that we believe the state more than we believe ourselves. Unwavering loyalists like my grandfather blamed the state's own mistakes on the never-ending supply of the subversive elements—class, imperialist, and bourgeois antagonists. And by the mid-1930s, the hunt for these supposed enemies became an all-encompassing policy. As the historian Richard Pipes explains:

> At the pinnacle of Great Terror, the Politburo issued
> "quotas" to the police authorities, instructing them as
> to what percentage of the population in their district
> was to be shot and what percentage sent to camps. For
> example, on June 2, 1937, it set a quota of 35,000 persons
> to be "repressed" in Moscow city and Moscow province, of
> which number 5,000 were to be shot.[40]

As the head of the Moscow communist party, Khrushchev also obediently requested quotas for jailing and executing "anti-Soviet criminals."[41] Moreover, afraid of becoming one of those criminals himself, he confessed to his mentor Kaganovich that Trotsky was once his hero. Kaganovich advised a disclosure to Stalin, who was surprisingly understanding. "Better to tell what happened [to the whole Party], because if you don't then, they'll be able to pester you; they'll bombard you with questions—and us with reports,"[42] Stalin said. In retrospect, it seems miraculous that both Khrushchevs managed to escape a grim Trotskyite's fate.

———

As I have learned more about my grandfather and his prodigal son, I have become more certain that Leonid's misadventures were a direct product of the despotic communist system. I came to see him as yet another victim of Soviet tyranny. His rowdy behavior was often inexcusable, but my grandparents' requirement of absolute impeccability from their children, especially their older son, made matters worse. In an inhumane communist society that bled its citizens to save humanity but didn't lift a finger to help a single person, in a country that viewed individuality with intense and ever-present suspicion, being human often had grave consequences. Soviet Supermen were not supposed to live their own lives but instead only labor for the good of the collective. In other more humane, individual-centered societies, Leonid's actions would have been commonplace and far less shameful. Today his short attention span might be diagnosed as attention deficit hyperactivity disorder. Or perhaps he was what we now call an adrenalin junkie—hence his infatuation with speed, from childhood bicycles to the ultimate machine of the era, the airplane.

But in the USSR during the 1930s, he was considered dangerous. He was not just a bad statistic; he was a menace, an antihero of the regime—a rebel within a cause. This was long before it became romantic to reject the Soviet system because of opposition to tyranny. Leonid was not Venichka Erofeev, now one of the best-known dissidents—an alcoholic philosopher (a pseudoautobiographical character of Venedict Erofeev in his 1970 novel *Moscow to the End of the Line*) who defied Brezhnev's regime by falling into a drunken stupor on a suburban train from Moscow to Petushki. Nor was he Andrei Sakharov, a developer of the Soviet H-bomb who later became a human rights activist and Nobel Laureate. Leonid can better be described as a Soviet James Dean of sorts, a disenfranchised young man, who broke the rules and disrupted social norms.[43]

After graduating from the Third Aviation School in 1938, the twenty-one-year-old rebel moved to Kiev with his family, where he continued to cause trouble. His aunt Arisha remembered there were heated disagreements about the move because her nephew wanted to remain in Moscow and felt he was old enough to live on his own. He ultimately lost the argument to Nina, who thought it was easier to keep an eye on her wayward stepson if he was still living under her roof.

Victor Gontar, Big Yulia's husband, was an avid observer of the Khrushchev family and documented the persistence of Leonid's rebellion in five, multicolored vinyl diaries. Like most other documents and family photos, I found them buried under Mother's bed. Gontar didn't write in the wooden Soviet jargon of *Pravda* editorials. Instead, his journal was more reminiscent of something found on page 6 of *The New York Post*, perhaps because he used to be the director of various Kiev theaters and dealt with celebrities and prima donnas. His comments on the family dynamic are vivid and spot on. Citing his wife's accounts, he recalled how the parents constantly worried that Leonid could spiral out of control just to prove his independence. "Leonya required an extra degree of attention," Gontar wrote. "In the space of a year he crashed two motorcycles, a boat and a car. His father was livid."

Not only was Leonid destructive, he also destroyed state property. For higher party members, their cars, apartments, *dachas*, furniture and other possessions were all given on a kind of state loan. "The loan from the people," Khrushchev used to say, also repeatedly reminding his son that when he was Leonid's age, he "hand-built a motorcycle from scrap and carried it over puddles so it won't get damaged." But according to Gontar's notes, "Leonid refused to play along. His response was always, 'Whatever.'" Decades later, in a rare open moment about her stepson, Nina told my mother: "As much blood as your father had cost me, my own children never gave me as much grief."

⬟

The elder Khrushchev had no time or patience for his son's antics. In Kiev, Grandfather's duties were extensive, as he himself explained: "In 1938 Stalin called me in and said, 'We want to send you to Ukraine so that you can head up the party organization there...' I began trying to refuse because I knew Ukraine and figured I would be unable to cope."[44]

Leading the Ukrainian communists was no easy task. Khrushchev was overseeing almost ten times more people than the 3.8 million he had been in charge of in Moscow.[45] But most importantly, Stalin needed him to pacify the republic after the *Holodomor*, the Great Famine of the early 1930s, which occurred after the authorities forced farmers to relinquish all their land and crops to the state.[46] For decades, the *Holodomor* was a state secret, which explains a disparity in the victim count—ranging from 2.6 to 10 million lives, including those who perished from widespread cannibalism. But here are some impartial statistics: In January of 1932, at the start of *Holodomor*, Ukraine's population was listed as 32.7 million.[47] In 1937, one year before Khrushchev took over, the census reported its inhabitants at just above 28 million,[48] a decrease of more than ten percent—a literal decimation.

By then, international outrage over the famine was becoming a major problem.[49] But even more than public opinion, Stalin was concerned with replenishing the vast Ukrainian wheat fields, which he needed to feed the rest of his Soviet empire.

An eager devotee like Khrushchev seemed the perfect man for the job, and though historians often omit it, it is clear that Stalin sent my grandfather to Ukraine to save the country from the horrors of hunger. Khrushchev had already achieved great success spearheading the construction of Moscow's bus and subway systems, among other posts. Milovan Djilas, Yugoslav politician turned dissident famous for his book *Conversations with Stalin* explained: "In Soviet top echelons [Khrushchev] was held to be a very skillful operator with a great capacity for economic and organizational matters... He did look into matters and remedy them, while others issued orders from offices and received reports."[50]

So it is no surprise that now Stalin wanted his trusted lieutenant to "pay more attention to agriculture, because for the Soviet Union the agriculture of Ukraine is of greatest importance."[51] Is it possible my grandfather didn't know why Stalin wanted him in Kiev? Like many at the time Khrushchev attributed the famine to the Western propaganda.[52] But even he couldn't hide his shock at the speed with which hunger hit Ukraine in the early 1930s: "I simply couldn't imagine how there could be famine in 1932. When I left there in 1929, Ukraine was in excellent condition as far as food supplies went...Now suddenly there was famine!"

At the time though Khrushchev stuck to the Bolshevik line—communists don't kill peasants; they help them. Never mind that people were disappearing and dying from hunger or hard labor, his delusion was more real than the truth. "In those days," Grandfather remembered, "I looked at things idealistically: if a person carried a party card and was a real Communist, then he was my brother...In my view we were all bound by the invisible threads of ideological struggle, the idea of building communism, which was something elevated and holy."

And so he obediently charged on to deliver results to validate Stalin's patriotic claims that the Soviet Union was creating heroes of industrial and agricultural production.[53] Ukraine, the USSR's second largest republic after the Russian Federation, with its fertile land and skilled population, was supposed to be an example of obedience and success for the rest of the nation—and the world. Raised as a peasant with a knack for agriculture, Khrushchev promoted various types of farming techniques, as opposed to a one-size-fits-all collectivist method. He personally "inspected the garden hotbeds, peeked into the pigsty...discuss[ed] practical problems...[of] the collective farms," all with garrulity and a lively sense of humor.[54]

Watching the elder Khrushchev's dedication to rebuilding Ukraine, Leonid seemed to make a renewed effort at shaping up. In 1938, he was quickly hired at the Kiev airport as an instructor with a Society of Friends of Defense and Creation of Aviation and Chemical Strength of the USSR (OSOVIAKhIM—Soviet acronyms tended to be long in communism's unsettled early days). This nonprofessional organization provided ordinary citizens with flying lessons, and skilled pilots like Leonid were in great demand, regardless of the quality of their grades.

Was this a good job for Khrushchev's son? In Gontar's notes I found evidence that he thought of himself as a "cosmopolitan" Moscow dandy, and this was at the time when "cosmopolitanism" was a curse word, even a crime, as it implied a lack of Soviet patriotism. Leonid certainly didn't want to become some provincial *bon vivant*, forced to give boring lessons to the enthusiastic volunteers at the Kiev airport. I once posed this question to Mikoyan, who thought the title itself mattered little to his friend. He reminded me that being a pilot was a popular profession back then, and Leonid, at six feet tall, with confidence and stylish good looks—especially in his uniform—often boasted about his aviation skills.

Leonid also didn't wait long to pursue his next love interest. One April afternoon in 1938, he came to the airport director's office to sign up for the instructor position. The director rose to his feet and eagerly greeted the new pilot, but Leonid's eyes were focused on the other person in the room: a pretty, petite woman sporting a short bob haircut and a leather coat. She was repeatedly dialing a number, trying to make arrangements for a car to take her back into town. Leonid handed in his paperwork and received his monthly flying schedule. He saw the woman's frustration and offered her a ride on his new German-made motorcycle. Coincidentally, they lived on the same street, Levashovsky (now Shelkovichny). She accepted and introduced herself as Lyubov "Lyuba" Sizykh. From that night on, Lyuba—then a young pilot in training—and Leonid became inseparable. And my family's fate was sealed.

⸎

For ten years, I have been talking to Lyuba about her past. Every summer, we sit in her cramped studio apartment in one of Kiev's cookie-cutter high-rises on Prospect Pobedy, a name which translates to "Victory Avenue," the name shared by thousands of other streets throughout the former USSR. She moved here in the 1960s, and the room is still decorated in the old Soviet style: a dark lacquered buffet, a small desk, a firm folding couch, two austere armchairs, and a few shelves scattered around one wall, which are covered with yellow flowery wallpaper.

My visits are always the same. The southern morning sun heats the apartment, but it stays cool and dark when the cheap Vietnamese bamboo shades are rolled down. The details of Lyuba's stories often change, but the essence of her narrative is remarkably consistent. She is a much-admired Soviet hero. End of story.

The daughter of a Russian father and German mother, Lyuba grew up in a religious family in Kiev. Her mother died when she was very young, and as a result, her father turned to God. He spent hours in the church and made Lyuba—the youngest of his four children—accompany him. She says that the worst moments of her life, "were in that gloomy space, with the *babushkis* (grannies) praying in their black kerchiefs, my father on his knees holding my hand." Her sense of smell overpowered by incense, she passed the time imagining herself as a fearless fairy princess.

Old enough to understand the Bolsheviks' slogan, "Religion is the opium of the people," Lyuba soon replaced her princess dreams with those of the proletariat. She imagined her future in exact details: First, she would cut her hair short, and with a long cigarette in her hand, she would don a red kerchief, not those long dark shawls that the *babushkis* wore in church. She would wear a black leather coat a la Felix Dzerzhinsky, the first Soviet secret police chief. After finishing school, she would get a daring man's job, performing it to perfection. She felt destined to become a Soviet hero, the kind described in "The Internationale," which they enthusiastically sang in class—*those nothings will become all!*

Upon high school graduation, the feisty young communist finished a yearlong program at the Mineral Resources and Geology Research Technical School and joined a soil excavation exercise just outside of Kiev in 1931. In choosing this masculine profession, she was the only female on the dig and quickly married the head of the team, a mature and well-established man named Efim Belonenko. The couple divorced soon after, and Lyuba, then twenty-one, returned to the Ukrainian capital with an eight-month-old son named Anatoly (or Tolya for short).

Enthusiasm was in abundance in the early Soviet decades, but young Lyuba's energy was particularly infectious, which helped her land a prestigious (albeit low level) office manager job at the Kiev Council of the People's Commissariat. Her poor family—her mother was a scullery maid and her father, a petty bank clerk—was an asset among the proletariat, and she used her humble origins to climb the communist ladder toward success.

But even for Lyuba, advancing through the Soviet bureaucracy proved to be a difficult feat without a husband's help along the way. Communism had allowed women to have a job instead of just settling for the life of a homemaker, and to Lyuba's credit, she tried to succeed on her own, making ample effort to contest the primacy of men. Yet while the Soviet people had supposedly overcome its patriarchal past, this was easier said than done. Despite the call for female independence by Lenin's wife, Nadezhda Krupskaya, the Soviet Union had never become a place where women could freely build their careers without worrying about being single; the social pressures of marriage and raising a family often offset any notions of egalitarianism.

Lyuba's ambition—both for her career and for her future husband—brought her to the amateur flight school in Kiev and thus eventually to Leonid, her instructor. Once, during a training exercise, Lyuba sat upfront as the navigator with Leonid behind her in the U-2. She followed his instructions to perform a split-S, a barrel roll, a loop, a 360-degree turn. Every time she took the plane up or down, she heard him laughing vociferously, as he mocked her well-studied but ordinary performance. Afterward he made his opinions known: "Girls can't fly." Lenin's slogan that "every maid can rule the state," one to which his parents wholly subscribed, was apparently lost on their politically incorrect son.

Perhaps Leonid's new love wasn't as talented of a pilot as he was—Lyuba insists that "anything Leonya did, he did brilliantly"—but as a communist, she was his superior. Lyuba's Komsomol leadership of both the OSOVIAKhIM and the Council of the People's Commissariat made her important in the airport's political life. To use the language of the era, she was on the "ideological vanguard." And while being a good pilot was getting Leonid nowhere, his relationship with the ever-ambitious Lyuba helped improve his communist image.

Contrary to his treatment of other women in Leonid's life, Nikita was eager to make Lyuba's acquaintance, hoping her love would steer his itinerant son in the right direction. At the time, the younger Khrushchev, who always followed the latest trends, had taken up photography. Like flying, this was another fad of the era. Rolls of film and stacks of photographs were lying all over his room in the house on Levashovsky in Kiev. His father once walked in to find many images of the same woman on a table, on a bed stand, on a windowsill.

"Who is that?" asked Nikita.

"My friend, Lyuba, a pilot at the Kiev airport."

"I guess it's time for me to meet this Lyuba. She is what a Soviet woman should be," Nikita said.

Aunt Rada, almost ten years old at the time, was curious about her big brother's life and remembers a lot of excitement before the new girlfriend's visit. The young woman came dressed in her pilot uniform, ready to impress the head of Ukrainian communists with her seriousness. When she walked in, Lyuba was struck by the neat whiteness of the Khrushchev villa with its French curtains, plaster fretwork, and ceiling medallions. Crafted in 1912 to meet the wealthy tastes of the emerging merchant class of the Russian empire, these opulent homes were inherited by the Soviet *nomenklatura* after 1917. Dinner was supposed to start at 8:00 p.m., but Nikita called to apologize for being delayed in the office, and Lyuba got plenty of time to catch her breath. Nina came into the dining room where they waited, silently picked up something from the buffet and left. She didn't introduce herself. Lyuba explained that since Leonid had never accepted Nina as a mother, she wasn't welcome at this introductory dinner. But I think that Grandmother simply wasn't eager to meet another one of Leonid's flames.

Khrushchev finally came home at eleven o'clock, and the three of them sat down to dinner. "Nikita Sergeevich instantly liked me," Lyuba remembers:

> I told him about my Council job, which impressed him. We also talked about how important it was to conquer the skies. I said his son was the best instructor at school, and he lit up. But then I told him I had dared Leonya to a communist competition—who can fly more hours

in a week—and he refused. Nikita Sergeevich got upset. "Are you afraid to fail?" he asked. Leonya wasn't afraid of failure, but he told me later, he didn't want to assign Soviet ideological measures to the life he loved, the things he was good at doing. Khrushchev pressed Leonya to accept the challenge, but his son waved us off. After a short awkward moment, the conversation flowed again. For the rest of the evening Nikita Sergeevich was very caring, he insisted I should eat: "Eat, Lyuba, eat, or we'll make you take a doggy bag home." It was late, I don't eat late at night, but I couldn't tell him that.

In December of 1938, Lyuba made her first trip to Moscow. The young couple rang in the New Year in the Soviet capital, partying with friends. The elder Khrushchev kept his apartment from his Moscow days in the House on the Embankment, which was "a city within a city"—it had its own post office, school, supermarket, beauty salon, restaurant, even a cinema. Leonid was eager to show these amenities to his new girlfriend. To this day, Lyuba keeps a photo from that night. The group exudes happiness. One friend is holding a cigarette, another a glass of wine. Lyuba, in the middle, is pictured hugging a bottle of champagne.

Not long thereafter, Lyuba said she and Leonid married in Moscow with no witnesses and no celebration, then returned to Kiev to inform the family of the new Mrs. Khrushchev. This made sense: after two previous marriage attempts, Leonid didn't want anyone aware of his decision, fearing that it might be stopped or annulled. It was easier to tell the family after the fact. Aunt Rada remembers, "When Lyuba and Leonya returned to Kiev late January 1939, everyone simply assumed they had tied the knot." And Leonid's personal autobiography, dated May 22, 1940, seems to confirm this story:

> I was born in Donbas (Stalino) 10 November 1917 in a working class family. Before the revolution, my father worked as a mechanic in the mines and factory... I have no

relatives abroad. Married. Wife is a pilot in the Squadron flying club in Moscow. Wife's father—a worker. Her brother—Military Air Force serviceman in Odessa. Her sister—a homemaker... Wife has never been abroad...

The match apparently thrilled father Khrushchev. At last his unruly son had made a good decision: choosing to associate with a woman eager to perfect herself as a Komsomol member, even though it was suspicious that they had married in secret.

Khrushchev had other objections too. In February 1939, the couple permanently moved to Moscow, and one night, Lyuba says she arrived at her father-in-law's home to find Nikita visiting from Kiev. He sat in the dining room, a photograph in his hand.

"What is this, Lyuba?" he said.

"A picture, Nikita Sergeevich, of our New Year celebration. A joke, really."

"A joke? How could you? You are the leader of your Komsomol organization. An example to others, and here you are cheerfully posing with a bottle of champagne. This is so bourgeois. I have never expected such frivolity from you."

Despite the incident, Lyuba and the elder Khrushchev were united in their efforts to turn Leonid into a model Soviet. They persuaded him to leave civilian aviation, join the Red Army, and enter the high-status Zhukovsky Military Academy—a place where army commanders, air engineers, and later cosmonauts received training. I checked with Aunt Rada to see if his enrollment was a sign of awakening ambition; she suggested that it was Lyuba's "very positive" influence. Joining the ranks of the professional military rather than simply training volunteer novices was more suitable for Leonid's larger-than-life character. Lyuba, who by then had received her own instructor's license, meanwhile began teaching her own volunteers at the Baumansky district aviation club on the east side of Moscow.

Every morning, she walked to the recently erected Sverdlov Square (now Teatralny) subway station through the little

Zamoskvoretsky streets over the renovated Bolshoi Kamenny Bridge from which she had a breathtaking view of the Kremlin. The metro was a novel attraction. Built out of marble and bronze and ornamented with monumental statues, red stars, and hammers and sickles, the new subway vestibules resembled underground palaces celebrating the care and convenience the state provided to its workers. Together with other citizens filling the pristine "Sdelano v SSSR" (Made in the USSR) underground cars, Lyuba commuted to the airport, her final destination. In Lyuba's mind, these daily trips symbolized the rising greatness of her country. Even today, she is still excited about those promising times: "It was a great feeling to be part of the mighty Soviet state, and I knew Nikita Sergeevich built that metro."

But while Lyuba was filled with communist pride, Leonid always mocked the subways his father used to be in charge of before moving to Kiev. "People are like herring in a can," the younger Khrushchev would say, disproving of the group mentality and choosing to drive alone in his fancy black car (lucky for him he had this option).

Moreover, it soon became clear that the Zhukovsky Academy was not a good fit for Khrushchev's son. It required a lot of theory; the school was preparing the *crème de la crème* of Stalin's army— the Stalin *sokoly* (falcons) as they were called—and all students had to be on sound political footing. The goal of the academy was to make its graduates experts in Leninism, Stalinism, and Marxism along with aviation, operations, and navigation. But wasting time on the history of the communist party was cramping Leonid's style. This time he didn't wait to see whether he would be expelled for ideological shortcomings. Bored out of his mind, he withdrew in six months, again disappointing his father. It seemed he was never going to truly accomplish anything.

After quitting Zhukovsky Academy, the young man started drifting again. He became a flight instructor at one of Moscow's local aviation clubs but spent more time attending Bolshoi performances than doing work. In contrast, Lyuba decided to begin a real career in aviation. She joined a course offered by their city district OSOVIAKhIM chapter to become a professional bomber. Her training, however, didn't last long.

On January 21, 1940, the glamorous couple became the happy parents of a baby girl, and Lyuba quickly gave up her dreams of being a pilot. By then they were living in their own spacious apartment in central Moscow, which they received courtesy of Leonid's important father. Their new home on exclusive Bolshaya Polyanka Street included a large balcony, a fancy bidet in the bathroom, and a convenient location just a block away from the *nomenklatura* House on the Embankment. Access to other privileges, distributed to all Politburo family members, included superior health care and unrationed food products that were unavailable to the rest of the population—fresh meat, sausage, candy, and exquisite Georgian wines. All the years later Lyuba still nostalgically remembers these amenities.

I've always thought that with all her Soviet enthusiasm it was strange that Lyuba became a stay-at-home mom; she certainly didn't have to. Being married to the Ukrainian communist party secretary's son provided her with all sorts of domestic assistance including a nanny and a cook. In the USSR, ninety percent of women had jobs—the Bolshevik call for a maid ruling the state was a reality in quantity, if not in quality. But even an activist like Lyuba fell for an easy life of privilege. "Life in Moscow was a constant celebration," she often repeats longingly. "One big party, the happiest of times."

Leonid, she says, was a wonderful husband and a great father. When Yulia was born, he made no distinction between his own daughter and her son, seven-year-old Anatoly. Once Leonid even suggested little Tolya should call him father. "If one child does, so should another," she recalled him saying. But Tolya never did because Lyuba herself never followed up on this suggestion. For many years, I couldn't grasp her abandonment of flying, and just the same, I couldn't understand her resistance to Leonid's attempts to make her son his own.

It was only later that I would find out the truth.

—◁◁◁◁◁ʃʃ▷▷▷▷▷—

On the eve of war, strong-minded Lyuba, who settled for motherhood, insisted that the father of her baby should make use of his ace talents. Surrendering to his wife's pressure, Leonid, then almost twenty-two, entered the Fourteenth Military Aviation School in Engels, which was not preparing civilian aviators (a job the young man found too boring) nor military commanders (which he considered too political) but combat bombers, a job perfect for this lost Khrushchev, who seemed to have dealt with life as if it were some sort childhood game—bombing targets after all wasn't that different from crashing motorcycles. The school, founded in 1931 in the Saratov region on the Volga River, five hundred miles southeast of Moscow, offered a solid education for trainees from all over the USSR.

"Nonelite," Lyuba remembers the elder Khrushchev stating with pride. "He is finally a true Soviet."

Since school took Leonid away from Moscow and its big city distractions for most of the week, he seemed to concentrate on his courses more than ever before. The young man's transcript from the Engels School shows that, for once, he performed well. Out of twenty-two disciplines assessing the "elements of flying," Leonid received three 4s (A-/B+), the rest were the 5s (A).[55] There were no reprimands; instead instructors raved about the cadet's extraordinary flying skills—his initiative, ingenuity, and dedication. Upon graduation in June 1940 with a rank of lieutenant, junior pilot Leonid Khrushchev joined the 134th High-Speed Bomber Aviation Regiment in Podolsk, a city twenty miles north of Moscow.

The prodigal son had finally found his calling.

THE GREAT PATRIOTIC WAR

B ack at home on the quiet streets of Moscow, after months on the front lines, a documentary filmmaker by the name of Leonid Dultsev took pen to paper and wrote a somber letter to his friend's father. The words didn't come easy; it took an hour to compose a simple paragraph:

> Much Esteemed Nikita Sergeevich! Please allow me to present photographs of your son—my very good, unforgettable friend, a friend of great kindness and immense spiritual depth. Dear Nikita Sergeevich, I remain constantly hopeful and have faith that I will see Leonya again and will lock him in an embrace. I ask you to accept my most profoundly felt best regards.
>
> —With deepest respect,
> Leonid Dultsev. 17 July 1944.

My grandmother Nina preserved this letter and fifteen others like it after her stepson died. My mother inherited them in the 1960s and, of course, stashed them away so she could forget they existed. About ten years ago, I dug out these notes, hoping to wrap my hands around the obscurity of Leonid's death. Through the eyes of the younger Khrushchev's comrades, I saw a portrait of a complex man, not a simple "screwup," as his father once described. These handwritten letters are yellowed and tattered along the edges, stained with water or sweat (maybe even tears). Some of them are just a single sheet of paper folded into what is known in Russia as a "war triangle," with text written on one side of the page and an address on the other. These pages reveal more than a typical wartime narrative; they tell a moving story of a loyal friend and daring pilot who fought to defend our country. Sifting through these vintage notes in the modern era of sound bites and 140-character tweets, I find their antiquated language naïve, flowery, even laughably homoerotic. But that cannot blunt an appreciation that these soldiers fought bravely against the Nazis, died heroically, and faced hardships we can hardly conceive.

⚬⚬⚬

On the evening of June 21, 1941, Leonid came home from a Saturday performance of *Swan Lake* at the Bolshoi, and he and Lyuba settled into one of their usual weekend dinners with some of his friends. A breeze from the Moscow River wafted through an open window, and the men—all pilots—traded aviation secrets, the best way to perform spiral dives and reverse tailspins. After they finished eating, Lyuba started cleaning the plates. Darkness fell for barely an hour—early summers are light in Moscow—and for the rest of the night they proceeded to drink.

It was shortly after 4:00 a.m. on Sunday when they heard the news. The company was still partying, and Lyuba noted that the first signs of sunrise seemed particularly early this year. Just as they were about to leave, the phone rang, interrupting their good-byes. Lyuba picked up, and Arisha immediately started crying into the phone: "War! With Germany! The end!" Leonid rolled his eyes. His aunt was always so dramatic. As apolitical as he was, Leonid could have missed the signs of a looming war, but if the

Nazi invasion was coming, wouldn't their regiment commanders make them stay in the garrison over the weekend? He turned on the radio and heard a deep, lugubrious voice announcing that German tanks had invaded Soviet territory from the West, in the Belorussian city of Brest.

The invasion came at a bad time for the Soviets. The country was not ready for war. Fearful of being invaded by capitalist France and Great Britain, Stalin had relied too much on the 1939 Molotov-Ribbentrop Non-Aggression Treaty. But amid the chaos of the German advance, Leonid was imbued with a sense of purpose: to fight for the motherland. Without waiting for the next phone call from the regiment, he took off his fancy blue Sunday suit and put on his uniform—a pair of monochrome dark green fatigues, tall black boots, and a gun strap. Tolya, who had been peeking out from his room with a mixture of fear and curiosity, hugged his stepfather's knees. Leonid embraced him, picked up sixteen-month-old Yulia, who was half asleep, and gave her a kiss good-bye. The embrace would be one of their last.

When the war began, Lieutenant Khrushchev served as a squad leader in the 134th High-Speed Bomber Regiment of 303d Aviation Army stationed outside of Podolsk, a small town near Moscow. As the main aircraft navigator in a group of three, he also was responsible for the men of the three other bomber crews comprising his squadron. Judging by the views of his eleven subordinates, Leonid was a capable and caring commander.

On July 26, 1941, roughly a month into the war, he was wounded in an air battle on the Soviet Western Front. Flying his thirty-first military sortie in four weeks, Khrushchev's plane was attacked, forcing him to make an emergency belly-landing. The plane's chassis was seriously damaged when the aircraft hit the ground, and Leonid shattered his left tibia and fibula; the break was so bad that the bone stuck out through his boot. According to his comrades, while he hung upside down for an hour waiting to be cut out of the smashed plane, he entertained the crew with jokes and humorously vulgar doggerels.[56] Leonid then was taken to a large military hospital in nearby Rzhev, an ancient Volga town in the Tver region west of Moscow, where, by his own account, he pulled a gun on a field surgeon for suggesting that his leg needed to be amputated at the hip. After a grueling operation with no anesthesia, the surgeon saved his leg, and Khrushchev, wearing a heavy cast, was moved to the Barvikha sanatorium, a rustic medical center in Moscow's vicinity, which was reserved for the privileged *nomenklatura*.

During the crash landing, other members of Khrushchev's crew were also injured: the second pilot, Lieutenant Vladimir Elinov, suffered multiple wounds and the gunner, Junior Sergeant Nikolai Novikov, badly hurt his back. Elinov ended up in one of Moscow's military infirmaries, but in the chaos of battle, he was originally declared dead, which remains a generally accepted myth today.[57]

These were the first months of the Great Patriotic War, a devastating and unsettling period during which there was no coherent strategic command. Letters from Leonid's comrades convey the shock and disarray of the entire country. They also show an epic commitment to demolish the Nazi enemy. During the summer of 1941, the country's main slogan was "No Footsteps in Retreat," a battle cry that went hand-in-hand with another popular slogan of the time: "For Motherland and Stalin." These demands came at a heavy price for the Red Army. From June to December of that year, eight million Soviets lost their lives, three million of whom perished as prisoners in the German-occupied territories from Brest to Moscow. The German military losses numbered 831,000. Likewise, while the Soviets lost more than 20,000 tanks and more than 10,000 planes; the Nazis lost just 4,000 tanks and 4,500 planes.[58]

Rules of modern warfare generally dictate that the invader should suffer greater loses, but Russia defied such laws. The Red Army's tactical views failed to evolve; military commanders were still studying the strategies of the former czarist officers, despite rapid advances in technology and dramatic changes in the nature of war. The new Soviet commissars continued to act in the old tradition, attempting to win the war not with strategy or sophistication but with sheer manpower, a paroxysm of soldiers rushing the enemy.

In the Soviet Union, centered as it was around heroic national feats and with a population numbering more than hundred and fifty million, concern for individual casualties was *never* a problem; mass death was considered part of the obvious costs of victory.[59] Worse still, in Stalin's state, which stretched from Finland to Japan, people avoided reporting any trouble to higher authorities for fear of reprisals. Under harsh totalitarian rule, few citizens dared to think independently, convinced (not incorrectly) that individual initiative was a punishable offense. Throughout the early stages of the war, Stalin blamed excessive Russian defeats on his countrymen's unpatriotic behavior. Of course he couldn't accept the truth: the military failures were the result of inexperienced officers and the purges by the NKVD, which shortly before Hitler's invasion had wiped out a capable military command which included the gifted Marshals Mikhail Tukhachevsky and Vasily Blyukher. Indeed, many classified documents released since the Soviet collapse unambiguously point to "the great leader's" own incompetent supervision.[60]

The following, for instance, is Stalin's memorandum addressed to my grandfather, who in a rare attempt to defy his boss tried to show creative vision and save soldiers' lives.

> Kiev, to Comrade Khrushchev:
>
> I have received information that all of you, from the Front Commander to the Military Council members are panicky planning to move the troops to the left bank of the Dnieper. I am warning you, if you make at least one step in that direction, if you don't defend the areas of

UROV [fortified quarters] on Dnieper's right bank, severe retribution awaits you for being cowards and deserters.

Chair of the State Committee of Defense
(I. Stalin). 11/VII/41.[61]

Threatened by the consequences, Khrushchev, who at the time was the political commissar of the Southwestern Front, and the Front's Commander Mikhail Kirponos scrapped their life-saving efforts. The troops remained on Dnieper's right bank, and in September, all four southwestern armies were surrounded and destroyed—one of the worst catastrophes of the Great Patriotic War. Stalin, of course, blamed the local authorities, not himself.

In a letter to Leonid from January 13, 1942, Nikolai Novikov, the gunner, voiced his disbelief about the Soviet military's poor leadership: "Our bomber 'star' Vandyka moved to another battalion," he wrote. "Horrible what happened to him, his whole division was wasted"—the pilots and their planes were used as cannon fodder in defense of Rzhev and the nearby towns buffering the Soviet capital. In a later correspondence, Novikov draws a comparison between the beginning of the war and 1942: "Leonya, now the fighting is not like last year. We never fly out without a protective shield of fighter planes."

The gunner's eight letters, stretching for over a year beginning in August 1941, show a striking dedication to his former commander. Missing the days of special bonding brought about by the war's arduous beginning, Novikov wrote in November 1941:

Leonichka,

Hello, I write to you from human hell. I am in Kazan [city on Volga, four hundred and fifty miles east of Moscow] at the rotating membership battalion, with so many people, you can't imagine. Leonya how are things, how is your leg? Did you go through the medical commission? I am still hoping to work with you. Leonya! Our team was awarded the Medal of the Red Banner. If you get permission to fly please take me with you.

Six months later, in March 1942, the gunner continued with his pleas:

> Forgive me that I barrage you with letters but I've no one else with whom I can share the bad and the good. I wrote to you from Kazan of my little chance to return to aviation—too many people wait in rotation. Will you be allowed to fly? If so please, Leonichka, I beg you, take me with you or I'll sit here until the war ends where the only thing to do is to clean toilets. In aviation I can be very useful demolishing the Fritzes. Leonya! Now life isn't good so I won't describe it. Hope that you won't forget your gunner. I send you a spirited kiss, Nikolai.

Almost every month, Novikov sent Leonid similar requests. In February 1942, the loyal sergeant was as determined to reunite their unit, Team 11 Blue, Khrushchev's four-plane squad:

> Today I was happy to receive your letter. At least I have a link with one close person with whom I can talk about good and bad days of our combat life. I'm in Kalinin [now Tver, regional center hundred miles northwest of Moscow] but I think we'll go elsewhere tomorrow. We are like peasants without horses (with no machines) and will have to retrain. We stay in Migalovo [an airlift base outside of Tver] but you wouldn't have recognized it.[62] Everything is burned, broken; everywhere are signs of "German culture." The hangers are all blown up…Life here is boring with no action. And we've been living like nomads. Leonya! How awfully I want to fly with the old group, now I have no group. Wretched that your leg isn't healing, delaying our reunion.
>
> Can't wait for that happy day when you and I and Elinov will fly together. It'll be better than before, and

without tragic consequences. I think you should take me into any group you enter and I'll, as before and even better, defend the life of my beloved commander and demolish the hordes of retreating fascists. I tried to resurrect our combat missions, using paperwork from other groups to compare sorties. This may be useful when we renew the actions of our squad. That would be the happiest day of my life and grief for the fascists. I remain forever devoted to you, your gunner, Nikolai.

Bands of tight-knit comrades flourish in dangerous circumstances—the greater the adversity, the stronger the emotional connection—and the group's closeness was yet another testimony to the young Khrushchev's ability to cultivate trusted friendships. At the Third Civilian Aviation School, his alleged Trotskyism was based on a refusal to denounce two school instructors. The 134th Regiment was no different. All its men knew Lyuba, and Dultsev, the cameraman, was a weekend fixture in the Khrushchevs's apartment on Bolshaya Polyanka, along with Leonid's pilot friends.

One such pilot friend was George Ivanov, who was as much of a dandy as Leonid. Together they frequented ballet performances, and George never missed the Khrushchevs's Moscow gatherings. He sent his wounded comrade two touching letters. One, dated August 15, 1941, just a week before he was killed in a battle of Smolensk reads:

> Hello sweet friend Leonid!
>
> A fierce Bolshevik hello! This letter is from all your military comrades, but mostly from me, Volodya [Golovanov] and Feodor [Ivanov]. Did you get my earlier note and another one from Kiev, which I personally gave to someone who brought you from the place of the accident? I also forwarded your monthly wages. All your things we put away in storage.

Leonya, it's so unfortunate we aren't together. Trust me, my friend, I miss you as a lover misses a girl. Seriously! Now there's nobody to unburden my soul to. There's only *papasha* (old man) Feodor and Volodya, but Volodya is also leaving and I'll be left with only the old man. Also I miss music, without you there's no harmonica. We all miss you. But that's all for later, as you used to say. Recently I brought back my first shrapnel piece, so we were all in a good mood and even more determined to destroy the fascist bastards. We wish you a speedy recovery. Volodya will write separately from his new place. I am sending you one letter from Lyuba that arrived today. Please be sure to write, I won't delay my answer. I plant a kiss on you, your friend George.

Papasha Feodor Ivanov, George Ivanov's namesake, was an older pilot and a mentor to his fellow airmen. When Leonid and George joined the 134th a year before the war began, Feodor became the boys' dad, as the officers called him. He referred to them as my sons and, in his own letters to Leonid, recalls how the place had quieted down since the young Khrushchev's departure. There were fewer jokes, less laughter, and no more music. Instead, there was just the sorrows of war, the sadness that comes when friends die:

Dear friend, son Leonya.

Yesterday I got your note for which I am very grateful. It came when I needed it most. I want to share thoughts with a friend who was together with us when we pounded the fascist monsters that invaded our motherland. Leonya, on August 23 my beloved son and friend George died. He gave his young life for our country as a faithful soldier. The battle was unequal, our five bombers against thirteen of the fascist jackals. We hit four and then the fighter planes hit another five so we fulfilled our mission demolishing their big cluster of artillery and troops. We mix them up with dirt so they would never do it again. I came back but my wheels were hit, so I had to "belly-land."

I'm sorry for my son, he tried to land, which was a mistake. If he jumped he would have lived. His navigator died with him. George worked gloriously annihilating fascism and before death he hit more than a thousand tanks, artillery, and the scum that came at us. We will not forget him as a devoted son of the motherland.

Leonya, write to me. I wish you the best, to get better and to return to the front lines where you used to be with us. Also many others shake your hand. They all wish you a speedy recovery. I kiss you as a father. Your Feodor.

Two months later, Feodor Ivanov went missing and was presumed dead during an air battle on the Central Front (operations between Russia and Belorussia). Novikov's February letter related this tragedy: "Leonya, I have very sad news about Feodor who didn't return from a sortie. It's been two months, and we've heard nothing."

In another two months, Ivanov turned up in a field hospital far away from the front. Although he returned to aviation, his career stalled; his short-lived "missing in action" status had branded him "disloyal" for life. In August 1964, the retired pilot wrote a letter to the Soviet military newspaper *Krasnaya Zvezda* (Red Star).[63] He talked about his service alongside his two "adopted sons, fallen war heroes," George Ivanov and Leonid Khrushchev. The letter was never published. The elder Khrushchev was ousted in October, and there was no interest in the brave actions of the former premier's son. Ivanov's note also movingly described his own experience of being a postwar outcast who had once been missing in action. He never advanced above the rank of senior lieutenant and worked as a plumber in the tiny far off Kazakh town of Balkhash.

According to the war-era rule announced by Stalin, "There are no Soviet prisoners of war. The Soviet soldier fights on till death. If he chooses to become a prisoner, he is automatically excluded from the Russian community."[64] All MIA soldiers or former Nazi prisoners were considered traitors by definition. No proof of guilt was required. Later, post-Soviet statistics showed that the war claimed over four and a half million MIAs whose bodies were never recovered,[65] including those who died trying to get back to the Red Army across enemy lines. Would-be heroes in most other military cultures, they all had become victims of the USSR's inhumane POW policy; Stalin's own elder son was no exception. Yakov Dzhugashvili was captured in a battle of Vitebsk in 1941, and the Nazis offered his all-powerful father a trade: German Field Marshal Friedrich Paulus for Dzhugashvili, an artillery officer. Stalin refused, uttering what since has become an iconic statement, "We don't trade generals for soldiers."

Life in the Soviet Union was never easy, but after 1941, it was unbearable, especially for the men who had become such close friends. From Novikov's March 1942 correspondence, Leonid learned that his crewmate, Vladimir Golovanov and their Captain Solodenko, "are in a hospital. The captain was badly burned, chiefly his face and neck. Golovanov burned his hands. A missile hit them and the captain made a crash landing. Everybody jumped, but Golovanov forgot to unbuckle the right belt and got entangled. He didn't get out until after the gas tanks blew up."

Golovanov too was a close friend of Leonid's from the Moscow days. Unlike Solodenko, who lost his sight and had to relocate to a small field army base in the faraway Caucuses, Golovanov soon recovered from his wounds and then enrolled in the prestigious Zhukovsky Academy, which Leonid quit only two years prior. After that, Golovanov's fate is unknown. Did he perish like millions of others? Did he make it to May 9 Victory Day? Letters sent to Leonid in August and September 1941 suggested a fun-loving yet ambitious character. One of these letters read:

> I don't know, pet, how long the war will last but I may have an opportunity to escape to Moscow, meet with you and

party. Don't know the fate of other comrades, but George [Ivanov] and I speak of you often. I was also happy and proud to see your father's telegram. I thought, finally Leonka has proven that he and his friends are capable of not just having fun but also can give their all without extra words and swaggering on the job.

We now have a new plane I have examined, and love, of course, but not yet tried in action. Beyond this there is nothing new and cheery. Leonya get well, dearest, and I hope that you will come back to us. Your absence in our battle lines affects me enormously. It was with you I shared all that was laying on my heart.

I have another request, could you send me a "care package" from the capital?

P.S. I expect you to do more missions with me. So please don't waste any time getting better.

In this letter, Leonid's friend recalls Nikita Khrushchev's telegram, which arrived at the end of July while the lieutenant lay under the surgeon's knife in Rzhev. Khrushchev had learned of his son's brave leadership during the "river D offensive"—a mission that liberated the Podolsk area in mid-July 1941; it earned Leonid the Medal of Red Banner and commendations for the rest of the crew. Personal initiative was rather scarce and in great demand at that point in the war. Military successes were frighteningly rare, and in order to boost national morale, the event was written up in a few Soviet newspapers.

I found three articles about Leonid's courageous service in my mother's messy archives. One story from *Komsomolskaya Pravda* (The Komsomol Truth), "Leonid Khrushchev and his Team," described the operation:

Commander of the Komsomol squad of a high-speed bomber plane Leonid Khrushchev that morning showed a savvy tactical decision, which in combination with valor and bravery are signs of true communist heroism. If he had started by bombing the bridge, the noisy explosions would have warned the Nazis, handing them an opportunity to disperse. Yet Khrushchev with a sudden air advance crushed the enemy, making their defense impossible… The enemy ran… Solodenko's squadron turned their tanks into piles of metal… Khrushchev himself had a run in with 13 German fighters, three of which he took down. Even today, when Captain V. Solodenko is asked about his squadron he usually starts with the story of the River D mission, led by Lieutenant Khrushchev. This shows the mentor's pride in his best student, who had shown dazzling initiative during that mission.[66]

Reports about Leonid's valor brought the elder Khrushchev admiration from the fellows at the high command, and when another article in *Pravda* enthusiastically lauded his son as a "vibrant member of the communist society,"[67] finally Nikita seemed to think that the young man's troubles were behind him. As formal as the telegram reads, it was signed with the familial "your father," rather than the professional lieutenant general, Khrushchev's military rank:

> To Lieutenant L.N. Khrushchev. Happy for you and your military comrades. Excellent work, congratulations with the military successes. Continue to fight further the fascist scum, demolish them day and night. Your father N.S. Khrushchev.

Tense relations in the family were no secret to Leonid's friends, who thought that the elder Khrushchev was unfair to the young lieutenant. Leonid may have been a lousy Soviet, but he was a good soldier. The superhuman building of communism wasn't his greatest strength, but he was great at risking his life, albeit with no ideological motivation. The more I think about it, the more I agree with Aunt Rada: Nikita and Leonid were similar, which at least partially explains their tug-of-war. They were both social and personable. Both were constantly burning with inventive ideas, and had that ineffable something about their personalities, the charisma that attracted people to them. Nikita was always disappointed in his son because he thought he wasn't living up to his potential. And that potential, he felt, belonged to the party. In his view, only Bolshevism could provide people with education, purpose, and meaning—everything needed to elevate humanity. But Leonid seemed to believe just the opposite: that to preserve his humanity, he had to stay away from the party. On the face of it, it was a-not-so-original conflict between fathers and sons (in Russia described in an 1862 eponymous novel by Ivan Turgenev), but in our family, it turned into high political drama that reaches all the way into the present.

In twentieth century Russia, you simply couldn't have your own talents. Everything was in service to the state, and there was no love of motherland without love of Lenin, Stalin, and the party. But Leonid's immediate superiors needed good soldiers, not propagandists, and their genius was that instead of demanding sound ideology, they tapped into Leonid's true nature. As long as he kept coming up with creative ways to demolish the enemy, they had no problem with the lieutenant amending a slogan Soviet troops used marching into combat. According to Victor Fomin, a mechanic in Leonid's regiment, Khrushchev often used the slogan "For Motherland and Friendship," dropping the word Stalin from the popular battle cry.

Fomin never wrote letters to Leonid—as in all armies there was a division between officers and those "servicing equipment"—but in 1998, he sent my mother's half-brother Yury (Leonid's son with Esfir Ettinger) ten pages of hand-written notes describing "the real Khrushchev":

> A friendly, unassuming and considerate commander, who knew the planes and their technical readiness well...
> When he found out that I was an amateur singer and played the accordion, we became even closer. He also was

a good musician…and a great leader. We were unsure of what kind of commander he would be, being privileged, but he was good…Leonya often stayed in Moscow, not in the barracks, and other pilots were always welcome to stay with him. They always returned by car. This also added to Leonya's reputation, not only his generosity, he knew how to drive a car.[68]

Fomin recalled how in war and peace the young lieutenant remained a dandy. As ever filled with originality, he invented a new "fashion." Because of his height, Leonid's head stuck above the armored seat of the navigator's cabin. To shield himself from shrapnel, he wore a soldier's metal hardhat over his pilot helmet. At first everyone laughed, and many were afraid to violate the strict military dress code. But Leonid laughed back. "Come on. If they [the authorities] can't protect you, do it yourself." Soon the whole squadron and then the regiment followed suit. And long after their commander was gone, they continued to wear this combination headgear, calling it Leonya's helmet.

⎯⎯◦◦⎯⎯

As the Nazi troops briskly advanced toward Moscow, most of the Khrushchev family, including Lyuba and her two children, departed for Kuibyshev, which served as the makeshift Soviet capital beginning in October 1941 and continuing for the next two years. Along with various ministries and foreign diplomatic missions, the city hosted facilities critical for Soviet defense and military—aviation and engineering plants and higher education institutions like Moscow University. For propaganda purposes, Soviet authorities considered state radio, the Bolshoi, and the music conservatory to be indispensable for the survival and continuity of the communist state, so they relocated to Kuibyshev too. There was even a riverbank bunker built for Stalin, but he remained in Moscow throughout the war.

Grandmother Nina, who always saw positive signs in everything Bolshevik, remembered Kuibyshev with admiration as a "melting pot, the best sacrifices the USSR had to offer." Many of those escaping the Nazi occupation in Kuibyshev received cramped accommodations in this temporary capital. But unlike the Soviet middlemen—workers ranging from engineers to artists—the *nomenklatura* members were well off. Ever a Soviet propagandist, Nina told me that during the war, she felt guilty that the Khrushchevs "affluently occupied two spacious apartments at 2A Vilonovsky Street, in a large building which housed other notable political families and was located a block away from the magnificent banks of the Volga River."

Lyuba recalled with a slight air of displeasure, "Nina Petrovna and her children had five rooms, all to themselves." Originally, the apartment was supposed to host Khrushchev's mother, Ksenia, as well, but she, along with her daughter Arisha and Arisha's two daughters, Irma and Rona, chose to stay in a three-bedroom apartment with Lyuba.

Compared to the rest of the war-torn nation, the elite maintained a cushion against hardship that commoners could not afford. My nanny Masha often remembered how in her poor Orel village, when all men left for the front, the women did everything in their absence, sowing and plowing the fields, among other things. But they were not allowed to keep anything. Whatever crops were produced went to the military or to the countrywide rations. Then a ten-year-old girl, Masha collected dandelions and wormwood as an appetizer and learned to make potato-skin pancakes for the main course—that is when she could find any potatoes at all.

But for the *nomenklatura*, there were special rations twice the size of those given to the average Russian. The Soviet population was divided into five categories, ranked by the importance of their job—party apparatchiks, military plant workers, and scientists were in the first or second tier; doctors and teachers were ranked in the middle as three or four; and plumbers were on the lowest end as 5s. Families in the highest category received a 4.9-pound daily meat ration, for instance, compared to 2.5 for the lowest.[69] Of course, for categories three to five, most of these items were nothing more than meaningless statistics; there were no products such as fresh meat available in stores.

My grandparents on my father's side have been long dead. But I remember when my grandmother Tatiana Blyumina, a Moscow dentist (category four) from an affluent Jewish family, told Masha how for most of the war she received only a pound of bread on a good a day. Her husband—my grandfather—Sergei Petrov, a professor of internal medicine (category three) recalled that sometimes they could get eggs instead of meat, sixteen eggs for two pounds, but they didn't once get butter. "In Kuibyshev," though Lyuba says, "we always had butter." She would have been even better off, but Leonid, with his stepmother's prompting, decided to send a portion of his monthly military ration to Yury and Esfir Ettinger, who remained in Moscow and were in dire straits.

Lyuba doesn't like to discuss this aspect of Leonid's generosity—an indication of jealousy about anything in his life that was not about her. But in Kuibyshev, Lyuba was not the only one who was jealous; there were other tensions in the family as the fight with fascism took its toll on everyone. According to Aunt Rada, Arisha too was constantly annoyed with Nina "for wasting help on anybody." She was even upset with her own brother—he had never done enough to help her. "He is so high up with everything provided for him, he doesn't know how difficult it is for ordinary people like us," Arisha used to say. Of course, her life was not ordinary. Like the rest of the relatives, her family had plenty of amenities provided by Khrushchev's position.[70]

"Every unhappy family is unhappy in its own way," Lev Tolstoy wrote in the opening line to *Anna Karenina*. My well-read grandmother used to reference this line, adding her own twist in a pensive tone: "War turns everything upside down and tests people even when the daily hardships are not present."

At first I thought she was referring to her efforts to rescue her parents from Western Ukraine before the Nazi occupation. To pass through the military checkpoints, she was advised to wear a Soviet Army uniform. "The rescue was successful," Grandmother said. "But when Grandfather learned of my misuse of the uniform, he was very angry. Looking back on it, I have no idea how I could have been so careless. But family comes first, especially during the war. Being so close to the front made me miss my propagandist's duties though. I could have been so useful to the soldiers." Now I am certain that it was just a side story, that without saying this directly, she was juxtaposing her family dedication with Lyuba's lack thereof.

The confirmation first came from Arisha's elder daughter Irma, who was our next-door neighbor in Moscow. In the 1990s, when I was briefly considering writing a book about Grandmother Nina and other Soviet first ladies, I asked Irma about her impressions of the family during the war period. Her view was that "by 1942 Lyuba became the most contested member of the Khrushchev household. Leonya was badly wounded. He could barely walk, and in October 1941 came to recuperate in Kuibyshev. At first she visited him in a hospital but soon stopped showing up. Nina Petrovna had to come in her place."

—⚞⚟—

After a month in Rzhev and another in Barvikha, Lieutenant Khrushchev was moved to the Kuibyshev hospital. His wounds had almost healed, but his broken leg was still in a cast and gave him trouble. Leonid wanted to fly, but the surgeons insisted on a third operation and gently advised him against further army service, *gently*, because the lieutenant often promised to shoot anyone who doubted his fitness for battle.

Stepan Mikoyan (incidentally also a friend of Stalin's younger son, Vasily, his classmate at the prestigious Kacha Aviation School), who also spent time in Kuibyshev recovering after war injury, attested to the young Khrushchev's boisterous antics. Despite the uncertainties of health and doubts of professional future—"the leg was healing very badly and his treatment continued for over a year"—according to Stepan, Leonid was never dour. To amuse himself and his fellow patients, the young Khrushchev constantly played pranks on people, his stepmother being his favorite target. "She is just so easy." He laughed.

A responsible parent, Nina visited him almost every day. Exactly at 4:00 p.m., she walked in the hospital lobby and into her stepson's pranks. Fresh from the surgeon's knife, he often tried to shock Nina—marching without a crutch, balancing on one leg and jumping on the windowsill, or greeting her while hopping up and down the stairs. His buddies were always in stitches over his tricks, and she, appalled by his behavior, was often in a hurry to leave, fuming on her way out.

In February 1942, Leonid, still on crutches, was growing impatient. In the early winter, he and Stepan began sneaking out to an airfield in the hospital's vicinity. Leonid, who used to teach OSOVIAKhIM amateurs in Kiev and Moscow, discovered that some of his former students were now stationed at the aviation training center in nearby Kirzhach. "Leonya was a guy who knew everybody. Everywhere he had friends from days gone by," Mikoyan remembered:

> Although he shouldn't be getting around with his injuries, his former students were too happy to oblige, they let us fly training planes for fun. At times we would get to the city. He was a showoff, I was a fighter pilot, a more prestigious profession than a bomber, but I was fresh out of school. And he was showing me what an expert aviator he was. Once, we made a bet to see who could get closest to the ground. Leonid wasn't only fearless—we all were—he was daring, buzzing over houses, almost touching the roof, especially the house on Vilonovsky, where our families lived.

Aunt Arisha told my mother that same story. During these barnstorming sessions, the whole building shook from the noise of Leonid's hovering plane, and Grandmother Ksenia would raise her cane in the air and shout at the ceiling, "Leonka, you hooligan! Come down at once! I know it's you."

During their time together recovering, Stepan remembered being in the courtyard at the Khrushchev's apartment when Leonid pointed out a chubby toddler playing in a sandbox.

"That's my daughter," he said proudly.

I asked Stepan if he knew Leonid had a wife.

The former pilot shook his head and then confided in me: "If there is a daughter there must be a wife somewhere, I obviously assumed," adding, "but between us, Leonya was very much in love with someone else." As Mikoyan wrote in his 2006 memoir: "There were two young ballerinas from the Bolshoi— Valya Petrova and Lisa Ostrogradskaya, with whom we became friends...these evenings made me love ballet to this day."[71]

Valya was Stepan's passion at the time, Lisa was Leonid's; although while telling me about them, Mikoyan immediately clarified (perhaps because his wife, Eleonora, had just entered the room), "I had platonic relations with Petrova, but Leonid's with Lisa, of course, weren't." Stepan winked at me. "He didn't believe in friendship between sexes."

Both women were background ballet dancers. And ten years later, already in Moscow, my grandmother took the two Yulias, Big and Little, to one of the Bolshoi performances. They were sitting in left side box near to the stage, and during a short pause, my mother overheard a quiet conversation. Big Yulia whispered: "Isn't this Ostrogradskaya in the back, Leonya's old heartthrob?"

Grandmother, examining the stage through binoculars to be absolutely sure, replied, "That's certainly her."

In the early spring of 1942, with snow still on the ground, Stepan regained his strength. Leonid didn't, and the two friends parted. Khrushchev's military file from the Ministry of Defense

Central Archive in Podolsk contains a February 18, 1942, postsurgical medical report, which states that the lieutenant "does not physically qualify for military service."[72]

The young man flew to Moscow for this evaluation. Rada, then thirteen, remembers he was still barely walking but forbade anyone to ask about his condition. Nina took Rada to the capital a few times during the war to see Nikita, and that February their visit coincided with one of Leonid's. All three stayed in the Khrushchevs's new home on 3 Granovsky Street (now Romanov) in a spacious apartment on the top fifth floor of this dark maroon house with many wings and an impressive courtyard. The building still stands on one of the most beautiful and quiet streets in central Moscow close to the Bolshoi, the music conservatory, and the Kremlin. Lustrous parquet floors and large windows in each unit brightened the pristine white walls, and the vaulted ceilings were lined with crown molding. Other political elites, including many in the military—Marshals Semeon Budenny and Semeon Timoshenko—lived there as well. Today the building sides are covered with commemorative plaques to all these late Soviet officials, but Khrushchev's name is still conspicuously missing from these walls.

In January 1942 theaters, factories and government offices began to return to Moscow after the Nazis were pushed away from Naro-Fominsk, a city forty miles southwest of the Soviet capital. A cheerful atmosphere pervaded the city. The Bolshoi's gold and crimson baroque auditorium was filled with plain green military fatigues. Everyone exuded hope: if Moscow hadn't fallen, neither would the motherland. Rada remembers being very proud to be seen there with her big brother, the war hero.

In Leonid's personal documents, along with his comrades' letters, his father's telegram, and other papers—a military identification card, an address book with Moscow phone numbers, war orders and medals, all carefully preserved by my grandmother—there is another medical report from July 21,

1942, five months after the earlier document. In faded blue ink, written on a crudely stamped form of a math school notebook, it reads: "Khrushchev is ready to continue his service with no reservation in the 134th High-Speed Bomber Aviation Regiment or in another regiment, following his military assignment." Who did he charm to get this positive assessment? I was never able to find out.

As if health troubles weren't enough, Leonid decided to return to the front not as a bomber but as a fighter pilot, thanks in part to Stepan's influence. Fighters were the kings of the air force, and Leonid too wanted this royal status. Stepan confirmed to me that his friend had to go through a grueling process—writing to various authorities to get permission to retrain. The young Khrushchev was determined: he had been flying for seven years now, and he simply couldn't fail.

Retraining wasn't unusual during the war—his bomber comrade Golovanov went to the Zhukovsky Academy. And Leonid, eager to fulfill his own romantic dreams, filed nine notes requesting to become a fighter pilot. A draft of one handwritten petition remained in his papers:

> To the Air Force Command of the 22nd Army: I, Lieutenant Leonid Khrushchev, respectfully inquire about a possibility to intensify my qualifications as a military pilot. As a bomber aviator I completed 31 battle missions. For the suffering motherland I was avenging my comrades so the enemy should remember what it means to go against Stalin Falcons. I will bring even more damage to the fascists as a fighter. We, Stalin's Falcons, have steel blood and the fascists will not escape us. In becoming a fighter pilot I will not only be pounding the enemy, I will step up in the front lines responding to the call of our leader and our commander, Father Stalin.

Writing "Father Stalin" wasn't typical of Leonid. As I read this note closely, I discovered that most of the wording had been taken from one of *papasha* Feodor Ivanov's letters, which was replete with the jargon of the era. The young Khrushchev was not well versed in Soviet propaganda (his stepmother's professional expertise failed to rub off), so instead of trying to formulate the right communist sentiment on his own, he borrowed his older mentor's enthusiastic words.[73]

Leonid's persistence paid off. That spring, Lieutenant Khrushchev, who was freshly promoted to the rank of senior lieutenant, left Kuibyshev for the Third Training Joint Aviation Regiment in Sasovo, a small town in the Ryazan region some two hundred miles southeast of Moscow. And on December 19, 1942, following several months in Sasovo, where he trained to fly a Yak-7B fighter plane, he was deployed to the southwest Smolensk (now Kaluga) region as a squad commander of the 18th Vitebsk Guards Fighter Regiment of the First Aviation Army. Official documents stored in Khrushchev's file in the Podolsk military archive show that this appointment was supposed to have come sooner but was delayed first because Leonid was wanted back in the 134th Bomber Regiment and then because of an offer to hold a military staff position in Moscow.[74] But Leonid couldn't wait to get to the front and kept filing requests to be assigned to a fighter pilot division.[75]

Authorized travel instructions from the 18th Regiment, kept in Khrushchev's posthumous papers at home, show that even as a squad commander during the first two months of 1943, he mainly delivered planes from provincial towns like Khimki and Kaluga back to his base, the Khotenki airfield, in the Kozelsk area hundred and forty miles southwest of Moscow. Some orders indicate a few stopovers in the capital. Gontar, Big Yulia's husband, wrote in his diary: "These seem to make Leonid's lack of combat a bit more tolerable. I ran into him while on a theater business in Moscow. He was eager to fight, but the city certainly provided some nice distraction."

That distraction I learned was yet another love interest. Long after the war, my teenage mother joined her friend and neighbor, Nina, Marshal Budenny's daughter, for tea at Marshal Timoshenko's apartment, on the second floor of their elite Granovsky Street building. When Olga, Timoshenko's daughter, saw my mother she immediately blurted out: "My God, you have Leonya's face. You walked into the room just like him and sat right where he used to sit. You know he was in love with my sister Katya, but after his death, she married Vasily Stalin in 1944."

It's not clear exactly how intimate Leonid's relations with Katya were, but Olga told my mother that her sister was noticeably heartbroken when Leonid went missing in action. She even tried to find details of his death on her own, attempts that her family apparently quickly discouraged. What makes me also believe that their relations were more than just innocent courtship is that the USSR was far from puritanical. Though Soviet culture remained patriarchal at its root, sex with multiple partners was certainly not as stigmatized as it was in the Anglo-Saxon West.

Maria, Nina Budennaya's mother, was a neighbor of the Khrushchevs, not only in Moscow but in Kuibyshev as well. Before she passed away in 2006, she and I had many lengthy conversations over the course of a decade about my family. One time Maria said, the Stalin-Khrushchev rivalry over Katya always concerned her immensely. Ever since all three met in Kuibyshev— Leonya in the hospital, Vasily briefly visiting his then first wife Galina Burdonskaya at the birth of their son Alexander, and Katya Timoshenko in evacuation along with other *nomenklatura* families—Mrs. Budenny didn't think their "'friendship' was appropriate." She regularly saw the trio from the window of her Vilonovsky apartment:

> Everyone knew that both boys were courting Katya. They sat on a green bench next to the entrance, smoking, waiting for her to come out. She would exit in the cloud of perfume, little fancy hat and all. Leonya's black car was

ready to take her wherever, but Vasya had more than a limousine; he had a driver. Vasya, what a scandal, just had a newborn! But he thought no rules ever applied to him! And Leonya too! He could only walk with a cane but still wanted to compete with Vasily.

Only a few months before and with the same lack of embarrassment, Leonid was spending time with Lisa, the ballerina. Maria worried about Grandmother, whom she always admired for her firm character and principles. Nina was quietly upset about Leonid's promiscuity and feared it could harm our family's reputation.

"And what about Lyuba?" I asked. "How did she feel about him jumping from one woman to another? It's humiliating to be an abandoned wife for the whole world to see."

To this, the usually candid Mrs. Budennaya cryptically replied, "You'd better ask her." Eventually I did.

Now one hundred years old, Lyuba never eats before noon. "I only drink lemon water. It makes my skin look better, and I don't want to gain weight," she explained to me during my last visit to Kiev in 2013. For decades, she spent thirty minutes of every day doing calisthenics: 1,100 months, 4,350 weeks. "Never have I missed a morning," she said, looking at me with disapproval as I finished my third cup of coffee.

Every year that I come here, we sit in her living room and flip through old photographs, which are painstakingly arranged in two enormous photo albums. Considering all the hardships she has endured, these scrapbooks with glossy covers, decorated with sunny beach vacation scenes, seem unsuitably bright. Lyuba is always excited to share the ever-expanding details of her past. "What else can I tell you?" she asks, treating me as her own personal biographer, the sole chronicler of her "glamorous" life, in which Nikita and Nina, Leonid and my mother are just the *corps de ballet* that enhances her greatness.

Yet attempting to reconstruct Lyuba's life story is a challenge. Not because the information is as unavailable as it is with Leonid—his life was short and his parents, embarrassed by their son's flaws, were determined to keep his adventures out of the public eye. With Lyuba, the information is too available. Older than the USSR (and having survived the Soviet empire), she is still full of life, vigor, and optimism. She seems frozen in time, the model communist of the 1930s. Her sunny disposition is now only illustrated on old propaganda posters, those icons of Soviet triumph, which convey the same sort of falsely fervent sentiment as something Stalin said in 1935 as famine ravaged Ukraine: "Life has improved, comrades; life has become more joyous."[76]

Most of Lyuba's narratives, I've learned, are a balancing act between her reputation as a saintly Virgin Mary type and an entrancing woman that no man could resist, a Mary Magdalene of sorts.[77] Other aspects of her life are mired in inconsistency, even if in recent years Lyuba has refined her life's story and ironed out many of the messy details. Growing up, I knew that Lyuba had married once before her relationship with Leonid and once after him. Now, however, she says Leonid was her *only* husband and has written letters to newspaper editors expressing this sentiment in response to their articles about the young Khrushchev.[78] If anyone happens to bring up Leonid's other women, she will invariably argue that she was the *only* woman he ever loved. "He had just one official wife," she said. "*Me*, the one accepted by his family."

Several years ago, I learned otherwise. It was 2:00 a.m. in New York when the phone rang. Like most people today, I keep my BlackBerry right next to my pillow. And so when I saw that it was my mother calling, I suddenly became worried. What could possibly have happened in Moscow? Or has she just forgotten the time difference?

I picked up.

"What? Did Lyuba die? It's the middle of the night here."

All I heard on the other line was my mother's heavy breathing. She couldn't even get the words out. Like many Russians, my mother tends to be overtaken by emotions (our literature well attests to this tendency). Once, she was in tears when I told her that I no longer liked poetry—so I wasn't sure if something was actually seriously wrong.

"What's going on?" I asked again.

"Imagine! No marriage!" my mother cried.

"No! It can't be!" I exclaimed, knowing she meant Lyuba and Leonid and ready to cry myself.

Mother was still hyperventilating, hardly able put together a sentence, and my heart sank. We are all illegitimate; what am I doing writing about the Khrushchevs?

I didn't even know who we were anymore. Listening to my mother slowly regain her ability to speak, I stood up, turned on the lights, and paced around my East Village apartment. Finally calming herself, my mother tried to justify Lyuba's actions: "Mother and Father were never married after all."

Not marrying after the revolution is not the same as being unwed in the 1930s in the midst of Stalin's order to return to traditional family values. But I didn't want to upset her more, so I held my tongue and let her talk.

> Vasily Stalin thought of many women as his wives. His sister Svetlana called her relations with Brajesh Singh [an Indian diplomat] a marriage. Anastas [Mikoyan] later told me, in 1964 Svetlana really wanted to make it official, but in the USSR even Stalin's daughter couldn't withstand the antiforeign ideology. So he encouraged her to just *act* as if they were married, live together, and so on. If this didn't matter then, in our day and age it's really irrelevant.

"You are right," I finally replied. Yet for me the issue isn't that Lyuba and Leonid hadn't actually married. It's that she had lived a lie, deliberately and consistently, for more than seventy years, "all for the sake of my daughter," as she explained to me next time I talked to her. Mother never discussed her parents' nuptials; the relations were simply assumed. I, on the other hand, repeatedly interviewed Lyuba for this book, seeking details about their wedding. Always making me feel that my questions were somehow inappropriate, she would elusively respond, "I don't remember," lying to my face over and over again.

This was the most egregious instance of Lyuba's dishonesty—or maybe self-delusion is a better word—but it certainly wasn't the first. Leonid did have numerous affairs, but for years, there were rumors that Lyuba, her Virgin Mary image notwithstanding, too had initiated flings, most notably with a French military attaché named Raymond Schmittlein. This relationship was in fact a root cause for her future life's unraveling; her decision to get involved with the Frenchman in the middle of war affected our whole family for decades to come.

Lyuba has always denied the affair, and I understand why. A relationship with Schmittlein would interfere with her image of Leonid's grieving widow. For example, in his 2004 widely acclaimed biography of Khrushchev, Amherst college professor William Taubman only writes of this vital French encounter, "After Lyonia (*sic*) returned to the front, Liuba (*sic*) dared accompany a French military attaché (whom she described as 'an amazing attractive man') to the theater."[79]

Once, more than a decade ago, I caught a glimpse of the real story though. "Raymond was irresistible, and he couldn't resist my charms. We were destined to have a passionate *roman* (love affair)," Lyuba said. That conversation was for the possible book about Grandmother Nina's role as the Soviet first lady, so I had the tape record running. Despite her clear confession, since then Lyuba has never repeated that admission ever again.

"In Kuibyshev," she recently recalled, as we flipped through a photo album, "I had no friends. When Leonya was released from the city hospital in the winter of 1942, he wanted to introduce me 'to the splendid people,' he said. That's how I met Vera Chernetskaya, the wife of the French journalist, Jean Nau."

Stumbling upon a page in the middle of an album, Lyuba paused. On one side was a picture of her and Leonid in 1940 on the Moscow River beach. She is wearing a weightless white chiffon dress and stands on a large rock, towering over the young Khrushchev. She looks confident with her hands held firmly on her hips as though she, a superwoman, were about to take off in flight. He seems cold in a pair of long, black, satin trunks, bony and boyish looking with his shoulders hunched and his fingers knotted together. On the opposite page is another photo of Lyuba; this time she is wearing a sexy black swimsuit as she stands on the shore of the Volga in 1942, making eyes at the camera. "Schmittlein took this photo," she said flirtatiously. Sometimes, I guess, she just can't help herself.

"We walked into Vera's luxurious suite at the high-end Bristol hotel, just a few blocks from the *nomenklatura* house on Vilonovsky Street. It was a reminder of the fun, fancy life we used to have in Moscow," Lyuba continued. "The party was for the Normandy Neman, a French-Soviet allied fighter Air Force squadron, serving on the Western Front. As a distinguished pilot, Leonya was asked to greet them."

Lyuba found the time she spent with her French friends incredibly exciting. These people must have served as an escape from her complex family life with the man who enjoyed his own friends and parties, didn't seem in a rush to marry, and left Kuibyshev shortly after anyway.

Most of the French spoke no Russian, but Raymond Schmittlein did. The handsome attaché was very attentive and immediately invited her to see "The Fountain of Bakhchisarai" at the Bolshoi ballet.

According to French researcher Corine Defrance, Schmittlein was Charles de Gaulle's representative of France Libre in 1942 and was thus responsible for relations with the Soviet military and the press;[80] Defrance confirmed that there was indeed a passionate fling between the French diplomat and the young Soviet. In 2009, Corine and I met at a lovely Parisian bistro in the Marais district, and over several espressos, we compared notes on Raymond, Lyuba, and Leonid. "These three were made for each other," my new friend said. "Schmittlein was someone who had a girl in every port." He married a German woman while working in the Baltic States before the war. After leaving the USSR in 1943, he went to Algiers where he had another relationship with Irene Giron, a Brit with a German mother.

The Frenchman's German sympathies prompted suspicion that he was a spy, though it was unclear for which country. "His position was blurry," Corine explained. "France hated Germany, but he spoke German fluently, had a Germanic name being from Alsace and a German wife. He may have been interested in Lyuba, also half German on her mother's side, thinking she could provide some valuable inside Politburo information. If he was a spy, he may have thought to recruit her, turn her into the Russian Mata Hari."

Despite the rumors, Schmittlein's ability to deal with complex diplomatic issues made him attractive to De Gaulle's war efforts.[81] Such a respected diplomat would have been an amazing catch for Lyuba. That is, if he hadn't already been married.

Lyuba's affair with the Frenchman is a striking omission in her narrative, an omission that pervades historical accounts of those writing about Khrushchev and has become accepted academic fact—reference William Taubman for one. Yet the relationship was well known around small Kuibyshev. Jean Cathala, a wartime representative of the Alliance Française, whom Lyuba doesn't remember meeting, in his memoir *With Neither Flowers Nor Guns* details how Schmittlein once showed him Leonid's military identification. "His wife spent the night with me,"[82] Schmittlein explained. Moreover, Arisha's daughter Irma insisted that "it was much worse with Lyuba": there was not just this Frenchman, but another one, Jean Nau, Vera Chernetskaya's journalist husband, and also a fling with the Moscow music conservatory conductor.

Even if I was never able to confirm these latter love interests, Irma's indignation is not without Soviet logic. Women's liberation was a big part of the vocabulary of the period, but in reality, machismo was never uprooted. Men could have a wife and multiple mistresses on the side, while women were judged harshly for that same behavior. In communist society, which scrappily slapped together the extremes of patriarchy and progress, Lyuba couldn't win. She was a woman and an individualist (Irma thought of it rather as selfishness) in a country that recognized no individual interests in serving grandiose causes—be it the dictatorship of the proletariat, the war with Germany, or world communism.

By 1942, the glamour of being a Khrushchev had entirely worn off, and Lyuba felt she had to do something about it. Leonid was away retraining, and she was lonely and unmarried in a family that had little chance to become her own. Meanwhile, the courteous Frenchman described the charmed life one could lead in stylish Paris, with proper credentials and the right education. And so as Lyuba explained to me, Schmittlein influenced her decision to enroll in the Military Institute of Foreign Languages, which primarily prepared Soviet foreign intelligence officers.[83]

Surveying a history of female espionage in his 1959 book *Sisters of Delilah: Stories of Famous Women Spies*, retired MI6 agent E. H. Cookridge (also known as the popular spy author Edward Spiro) wrote: "The prize in the eyes of most women spies has been…the capitulation of men…Women agents whom I have met admitted that they have been unable to resist a life in which the main object was to subdue men whose very positions should have made them impervious to feminine charms and seductions."[84] This description neatly fits Lyuba's reputation as a "vampire woman," as my sister Ksenia likes to call her—someone who desires to reign over men. Learning a foreign language was

Lyuba's ticket to power and a new romantic career in covert operations. But to acquire this power, she would have to leave her children behind.

When Nina learned of her daughter-in-law's decision to attend the language institute in a nearby town of Stavropol-on-Volga (now Togliatti), she tried to dissuade her. "Lyuba, you can't leave your children in bad times. You never know what might happen to them, to you, to us..." This wisdom came from a woman who had evacuated as many of her family members as she could and had almost twenty people in her care during the war.

But Lyuba was unrelenting. "I am a free being. Don't control my life," she told Nina. "My husband is at war, and I am uncertain about my children's future. I need to get an education to care for my family. Flying is not an option, and my geological work is banal."

Obviously, Lyuba's old professions didn't seem glamorous anymore. But the mystery for decades was the oddity of her logic: she wanted to go away in order to be a better mother. Why? The Khrushchevs would have supported her whether Leonid was dead or alive—as far as anyone knew, she was their son's wife. Now I know that Lyuba wasn't leaving because she needed a job or feared to lose her husband; she was leaving because she didn't know whether he would become her husband at all. Studying French was a path to success she always desired. If the men in her life (Schmittlein married, Leonid off having affairs and fighting war) were unavailable, she would take care of herself.

The lie that the young couple told the family about their marriage three years prior came back to haunt Lyuba in Kuibyshev. The best option was perhaps to explain everything to Nina, who would have been empathetic, as she was also unmarried. She would surely have blamed Leonid. After two unsuccessful unions, he clearly had reason to lie. But a proud and angry Lyuba settled on revenge, which she took in the form of an affair with the Frenchman. For a wife of a Soviet officer and daughter-in-law of the political commissar of the Red Army, that was an obvious path to scandal.

The scandal was even greater as she was also abandoning her children. My mother, then two, stayed with the rest of the Khrushchevs kids—"She would be better off with you," Lyuba told Nina. Tolya, who was nine, remained with Arisha. He never got to call Leonid father—Lyuba didn't allow it without a formality of marriage, but Arisha, who knew none of this, was happy to assist her nephew's "wife." After six months, however, she begged Lyuba to take her son to Stavropol—the neighbors in the Vilonovsky house were complaining. According to Maria Budennaya, his behavior worried many parents. Caught flashing his privates in front of girls and urinating in public, he was kicked out of school and had to be tutored privately. "At times Tolya seemed a flashback to Leonid, though he was gross, not charming," said Mrs. Budennaya.

The institute was only forty miles up the Volga, but a world away from Lyuba's old life. In leaving Kuibyshev she thought she was giving up all things Khrushchev. About five years ago, she told me the story of her departure: "It was early September morning. The weather was beautiful. I said my good-byes and was looking forward to my new life. The car came to pick me up, and while we were pulling out of the driveway, I saw Yulochka running after the car—she was only two and still wobbly, she fell down a few times—crying at the top of her lungs, 'Mama, mama, don't go away.' This scream still rings in my ears."

"You must regret that you left with Leonid dying and everything that followed?" I asked.

"I don't regret anything!" she retorted. "I wanted to become a professional interpreter." Of course, just a few years before she was as keen on becoming a professional pilot. And the memory of her little daughter chasing the car and begging her to stay is not a memory of remorse but of pride. "I was so loved by that girl. She didn't want to let me go," Lyuba said, her face lighting up as she recalled such filial devotion.

Lyuba didn't write her first letter to my mother until seven months into her Stavropol life when Leonid was declared missing in action. The actual letter has been lost, but Grandmother preserved Rada's touching reply from April 13, 1943. The note explained how happy Little Yulia was to get her mom's letter, how she made everyone read it until she knew it by heart, how errant the girl had become, jumping into every puddle and splashing water everywhere, how funny it was that she used adult words with great authority but was mixing up her Ls and Rs—*necessalily, appalently*. Concluding the letter, Rada asked Lyuba to write to Yulia separately—it would mean so much to her. But the next letter Lyuba wrote to her daughter was thirteen years later in 1956 following the twentieth party congress.

In the summer of 1943, around the time Little Yulia hugged her grandfather's knee recognizing him as her only family, the KGB searched Lyuba's modest room at the Military Institute of Foreign Languages for evidence of *svyazi s inostrantsami* (contact with foreigners). A playbill from the "Fountain of Bakhchisarai" ballet she attended with the French attaché was deemed incriminating material, and she was arrested for espionage. The security commandant of the Vilonovsky building, Vladimir Bozhko, wrote a report to the NKVD about Lyuba's consorting with foreigners while her husband was off heroically fighting the Nazis. This accusation was even more convincing, as Lyuba's mother was German-born and so was Schmittlein's father. And because the French diplomat was a suspected spy, Lyuba's decision to study French at a military intelligence school became further proof of her guilt. Article 58, Section 1b, of the USSR Criminal Code, signed in 1934 shortly before the Great Purges, pronounced it illegal to make contact with foreigners "with counter-revolutionary purposes" and was "punishable by the supreme measure of criminal sentence—shooting with confiscation of all property."[85] Essentially, that meant anyone in touch with a foreigner could be accused of betraying the country.

No wonder in his 1940 personal autobiography Leonid was very explicit, "Wife has never been abroad." "Abroad" always brought suspicion on any Soviet. Despite its declared policy of internationalism, the USSR disapproved of its citizens having contacts with those of other countries, particularly capitalist ones. In an ideology-driven, inward-looking dictatorial system, the Kremlin authorities feared open competition with the Western world and thus refused to grant basic freedoms to its citizens, including the freedom of choosing friends who didn't hold a red passport with the hammer and sickle on the cover.[86]

Over the years Lyuba's arrest became a core justification for everything in her life. It allowed her to maintain that leaving her daughter behind was beyond her control. "I was imprisoned and Yulochka had to stay in the grandparents family, and call Nikita Sergeevich father."[87] Yet in all Lyuba's conversations and interviews, she regularly omits the exact timeline: the fact that Yulochka had to stay with her grandparents long before the arrest.

Since Lyuba has never been fully open about the Schmittlein affair, a more explicable version of history has become a staple of reporters' and historians' accounts: her arrest was part of Stalin's political trend of punishing close relatives of his associates in order to keep those associates in check, and Nikita was just too afraid to defend her. Of course, in 1943, Nikita was not that important to Stalin; moreover, there was no such brave soul in the dictator's entourage dared to defend one's relatives, but the burden had been shifted—from Lyuba's character to Khrushchev's position.[88]

In her notes from the 1980s (included in the full three-volume edition of Khrushchev's *Memoirs* edited by Uncle Sergei and released in 2005–2007), my grandmother referred to Lyuba as a victim too. "Yulochka…grew up with us. Her mother…was unjustly repressed in 1942 and remained in the Stalinist camps until the middle of the 1950s."[89] Safeguarding the family against scandals, Nina mentioned nothing else. Leonid's and Lyuba's real past was papered over—don't speak ill of the dead or the gulag victims—which allowed the mystery of Lyuba's affair and imprisonment to go unquestioned. Aunt Rada explained these times as obeying the "ideology of silence"—when Leonid's "wife" was detained, she knew not to ask any questions. And after all these years, Grandmother's silence has backfired. Instead of shielding the family from the rumors, it created more of them.

During Lyuba's ten-month hold in the Lubyanka prison, Victor Abakumov, the ruthless Chief of NKVD Counterintelligence (SMERSH), personally interrogated her. Yet Lyuba still admires Abakumov as a "flirtatious and impressive looking man…despite his offensive questions. A *bon vivant*, dressed impeccably each day in a different suit." In her account, Abakumov sat on his desk, very close, and "playfully" asked her whether she and Schmittlein, "both Germans," had shared any documents or secrets. And then, appealing to her female vanity, threatened her with the loss of her "beautiful white teeth."

In the end, Lyuba was somehow able to keep her teeth. Did she court the infamous NKVD apparatchik just as she did Schmittlein? Rather than receiving a death sentence normally meted out for her type of "counter-revolutionary crimes," her punishment was five years of hauling trees in a prison camp called Temlag in the woods of Mordovia, a region four hundred miles southeast of Moscow. These camps were harsh—the convicts had to work eighteen hours a day, and many died from malnutrition and disease. Rape and assault were common, especially in the female brigades.

Yet Lyuba insisted that "nobody was raped in the Gulag."[90] Instead she offered me a version of prison that's only fit for a fairytale: "The guards were awfully nice, logging was hard, and we were young girls. The whole first week it was cold and they made us a fire so we wouldn't freeze to death during the day. They boiled us tea, gave us food. We were inexperienced and didn't have a stash of anything extra—snacks, clothes—like other already seasoned *zeks* (inmates)."[91]

I wanted to know what happened afterward. But this first week was the only memory Lyuba was willing to share: "Soon I began to suffer from lung disease, and when I got better, I was able to get a job as a nurse in the hospital's tuberculosis wing for the rest of my time."

While in the hospital with a high fever, life-threatening pneumonia and with her weight falling to roughly seventy pounds, Lyuba said she had a vision, "I am riding a white swan in the clouds, and suddenly, I hear Nikita Sergeevich demanding I should be freed. I woke up thinking, 'I will survive, no matter what.'" Did she really dream of Khrushchev or was this a later addition, an attempt to establish a greater connection between the Soviet leader and his "favorite" daughter-in-law?

Either way, she survived, but we will never know exactly what she endured.

⎯⎯⎯

During his assignments to Moscow, Leonid didn't stay in his own apartment on Polyanka but rather in his father's flat on Granovsky in order to be near his new love, Katya Timoshenko. His place on Polyanka, which he used to share with Lyuba, no longer felt like home. As relayed in one of the letters from Novikov, the gunner, Leonid just gave it away to the cameraman, Dultsev, who had his own girl troubles and used the residence during his time off from documenting the war. In February of 1943, Leonid had become intensely restless, even dismayed at his menial duties: he had fought hard to become a fighter pilot only to wind up shuttling equipment.

Judging by the correspondence with his comrades, reassignment delays were common during the war. In Leonid's case, according to Stepan, the delay was a special order from the top. At the end of the war, Mikoyan said, his friend Vasily Stalin confided in him that by 1943, with the number of Soviet casualties rising, particularly after the grisly battle of Stalingrad,[92] Stalin made a "quiet decision to keep the Politburo children out of harm's way."[93] The 1943 death of Vasily's half-brother Yakov in a Nazi camp, along with other high profile deaths, made the Generalissimus apprehensive about losing more notable figures. After Stalingrad, Stepan himself was moved to the safer 12th Regiment based in the capital because his younger brother Vladimir, also a fighter pilot, went missing in action during that devastating battle.[94]

Ivan Pavlov, Khrushchev's mechanic at the 18th Fighter Regiment, testified to his commander's "unhappy state of mind"[95] as he was kept out of the battle:

> My lieutenant was depressed that the regiment's command didn't let him fly combat missions, instead forcing him just to "iron air" over our airfield under the pretext of our protection. Khrushchev complained. "Why do they keep me still as a tree, am I not a citizen of this country? Why should I sit here, watching others return from a battle, and I am not allowed to go?"
>
> His voice trembled. We were in different parts of the plane, and I didn't see his eyes, but I felt that he was ready to cry. Khrushchev then firmly decided to complain to the commanders of the regiment, the division or even the army.

Leonid was so distraught that he was ready to accept a demotion and become a regular pilot if his superiors didn't believe he was qualified enough to lead a squad. According to Pavlov, Khrushchev kept repeating. "If I am forced to stay on the ground, I can't go on living!"

When the high command arrived for inspection in early March, Leonid went to talk to generals Khudyakov and Zakharov, the Chief of the First Aviation Army and the 303d Fighter Air Division respectively. Afterward, he was no longer leading the squad but was allowed to fly missions as an ordinary airman and a wingman to Senior Lieutenant Ivan Zamorin, the ace pilot in the regiment and commander of its second squadron. Pavlov further recalled: "My boss's behavior changed dramatically. He looked fresh and smiling…on 11 March 1943…in a good mood, he sat in the cockpit and, together with Zamorin in the lead, departed on a mission."

For Senior Lieutenant Khrushchev, the day couldn't have begun better. The sun was bright and melting a few patches of snow still on the ground. Finally assigned to a real squadron with ten other airmen from the Zamorin crew, Leonid took off at 7:00 a.m. in his Yak-7B, a single-seat aircraft. The most untested in the group—it was his first active mission as a fighter pilot—Leonid could barely keep up with Zamorin during the two morning battles, which occurred over the Bryansk region. Other fighters too were looking after him in the air. Leonid was the son of the political commissar, so no one wanted to be responsible for his death. At some point, Zamorin signaled that Khrushchev should finish off an already damaged Nazi plane, but the young lieutenant was unable to promptly down the aircraft, and it escaped to its own airfield.

When Leonid returned to the Khotenki base, witnesses remembered that he was brimming with excitement and gesticulating, showing off how he "drove off the Fritz." His comrades couldn't help but smile.[96] Stepan told me that he heard that Zamorin didn't relish having to babysit Leonid; the whole crew felt he could hold them back. "But you know," Stepan added with a grin, "everyone loved Leonya. He always got what he wanted, and they all had to cover the novice."

It was already late afternoon, and the sun was about to set when suddenly the fighters received another call to arms. The battle took place in the foggy skies over Zhizdra in the Kaluga-Orel regions, which was then occupied by the Nazis. It was the most serious sortie that day, and due to poor visibility, every fighter in the Zamorin squadron had to take care of his own Fritz, with little time to attend to their green comrade. Some chased the Germans toward Orel and Bryansk; others went as far as Smolensk. Zamorin and Khrushchev separated from the rest of the group. The battle became heated. The Soviets were outnumbered, losing sight of one another in a haze of smoke.

On that fateful day, Zamorin allegedly flew west alone and downed two Nazi planes. Returning to the Zhizdra area, he found neither his wingman nor any German aircrafts remaining. It was already dark when the flight leader came back to Khotenki, never to see Khrushchev again.

According to Zamorin's finely detailed description, on the last day of his life Leonid wore:

> A black leather radio-helmet, a dark brown leather jacket with an Astrakhan gray collar, tall boots with zippers (the wounded leg made it impossible to put on a regular boot) and dark brown fur-lined gloves. He wore a high collar drab grey shirt with pockets and senior lieutenant's epaulets. On the left, pinned the Medal of the Red Banner, on the right—the Guards badge. His knickers were the same color as the shirt. Instead of an undershirt Leonid always wore a seaman's striped-shirt. Belt with an officer star, holstered a Walther; in a shoulder strap was another firearm, a Mauser. Watch on the wrist seems to be Longines. He had a silver cigarette case, with a hunting dog and an inscription: "On your birthday from your wife."

Lyuba denies ever giving him this case. Could it have been a gift from Rosa Trevis, his wife from the previous, short-lived marriage? I have never found out.

Nikita Khrushchev and Efrosinia Pisareva, Yuzovka ca 1916

The Pisarev Sisters, ca 1914

Ksenia Khudyakova, Nikita's formidable mother, Moscow 1930s

Nikita Khrushchev, the young Bolshevik on the rise, early 1920s

Yulia and Leonid Khrushchev with their father Nikita, ca 1924

Yulia and Leonid Khrushchev are going fishing in Kiev

Finally on Iosif Stalin's radar. Grandfather, the leader of
Moscow communists, with his Kremlin boss, 1936

Lyuba Sizykh, pilot in training, is always a
lone woman among men, Kiev 1937

Lyuba, a pilot trainee, and Leonid Khrushchev,
her instructor, at the Kiev airport, 1938

Lyuba (middle) celebrating 1939 New Year in Moscow,
photo taken by Leonid

Lyuba, an exemplary young communist,
with *Pravda* newspaper, Moscow 1940

Lyuba and Leonid on the Moscow River beach,
August 15, 1940

Leonid at his airbase near Podolsk, 1940

Leonid and daughter Yulia (my mother) in 1941 before
Leonid leaves for the Great Patriotic War front

Leonid in Moscow to receive health evaluation in the winter of 1942

War letters to Leonid from his bomber comrades in 1941 and 1942

Leonid Khrushchev with Stepan Mikoyan and his
girlfriend, Valentina Petrova, Kuibyshev, 1942

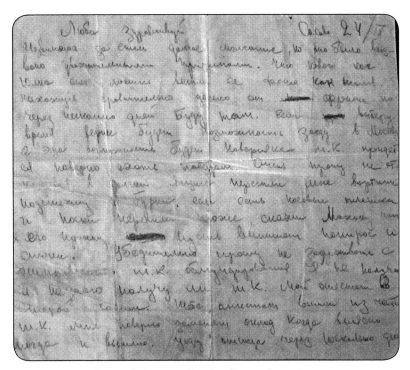

Leonid's letter to Lyuba, September 1942.
Cold and distant, it asks for matches and clothes
to prepare Leonid for the front

Lyuba on the Volga beach in Kuibyshev in 1942,
photo taken by Raymond Schmittlein

In the Kuibyshev evacuation in August 1943 from left to right:
[back] Grandmother Nina, Ekaterina Kukharchuk (Grandmother's
mother), Nina (Grandmother's niece), Rada, Berta Serebrier (Sergei's
nurse); [front] unknown boy, Sergei, Elena "Lena," Yulia (my mother).
During the war, Grandmother had over 20 people in her care.

Sergei, Lena and Yulia. The family always liked dogs

Leonid and comrades at the front, near Zhizdra in Spring 1943

Nikita Khrushchev and his future Kremlin successor,
Leonid Brezhnev, at the Ukrainian Front, 1943

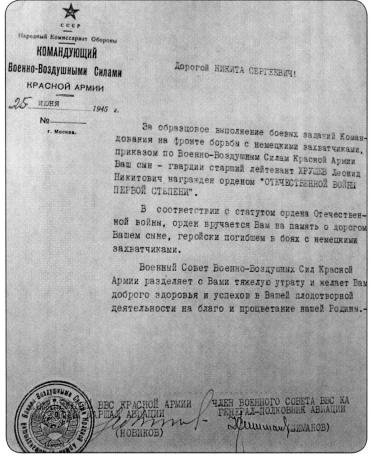

Letter to Nikita Khrushchev from the Red Army command awarding the late Leonid with the Great Patriotic War Order First Degree, June 1945

Leonid's Great Patriotic Order First Degree certificate, 1945

After Victory: Nikita Khrushchev in Ukraine, 1945

Little Yulia, my mother, with her new mother Nina
Kukharchuk (Khrushcheva) in Moscow, Spring 1946

Grandmother Nina cared a lot about children's health; they would take trips out to the sea for fresh air. With Rada, Big Yulia (Leonid's sister), Zina (Grandmother's niece), and Little Yulia, my mother, on the Baltic Sea, Latvia, July 1947

TRIBULATIONS AND TRIALS

In 1987, some two years after Gorbachev mentioned Khrushchev in his interview with *Time* magazine, Leonid reentered the public discourse. Only, unlike his father, the young man's reputation was immediately called into question. In October of that year, on the thirtieth anniversary of Sputnik, when the first satellite launched into space, my mother and I were sitting in her bedroom in our apartment, watching a television show commemorating the watershed event. The 1957 launch was considered one of my grandfather's greatest achievements; it led to a host of breakthrough scientific discoveries and a heated space race between the world's two superpowers.[97] Mother tuned into the program hoping to hear her father receive praise, which he did. But the show also made a series of vague accusations against Leonid—that he was a member of a notorious Kiev gang, that he'd killed a man in a drunken incident during the war, and, worst of all, that he collaborated with the Nazis.

Mother was horrified. She had heard muffled rumors of the drunken incident before, disseminated, she thought, through a brief mention in Solzhenitsyn's dissident novel *The Gulag*

Archipelago.[98] But learning of these allegations from official Soviet television and during the Gorbachev era of all times was beyond the pale.

"Glasnost is glasnost." I tried to console her. "After complete censorship, it is going to be complete openness—the good and the bad will come out."

I reminded her of our conversation six years prior, of Molotov's warning about the KGB and its *versiya*. Then she had brushed it aside, and neither of us had spoken of it since. Silence was a critical component of Soviet society, and our family constantly lived in fear of saying something that could lead to more embarrassment. Any negative remarks about Grandfather or his fragile legacy were strictly forbidden. After the Sputnik program though, I hoped things might change and I would finally learn the truth about the real circumstances surrounding Leonid's death. But once again my mother ignored me. Instead she called Aunt Rada, and for more than an hour, they whispered on the phone behind closed doors. Rada—I later learned—was unaware of the rumors. "Leonid was adventurous, disobedient," she said, "but a traitor? A gang member? A drunken murder? No. It couldn't be true."

Upset, my mother and aunt went to see Stepan Mikoyan, expecting he would discredit the report. Mikoyan indignantly dismissed the possibility that Leonid was a gang member or involved in treason. But to their dismay, he said he knew of the shooting. Leonid, he claimed, had accidentally killed a man. I later read that same account in the Russian language version of his memoir, published in 2006:

> In the last months of 1942, Leonid was unexpectedly in Moscow. Even with his bad leg, he rode to the front… Later…I met with Peotr—Leonid's friend—who spoke of the tragedy that took place in Kuibyshev that fall. A sailor visited from the front. When all were very drunk, someone said Leonid was a good shot. The sailor asked Leonid to knock down a bottle from his head. Leonid first refused,

but then shot off the bottleneck. The seaman found it insufficient, asking to smash the bottle. Leonid fired again, hitting the sailor in the forehead. He was sentenced to eight years spent at the front (during the war this was a form of punishment for the military). That's why he went to the front with an unhealed wound. At our meeting in Moscow, Leonid kept silent about this story.[99]

In the mid-1990s, after the USSR had dissolved and as I was continuing my studies in America, the nasty allegations about Leonid began to circulate once again, partly due to the postcommunist rush to document the miseries and the glories of the Soviet past. In 1994 Sergo Beria, the son of the former NKVD chief, Lavrenty Beria, published an obsequious book about his father in which he claimed that from 1935 to 1937, Leonid had consorted with "a Kiev gang of criminals [which was] hunted for looting and murder."[100] When the gang was arrested, Nikita allegedly asked Lavrenty to pardon Leonid. "But the case had already gone to the public prosecutor," the younger Beria wrote. "Thousands of people knew about their horrible crimes…Khrushchev insisted it be closed, but the case went to trial. Members of the gang were sentenced to capital punishment and shot. Khrushchev's son got away with ten years of prison."

The following year, former KGB General Mikhail Dokuchaev released his own then rather obscure memoir, called *Moscow. Kremlin. Security Guard.* Denouncing Khrushchev for his son's "treasonous fate,"[101] Dokuchaev alleged that Leonid defected to the Nazis only to be recaptured by the Red Army. In this supposed eyewitness account, the elder Khrushchev is described as hugging Stalin's knees and begging forgiveness for his son's crimes. Caring and fair (the way he used to appear in old Soviet propaganda), Stalin wisely replies: "What would I tell the other fathers whose sons have died as heroes?" He then ordered the pilot's execution.[102]

Both books read like bad detective novels, and few took them seriously at the time. Those who did, such as members of Russia's Chief Military Prosecutor's Office, quickly determined that the stories were far-fetched. In 1999, the office released a statement saying that an investigation had not uncovered any evidence "that Leonid Khrushchev had ever been sentenced to prison or ever committed any crimes."[103] And while the bottle shooting incident may have gained some credence in private conversations (mostly due to Mikoyan's occasional testimonies), the treachery and gang charges by and large were dismissed in the larger public sphere as little more than a KGB vendetta against Khrushchev.

When Putin came to power, however, the allegations about Leonid serving the Nazis suddenly went mainstream. And it was Molotov, who became an undisputed source of the treason *versiya*. *My teenage assumption was correct*, I thought, *in saying that Leonid was innocent, Molotov was just toying with me, employing a form of double speak to make me question the Khrushchevs's reputation.*

In 2000, long after Molotov's death, the Stalinist poet, Felix Chuev, published a collection of interviews that he said had been recorded in the 1980s, under the title *Molotov: A Semi-Czar*. The former senior Soviet apparatchik supposedly told the poet that: "Nikita was angry at Stalin for killing his son during the war. Nothing would have stopped him from dirtying Stalin's name... What kind of a political leader is that whose son was some sort of a traitor."[104]

But even that was not the worst: the most widely cited and circulated account of my family's betrayal was detailed in Soviet Marshal Yazov's memoir *Blows of Fate*. Soon hundreds of other publications, films, and news reports followed suit. The floodgates had opened. Many of these books were written by former Soviet brass turned Stalinist historians who deliberately aggrandized Leonid's herculean qualities, making him into such an antisuperman that the KGB (and its precursor, the NKVD) looked like a mythically powerful force in opposition. In an earlier and lesser-known description of Leonid's treason, for instance, former KGB General Vadim Udilov wrote that after purposely crashing his airplane, Leonid purportedly dragged it on a rope through the thick forest in the deep snow in order to offer it to the Nazis.[105]

Later, in 2002, the notoriously pro-Stalinist writer Vladimir Karpov published his monumental bestseller *Generalissimus*, which returned Stalin to the pedestal the dictator hadn't been on since his death. Citing Udilov, Karpov claimed to have proven Leonid's treason. Then in 2004, retired Soviet Aviation Marshal Ivan Pstygo shocked the public with more staggering details of the young Khrushchev's misconduct:

> Leonid's plane was shot at the front, he jumped out, was captured by the Nazis and began to work for them, walking proudly with an SS armband. Stalin ordered the commander of the partisans' brigade to catch Khrushchev, and bring him back in a potato sack. Remembering that Leonka was a huge guy, the partisans had to sew two sacks together. They brought the traitor to Moscow, and the Tribunal sentenced him to death…Khrushchev in tears on his knees begged Stalin, but to no avail—Leonid was shot.[106]

Elsewhere, Pstygo also claimed that on his deathbed, Ivan Kozhedub, the legendary Soviet war aviator, professed his personal participation in Leonid's execution.[107]

As I have read these accounts, I wondered: *There was such a code of silence surrounding Leonid, such a sense of shame for his human flaws. Today it seems easy to fill this silence with slander.* It is always the case that when you don't put the facts out there other people would step in to create them. And after all these years, who would dare to argue with the decorated militarymen who now say they were eyewitnesses to Lieutenant Khrushchev's dishonor?

Never mind that I knew just the opposite growing up. The proof of Leonid's valor was always in front of my eyes—the medals that my mother had hanging on the living room wall. They were among the few relics of the past that she kept in plain sight. It was if she knew what would come later, as if she could predict that the burden of proof would fall on our family. Leonid was nominated for the First Degree Order of the Great Patriotic War on April 18, 1943, and the medal was posthumously awarded to his father with an accompanying note dated June 25, 1945: "According to the status of the Patriotic War, this award is given to you in the memory of your dear son, who heroically died battling German invaders. The Council of Military Aviation of the Red Army shares your heavy loss and wishes you health and success in your fruitful activity for the flouring of our motherland."[108]

If Generalissimus Stalin had declared Leonid a hero, how could he simultaneously have been a traitor as the old brass alleges? I kept racking my brain: Why is the story so persistent?

—◦◦◦◦◦—

During the 1990s, following years of Soviet-era repression, Russians became obsessed with everything that had been denied to them for so long. Just as sushi became all the rage in Moscow, so too did lawsuits, as a growing number of Russians sought both exotic Japanese food and access to justice through a democratic system, not so much for their own merits, but because now they could. Yet just as sushi in Russia is subpar, so too is justice.

When the general public appeared to accept Leonid's treachery as fact, my mother's half-brother, Yury, followed his countrymen's lead and went to court, suing the writer Nikolai Dobryukha for factual shortcomings in an article about the young Khrushchev, published in the Russian magazine *Versiya*.[109] In 2000, Yury argued that accusing Leonid of a crime as serious as treason should require proof. The court didn't dispute Leonid's innocence—the 1999 verdict by the Military Prosecutor's office was clear enough on that matter. Yet it still ruled against Yury, saying that because Dobryukha claimed he learned about Leonid's "crimes" from a conversation with a fellow journalist, he was "exempt from responsibility for disseminating information and for hurting the honor and dignity of citizens if this information is comprised of the exact quotes from conferences, other authors' works, reports, materials and fragments used by other media sources."[110] Of course, Dobryukha's article never used any direct quotes.

The failure of Yury's lawsuit hurt my mother deeply; she was always hypersensitive about anything critical of the Khrushchevs, but she found the now constant stream of allegations especially hard to handle. They brought her back to the Brezhnev era, when Grandfather fell from grace. Deep down, she wanted to fight back, but years of growing up under dictatorial Soviet rule convinced her that resistance was futile. She had vivid memories of her father's exile, of the long walks they'd take around the property in Petrovo Dalnee, listening to him grumble about Stalin's show trials. These trials were huge public affairs in which judges decided the verdicts before the indictments were made. And in the audience, hundreds of obedient communists, including Khrushchev himself, condemned the so-called crimes. She recalled what the fallen premier had admitted to her in the fall of 1969 as they surveyed the forest for maple leaves (it was their autumn tradition to collect the bright orange foliage for my sister and I):

> It wasn't enough to eliminate the old Bolshevik generation who posed a potential threat to Stalin's rule. They knew Lenin, they knew Leninism. But Stalin cynically wanted to pretend that the accused were treated fairly in the USSR. The most serious charge was that everyone conspired with Trotsky—who by then had been exiled—to assassinate Stalin. It was that or spying for the West or sabotaging the economy, a bogus allegation that Bukharin confessed to in 1937.[111] The show trials proved no guilt. I should have

rehabilitated all of the old guard in 1956. But I was asked not to embarrass other communist parties. The French with Maurice Thorez, the Italians with Palmiro Togliatti were on their knees—they were, like me, all participants in the Stalin "law."

This conversation was the first time that my mother had heard of Nikolai Bukharin, an erudite editor of *Pravda*, who was once known as the Heir of Lenin. She was thinking of Grandfather's remorse and the long history of Russian injustice when she finally decided to go on the offensive. In 2004, the Russian website, *Khronograph*, published an article that quoted Aunt Rada as saying that the bottle story was true. (Rada insists she never spoke to *Khronograph*.) That same year, Putin honored Marshal Yazov—coup leader against Gorbachev and political criminal two decades ago—with a prestigious state medal for his "high achievements,"[112] increasing his public standing and assuring yet another edition of the former Defense Minister's memoir. As the flood of books and movies continued, my mother began sorting through her old files, reckoning with the ghosts of her past, trying to tackle all those wrinkled and yellowed articles and letters, which for years she had pushed under her bed. At one point, the stress caused by all the media coverage of our family made her ill. Her chest and arms broke out in sores, and none of her doctors could explain why. All they could say is that the disease was similar to a mysterious skin condition that plagued the British monarchs Henry IV and George III.

What really pushed my mother over the edge was Vladimir Sukhodeev's encyclopedia of people and events during the Stalin era, which was also released in 2004. Encyclopedias, of course, are supposed to hew as close as possible to historical objectivity, but this book, published by Eksmo, one of Russia's largest publishing houses, provided no sourcing. Out of the six pages devoted to Khrushchev, only half deal with his forty-five-year political career; the other half offer "facts" about Leonid's unpatriotic behavior and ultimate disgrace.[113]

After learning of Sukhodeev's assertions, my mother finally put aside her disappointment with the failure of Yury's lawsuit. His 2003 death after a car accident brought her to the sad realization that she had to take matters into her own hands. And so she turned to the courts, wanting the justice system to stop these false accusations from being published or aired, and perhaps recall the already released books. She hoped that if she meticulously collected all the necessary documents and offered indisputable proof of Leonid's honorable military service, the courts would have to rule in her favor.

Around the time she began looking for legal representation, she bumped into Boris Kuznetsov at a party. In the early 2000s, Kuznetsov was one of the most famous—or perhaps infamous—defense attorneys in Russia. Self-assured to the point of cockiness, he felt he could win any trial, regardless of the odds or evidence. He had garnered acclaim in part due to his eccentricities. Kuznetsov looked like a cross between Popeye and Ernest Hemingway, smoked a captain's pipe, wore a seaman's striped shirt, and lived in a posh sailboat-shaped house in the middle of a large forest outside of Moscow. But his growing list of renowned clients cemented his professional reputation and with good cause. At that time, Kuznetsov represented, among others, a number of military families who were suing the state for its allegedly sluggish reaction to an explosion on a Russian submarine called *Kursk*, which killed more than one hundred on board in 2000.[114]

In June 2004, my mother asked me to join her and meet Kuznetsov at his home some forty miles west of Moscow, in a neighborhood where the political elite reside alongside of those who aspire to be like them. His house was enormous, but right next door was a large ditch in which lay an old tire. Nearby I also spotted a rusting Soviet-era Fiat under a birch tree. In typical

Russian fashion, Kuznetsov ignored both the tire and the old car, and with his pipe between his lips, he proudly showed us around, trying to impress us with his wealth. He was clearly showing off in front of my mother because of her last name, talking at length about his chic vacations in Italy and France. Within the course of several hours, he convinced my mother to ask for one million rubles ($30,000) in financial compensation, predicting a grueling legal process.

After visiting Kuznetsov, I immediately called my sister to tell her about the lawyer and his bizarre boathouse. "Mom thinks he is going to save us," I said. "But in Russia, the law is like celebrity journalism: it has nothing to do with justice and everything to do with showing off. Khrushchev is a public figure, just as Kennedy or Nixon. And everyone writes speculative accounts of their lives. It's worse here in Russia maybe, but really we aren't that original." My sister agreed but was more open to a legal challenge. "As long as we don't end up doing it," she said, "maybe it's good for Mother to confront the past."

"Easy for you to say," I replied. "If anyone is going to do it, it will be me." My sister has her own family to deal with; her two children are still in school, and as a grant manager for what's commonly known as the Soros Foundation, she is often on the road. And I have always been more interested in our family's history, perhaps because of my early encounter with Molotov.

———

Up until my mother hired Kuznetsov, I had no plans to formally defend the Khrushchevs's honor.[115] Nothing was likely to change, I thought. It was only a matter of time before my mother gave up.

To this day, she remains haunted by the memory of what happened to our family after the release of Grandfather's memoir. My father, Lev Petrov, had encouraged his father-in-law to write the book. Having lived in the West as a journalist and unofficial spy, he understood the value of leaving something behind for posterity. He knew Khrushchev felt he hadn't gone far enough in rolling back Stalinism. The former premier feared being misunderstood and was eager to explain that the secret speech was neither a cover up for his own participation in the despotic regime nor was it a cunning plot to get back at his former boss, or a distortion of communism as the Brezhnev state now portrayed it. He simply wanted the party to allow for more openness—a less controlled exchange of ideas, some access to foreign visitors and products. He saw no shame in admitting that communist leaders can make mistakes, and he regretted that during his time in power that he had failed to eliminate censorship or unseal the Soviet borders. He felt that reckoning with Stalin's tyranny—the murders, purges, and coerced confessions—was his moral obligation. He was so confident that he wasn't doing anything wrong that in 1966, he actually told the party he was writing a memoir and asked for an official typist, a request the party declined.

So my father gave Khrushchev a German-made Uher tape recorder with which to dictate his thoughts. Nikita began recording his reflections on Soviet history, starting with Stalin and continuing through the early 1960s.

My father did the early transcriptions, transforming Khrushchev's bureaucratic language into clear and captivating prose. An admirer of Ernest Hemingway (and one of the first Soviets to translate his books into Russian), my father wrote in short declarative sentences; he wanted the former premier's words to be easily understood. But after reading the first few entries, Khrushchev felt uncomfortable—the book was not going to be written in the dense Soviet style of the era, the one to which he was accustomed. So in 1967, he asked his son, Sergei, to take over the project—from then on Grandfather's thoughts were transcribed almost verbatim.

In 1970, when Time, Inc. announced it had acquired Khrushchev's memoir and would soon publish excerpts, in *Life* magazine Grandfather was stunned, my mother says. So stunned he suffered a heart attack. He was rushed to the hospital and survived, but his healing process was slow as the scandal ensued.

According to my mother, the Politburo was outraged by his "unpatriotic action of writing the book," and after Khrushchev finally got better, Andrei Kirilenko, Brezhnev's close associate, lambasted the former premier for his criticism of Soviet policies under Stalin. Khrushchev still didn't give in and boldly defended himself:

> What are you complaining about? I asked for your assistance, but you didn't give it to me. If you had helped me, we wouldn't have had a problem. I never planned to trick you. As a citizen of the USSR, I have the right to write my memoirs, and you don't have the power to deny me that right. My notes are intended for the Central Committee, for the party, and for the whole Soviet people. I want what I write about to be of use to the people and to our nation. The events I have witnessed should serve as a lesson for our future.

An enraged Kirilenko threatened Khrushchev: "You live too well. A pension, a *dacha!*"

"What can you do to me?" Khrushchev replied. "You'll take the house. I will go across the country in rags with my hand out begging for alms. And the people will reciprocate."

That was a scary proposition, to publicly test the powers of the architect of the Thaw. Eventually, Kirilenko calmed down and let Nikita off with a warning. But as Gorbachev told me some ten years ago, that conversation has haunted many high-level KGB agents to his day. The 1980s security chief Victor Chebrikov cautioned Gorbachev about "reintroducing Nikita to the nation"—it had to be done gradually "to avoid creating possible instability." "The country," Chebrikov said, "may want another Thaw."

"His almost absurd fear of liberalism prompted the start of my own perestroika," Gorbachev explained to me.

As usual, the secretive Soviet system feared criticism simply out of despotic habit. The memoir, though damaging to the regime's attempts to resurrect Stalinism, remained silent about Brezhnev and was by no means anticommunist. Although Grandfather's views often stood in direct conflict with official Soviet policy he was just offering his personal opinions, and no state secrets were revealed. [116]

Grandmother, never a fan of the project, always felt that the stress and turmoil brought on by the book's release, if not killed her husband, most certainly shortened his life. When he died in the hospital on September 11, 1971,[117] true to her communist self, she did not blame the state; she blamed my father, whom she believed had been the source of the leak. The family had never fully accepted my father. Tall, dark-haired, handsome, and part Jewish, he was eighteen years older than my mother, and she was his third wife. Perhaps the memory of Leonid's womanizing made made my grandparents mistrustful. Or maybe it was his time living abroad they feared, that somehow the West had corrupted him. And certainly they didn't want to—they couldn't—suspect their only son, Sergei, of causing the memoir mayhem.

Grandmother wasn't the only one who thought my father had leaked Khrushchev's recollections; by 1971, a number of Western news outlets ran highly speculative stories about my father's alleged role in the affair.[118] By then, he had already died from kidney failure, but the KGB still came to our house and rifled through all our possessions. They found nothing, but Mother, terrified, decided not to defend her husband's reputation. Making a fuss, she felt, would only make matters worse. Already scarred by her father's disappearance from public life, she worried what would happen to my sister and I if she spoke out (we were six and seven at the time) even though she knew her late husband couldn't have been responsible for the leak. In 1969, he was so sick he almost never left our house.

Today of course it is well known that Uncle Sergei was the family contact person who transmitted the memoir to Victor Louis, a flamboyant and enigmatic Russian journalist for Britain's *Evening News*,[119] indeed an acquaintance of my father. Strobe Talbott, at the time an Oxford University graduate student who went on to have a prominent career first as deputy secretary of state under president Bill Clinton and later as president of the Brookings Institution, verified and translated the book's early 1970s versions. He worked on *Khrushchev Remembers* at the request of *Time* magazine's Moscow bureau-chief, Jerrold Schecter, who first acquired the original from Louis. Like my father, Louis was an unofficial Soviet spy. But unlike my father, he was an actual KGB employee, who sometimes let information out as a way to perform damage control or to test the West's reaction. According to my mother, Louis, for instance, first came by the scoop of Khrushchev's ouster in 1964. In 1967, without the author's permission, he leaked Svetlana Alliluyeva's *Twenty Letters to A Friend*, Stalin's daughter's account of her life in the Kremlin. Solzhenitsyn's 1967 novel, *Cancer Ward*, met a similar fate.

Because of his access to the agency, the West found Louis useful, although nobody could ever prove he was a double agent, even if rumors about him serving both sides persist to this day.

Originally Louis learned of Khrushchev's tapes from my father. As a KGB operative, one would assume, he could have been motivated by a desire to make Grandfather look bad. Yet the memoir made Stalin look bad, not Khrushchev. Such was the reality in the post-Thaw USSR—often those who served the state were also against its monolithic nature. As historian Roy Medvedev, who studied the KGB in great detail, told me, Louis belonged to a faction inside the agency that did not want to see a complete return to Stalinism. Most of them weren't necessarily liberals or even supporters of Khrushchev. But they—and Louis among them—feared that Brezhnev would go too far.

Money was also part of the KGB man's motivation. He surely profited from his job for the agency, and working for a foreign paper (and having a British wife) had its perks in the USSR. His three-story country house featured luxuries that were unimaginable to most Soviets: a swimming pool and tennis court, a perfectly manicured lawn, and a collection of fancy cars including a Bentley and a Mercedes convertible. According to Schecter, Louis received hundreds of thousands of dollars for brokering the memoir deal, and he had originally asked for much more than that.[120]

Some of this money, Louis explained to Schecter, would be for the Khrushchevs, although my mother insists that neither she nor my grandparents ever received a dime he got from the publishers. Louis also wanted full guarantee that Soviet authorities couldn't directly tie the memoir's release to Nikita, his children, or even himself, which is why, I assume, my dead father became the convenient scapegoat—he was not an immediate family member after all.

In the 1960s Time of course only dealt with Louis and wasn't privy to any Khrushchev family dynamics. Their main goal of publishing the memoir was to reveal the inner workings of the Kremlin. The Thaw had already changed perceptions: Stalin was absolute, but Grandfather's secret speech showed that leaders could make mistakes; it proved that the Kremlin didn't have to be god-like and distant from an average man. Releasing the memoir fourteen years later helped to further expose glaring defects of the communist system, perhaps speeding up its eventual collapse. Another Time's objective was the sacred principle of journalism— to always protect the source, especially Khrushchev—which was achieved.

But the unintended consequence of this Cold War daring endeavor was that my mother's sense of futility to fight for fairness only got worse. Feeling powerless she never confronted Louis and even continued her cautious friendship with him. More so, today she remains cautious about the consequences, almost reluctant to mention Louis and doesn't want me to write too much about him. This is perhaps because he was not without compassion and was very kind to us after my father's death. Not in the least for having tarnished his memory, I am sure. But regardless of how Victor Louis felt personally, in politics or espionage, especially during the Cold War, ethics, morality, and all else seemed to have taken back stage. Results were all that mattered.

I myself remember Victor, our neighbor in the country, as tall and charming—at the time I thought all spies were good looking—though not as tall or charming as my father, whom I missed dearly. The Louises used to let my sister and I swim in their pool. It was an improbable treat; we thought we could never travel abroad so visiting their dacha was like seeing England firsthand. And Victor occasionally bought us fancy dresses or chewing gum from his foreign trips.

Looking back I recognize that my father was responsible for at least one thing: undoubtedly looking to score some career points, he had introduced Victor Louis to my grandfather and uncle. In 1966, my father and Victor Sukhodrev, once Khrushchev's interpreter, brought Louis to Petrovo Dalnee to meet Nikita. My father had already begun working with Khrushchev on his political recollections, but this visit supposedly had nothing to do with it. Louis had simply wanted to meet the former leader. Looking back on it, I think my father should have realized what that simple meeting might lead to. Sukhodrev was Brezhnev's interpreter by then but remained fond of his previous boss, and Louis, his friend (and likely KGB contact), was excited to witness history in action—the ex-Soviet premier as pensioner, walking through his pumpkin patches and along the little paths under the pine trees at the *dacha*. My father took pictures, and Louis shot video that he said was for his personal use.

To my mother's dismay, the footage appeared in the 1967 NBC documentary, *Khrushchev in Exile: His Opinions and Revelations.* There was nothing controversial in the film, but with unapproved foreign contacts as prohibited as ever, the title and the timing of the release were enough to worry Soviet authorities about what the former premier was doing on his *dacha*. They immediately replaced one of his guards with another more hardline security man, who was expected to be more vigilant. Moreover, every time Grandfather visited us in our own country house in Peredelkino on the other side of Moscow, my mother never invited Louis, even though he lived nearby.

Nevertheless, for years after the book's release, Louis and Uncle Sergei allowed the rumors about my father to continue. It was only in 1990, when publishing a memoir was seen as a heroic deed rather than an act of treachery, that Sergei finally admitted Lev Petrov wasn't involved. In his book *Khrushchev on Khrushchev*, my uncle wrote that he was the one who had given the memoir to "colleagues" (read Louis).

When Sergei's book was about to come out, he picked up my mother late one evening, took her home and read her the parts about the handover to test her reaction:

> The publisher was worried that some might be palming off a fake…We weren't in a position to write to them ourselves; it would have been too dangerous. Our colleagues found a solution involving the use of a camera. Father received two wide-brimmed hats from Vienna, one bright scarlet and the other black. In order to verify that they were dealing with us and not some imposter, the publisher asked us to send photographs of father wearing these two hats… [Father] got a big kick out of the situation… he liked witty people.[121]

My mother was despondent and in shock.

"You know it's not true," she objected. "Dad would have never approved the transfer. And this silliness with the hats? How clever you think you are! Dad was known for his hats, and everyone knew he loved to get them as gifts. So I guess it was easy to construct the story and get a picture to attach to it."

"Lev was sick," Sergei shot back. "You weren't in Petrovo Dalnee very often, so you can't really know. Lev and Father are dead, so what difference does it make?"

But my mother did know. Khrushchev wanted the Soviet Union to read his book, but he would *never* have willingly given his memoir abroad.[122] He was directly involved in the unfortunate fate of Boris Pasternak and his 1957 novel *Doctor Zhivago*. After the book was scandalously published in Italy and banned in Russia, Pasternak was forced to refuse his 1958 nomination for the Nobel Prize in literature. Khrushchev, a communist to his last breath, would not have agreed to become another Pasternak by willingly releasing his memoirs in America. Doing so was akin to immigrating, the ultimate betrayal of the motherland—something Sergei did in 1991, a move, he admitted, that would have shocked his father.[123]

"For years, you had my husband take the blame. Now you are letting our father take the blame as well," my mother thought, powerless to fight with her brother. As always, she remained silent, hoping that it would all go away.

As the accusations mounted against Leonid, my mother—to my surprise and to her credit—persisted in her quest to rebut them, even as her skin condition worsened. It was that same pit of rebellion, that same revolt against despotism she displayed when she circulated anti-Stalinist literature around Moscow in 1960s and 1970s. "We can't let it go," she said. This was Uncle Sergei's line. Despite their past disagreements, his opinion holds considerable sway. And he has always believed her lawsuit was a worthy endeavor.

As much as my mother wanted to fight on, however, I could tell it was hard for her to go it alone. I simply *had* to help. I already felt guilty for only coming home to Moscow once a year, for being so far away from her. How could I not take part in defending our Khrushchev name? So in the fall of 2004, having almost finished the first draft of another book—an examination of the links between Russian politics and the novels of Vladimir Nabokov—I started sorting through our family's history and the allegations against Leonid, beginning the research that would eventually become this book.

The experience proved to be more traumatizing than I had expected in my worst dreams. I too developed a strange rash all over my hands and often stayed awake at night, wondering why Russians have such visceral hatred for Khrushchev—a flawed but sensible leader, at least in the context of his times—and yet they remain smitten by Stalin, one of the worst dictators the world has ever seen. Compelled by this peculiarity of our national character as much as by a desire to help my mother, I delved deeper into my work, reading anything and everything I could, setting up sundry interviews with people who might be able to offer clues. Very soon my question has shifted. It was no longer "is it at all possible that Leonid was some sort of a Russian Benedict Arnold?" It was, what lay at the root of the treason allegations, "Who was behind them and why they had proliferated so easily?"

As always, Roy Medvedev provided me with valuable insight, explaining that the rumors dated back to when my grandfather was forced to step down:

> Khrushchev tried to demilitarize the USSR. He made an early crack in the tightly sealed Soviet borders inviting foreigners to the 1957 International Youth Festival. He hosted the first American National Exhibition in 1959, which allowed Muscovites to taste "bourgeois" Pepsi-Cola and admire a model American kitchen. From his 1959 US visit, he brought a washing machine, and in 1960, he announced a drastic cut to conventional ground forces, shifting money from defense to economy. This produced predictable contempt among those in epaulettes, who began fabricating intrigue, a "diversion" legend to discredit Nikita Sergeevich. Leonid's name only surfaced when

we began to hear these muffled tales in the late 1960s. Brezhnev was gearing up for 1968, Stalin's ninetieth birthday rehabilitation efforts, and the political order of the day was to discredit the secret speech. After Khrushchev's exile, internal security was told to reveal "his shameful anti-Party activity in exposing Stalin." One element of slander was his son's story—from a criminal gang to Nazi captivity—the "apple doesn't fall far from the tree," as the Stalinist saying goes.

After 1964 Grandfather's name was stricken from the public record. But KGB officials began a whisper campaign for loyalists to disseminate, contrasting the alleged bravery of Stalin's son with the cowardice of Khrushchev's. In 1943, Yakov Dzhugashvili was shot while trying to escape from a Nazi concentration camp, and his fate eventually inspired the crude KGB *versiya*: "It is well known that Stalin's son categorically refused to cooperate with the enemy. Khrushchev's son, because he felt he was mistreated by the Soviet regime, sided with the Nazis."[124]

Pairing the Stalins and the Khrushchevs was a no brainer, but since the orders to spread rumors were never given in writing, there is no written record of the intention to slander. Ranking party members simply traveled around the country speaking about important Politburo policies and mixing murky suggestions about the Khrushchevs's betrayal along with lectures about the Cold War, Eastern bloc military superiority, and international communism.

Some of these rumors went beyond Leonid and his father. Arisha's daughter once told me that at a party lecture in our Kutuzovsky apartment complex, she had heard of the "anti-Soviet, bourgeois" behavior of her cousin Rada Khrushcheva, who twice a month allegedly flew to Paris to have her hair done. Whoever was spreading this rumor had never met Aunt Rada, who has always been a model of modesty: she worked her whole life as a deputy editor of the science journal *Nauka i Zhizn* (Science and Life) and hasn't changed her hairstyle since college.

Regardless of the silliness of the stories, the KGB succeeded; the Soviet Union was a closed society, so people were starving for information. Thrust from the womb of communism, the public suddenly discovered the truth about the famines of the 1930s and the lies about the crimes people had allegedly committed against the Kremlin. When Russians learned how much information the Soviet authorities fabricated to support the ruling ideology, they became immensely cynical. As a byproduct of glasnost, people became willing to believe anything about government officials; the more outlandish the gossip, the more interest there was. In every country, the media tends to be sensational, but in postcommunist Russia, it's even more so. For seventy-five years, *Pravda* editorials were the only source of "truth," so today people jump at any opportunity to have their own "truth" be heard, real evidence be damned.

This post-Soviet cynicism reached a climax during the Yeltsin era, when chaos and corruption ran rampant. Initially inspired by Yeltsin's anticommunist drive, Russians welcomed the demise of the planned economy and the unrestricted access to goods and products. But within a few years, these advances could no longer keep people happy; they had grown tired of Yeltsin's brand of unruly democracy and unbridled capitalism. Ruling by decree and with little oversight, this former party apparatchik sold Russia's valuable natural resources piece by piece to a minority of politically-connected individuals for bargain basement prices, explaining the decision as a necessary evil, a way to make sure that communism didn't return.[125] The unnecessary fire sale gave the impression—correct I believe—that a cynical and corrupt communist regime had given way to an even more cynical and corrupt capitalist one. During Yeltsin's reign, more than 50 percent of Russians—teachers, scientists, workers, and doctors— saw their quality of life fall as their benefits disappeared.[126]

Millions, including my mother, lost their savings in a variety of Ponzi schemes and other financial scandals and were forced to sell their belongings to those enriched by privatization.

Before long, many Russians fell back on what they knew best—their addiction to strongmen, who could prevent further chaos according to the myth. In this atmosphere of insecurity brought about their country's ignominious collapse—with sacrifices of collectivization and industrialization or victories in the space race with the United States no longer relevant—only one event in the twentieth century was able to energize Russia's sense of national pride: the Great Patriotic War, which most people associated with Stalin.

When Putin replaced Yeltsin in 2000, the former KGB man seemed to fit perfectly into Russia's "strong man" desires.[127] Arriving at the Kremlin with a cohort of *siloviks*—security and military officials turned energy, oil, and defense executives whose moniker refers to force or muscle—in the name of fortifying power and fighting corruption after the 1990s disarray, Putin quickly assumed total control of Russia's vast natural resources.[128] Seeking to reinstate the country's Soviet-style "military-industrial complex"[129]—an intricate relation between the government, its armed forces, and supporting businesses—the new administration needed a scapegoat to explain the country's weakened state.

Khrushchev (and Leonid by association) became one of the primary targets. He was blamed for the "destructive bourgeois influence" on Russia, as Molotov had alleged during the early days of perestroika.[130] The only way to rid the country of this influence was to resurrect Stalin, to once again anoint him as the caretaker of our glorious past. And so Grandfather was made responsible for most of the "post-Soviet evil," even more so than Yeltsin or Gorbachev under whose leadership the USSR actually collapsed. In 2003, the writer Elena Prudnikova complained that it was Khrushchev's fault that "homosexuality is rampant and Tampax commercials are allowed on television."[131] "If it wasn't for the Khrushchev execution [of Stalin in the secret speech]," Prudnikova wrote, "we wouldn't have come to such a sorry state, when every foreigner could teach us life...The country, deprived of high ideals in just a few decades has rotted to the ground."

The nationalist newspaper *Otchizna* (Fatherland) assessed Khrushchev's contribution to the state of Russia in even harsher tones:

> Who he truly was became clear after his followers, "reformers" destroyed our country and people in the 80s-90s. In his "exposé" of Stalin, Khrushchev was not guided by truth, but by the Herostratus-like vain longing for fame and a vengeful desire to mix the great leader with mud. In comparison he was an ugly pygmy...Stalinist barracks, built to save the nation from the Nazis, may have passed on in time. But Stalin laid the solid foundation for all subsequent Soviet achievements...On this foundation, it was possible to build a prosperous and equitable society. Those who came after, beginning with Nikita, failed. Khrushchev was fully rotten, so his children ended up traitors.[132]

With Putin in power, Stalinist supporters suddenly had a chance to redress their self-inflicted wounds with bandages of glory. But an average Russian too was equally eager to make sense of the new, unsettling capitalist reality by reducing our complicated history to a simple narrative of good versus evil, us versus them. And now when Khrushchev was firmly assigned guilt for the Soviet collapse the lack of evidence presented by the revisionist "historians" is excused by the "secretive nature of their jobs." But when the KGB's files were opened up twenty-five years ago, exposing the horrors and truths about the agency's dark dealings, wouldn't the so-called evidence against Leonid have come to light? Why did they have to resort to insinuation if they truly had that evidence? The answer, I am now fully convinced, that there was no evidence.

Take, for instance, Beria's claims that Leonid was affiliated with a murderous Kiev gang. Without even a shred of proof, the son of Stalin's NKVD chief wrote that "thousands of people" knew of this gang and Leonid's crimes. But who were these people? Where was their testimony? And what specific crimes had Leonid committed? According to the military prosecutor's office, there were none. More so, as I researched the timeline, I discovered that the gang membership was not only improbable, it was impossible.

From 1935 to 1937, when Leonid's crimes allegedly took place, he was living in Russia, not Ukraine. The young Khrushchev was a cadet at the Third Civilian Aviation School in faraway Balashov, where for better or worse, his instructors recorded all his misadventures; gang affiliation *was not* one of them. And finally Beria's father was not an NKVD functionary until 1938. He couldn't have been involved in any alleged investigation as he was heading Georgia's communist party in Tbilisi at the time. The most obvious conclusion to draw is that these charges stemmed from a decades-old grudge by the son of a man my grandfather condemned to death in 1953 for his "anti-state activities."[133]

Getting to the bottom of the bottle shooting incident proved far more difficult. Using Mikoyan as a source (not directly but citing Sergei Khrushchev's 2000 book *Nikita Khrushchev and the Creation of a Superpower*), Grandfather's biographer William Taubman proliferated his own variation of the tale: "Lyonia was court-martialed, but instead of being sentenced to a penal battalion, he was allowed to undertake new training as a fighter pilot."[134] As further proof, Taubman writes that "Liuba Sizykh confirmed this account to the author."

Over the years, Lyuba has shared with me at least *three* versions of the "bottle" story. At first, she claimed she didn't witness that particular shooting game but had seen the trick on prior occasions. "Marksmanship competitions were common among officers then," she said. "And on the weekend, they had fun practicing their 'William Tell' skills into the wee hours of the morning." Another time Lyuba told me that Leonid confessed the shooting to her right before he left Kuibyshev for retraining. More recently, she changed her story again, saying she never had a conversation with Leonid but that she had heard about the incident from Arisha. Was this a ploy to cover up the real story? What was the real story?

Lyuba isn't alone in painting a confusing picture. Stepan Mikoyan's account has changed too. In the 1999 English publication of his *Memoirs of Military Test-Flying*, he makes no mention of the bottle incident or the alleged punishment. Instead he writes, "Leonid left for the front without waiting for his leg to heal and got retrained to fly the Yak-7 fighter. He and I met briefly in Moscow when he was passing through."[135] Around that time Stepan, however, told the writer Nikolai Andreev that he learned of the accident "from a ballerina friend,"[136] Valentina Petrova, not from Leonid's friend Peotr, as Mikoyan wrote seven years later in his Russian book.

Petrova herself gave interviews—all to Dobryukha, the notorious Stalinist writer whom Yury Khrushchev once sued—recounting her affair with Stepan, Lisa Ostrogradskaya's affair with Leonid, and the bottle incident. According to Petrova, Lisa left for Moscow, and Leonid, heartbroken, became infatuated with a circus girl: "I parted company with Leonid immediately. But Peotr told me that one time at his party, the circus gang, run by a ringmaster, surrounded Leonya and asked to perform shooting tricks on a bet—which one is a better shot, a military ace or a circus ace. After much pushing and nudging he agreed and accidentally shot a man. He was punished severely."[137]

Petrova's bizarre version is allegedly based on information from the same elusive Peotr, and yet it is entirely different from Stepan's account. Petrova passed away in the mid 2000s, so I was unable to interview her, but I did get in touch with her ex-husband, Alexander Shcherbakov, a decorated air force veteran with whom I had many lengthy conversations before he passed away in November 2013. In 1971, Shcherbakov received the nation's highest honor, Hero of the Soviet Union, but when I first met him at his unpretentious Moscow apartment several years ago, he looked more like a science professor than a war hero. At eighty years old, he spoke slowly as if he was considering every word. Unlike the children of other Kremlin officials like Beria, Shcherbakov has insisted on telling the truth about my family, despite Grandfather's disdain for his father, Alexander Shcherbakov Sr., the head of the Red Army's political division during the war.[138] "Leonid's fate," the younger Shcherbakov told me, "was an embodiment of war—tragic, messy, and confusing."

In 1943, the young Alexander, who was born nearly a decade after Leonid, lived in the same building as the Khrushchevs and Mikoyans in Kuibyshev. He married Stepan's ex-girlfriend Valentina Petrova after the war and has been adamant that his former wife had little real knowledge of the veracity of the bottle incident despite her claims otherwise. Shcherbakov had also heard of the "killing" rumor back then, but again, his version is different from Mikoyan's and Petrova's:

> Leonid must have made up the bottle story. I asked my father, who had to know, but he dismissed it as farce. I first heard of the bottle shooting from friend Lev Bulganin [son of Nikolai Bulganin, Member of the State Committee of Defense], who learned of it from Leonid himself. Lev and I were finishing high school. We both went into aviation. Leonya was "cool," a legend among the boys—a bomber, a senior lieutenant, the first in his regiment to get the Red Banner. He never failed to impress the teenage Bulganin, one time teaching him how to get rid of a clingy love interest. Lisa Ostrogradskaya fancied a more serious relationship, and Leonid wanted to spare her feelings by making up a story that after accidentally shooting an officer, he urgently had to leave for the front. To make it more plausible, Leonya added details about how he went

to the hospital to visit the wounded man. But the officer had died overnight, and as a keepsake, Leonya took his peaked cap, shot through.

The clearest evidence against Leonid's detractors is that the punishment didn't fit the crime. As Pavlov, a plane mechanic of Leonid's fighter regiment, explained:

> Today it's alleged—with no documentary evidence—that Leonid, after being wounded and [residing] in the Kuibyshev hospital, shot someone with a pistol in a drunken state. In the story, he was supposedly convicted by military tribunal and sent to the front—a lie from beginning to end. A person convicted by court-martial wasn't just sent to a penal battalion—pilots were sent to the worst divisions. And Khrushchev came to our fighter regiment, which was the best on the western front. While in the hospital, he was awarded a Red Banner and promoted to the rank of senior lieutenant. Also, there was a law that a person convicted of murder could no longer use a weapon. Khrushchev arrived with not one, but two pistols.

Shcherbakov agreed: "No one was punished by becoming a fighter pilot. Becoming a prestigious aviator, especially during wartime, *could never* follow a court-martial. This is a historical improbability." Shcherbakov took an issue with Mikoyan who, of course, "is aware of this all, but still talks about the court-martial. It's not his intention to discredit his fallen comrade, but repeating what he once heard, just to appear he is in the know, is irresponsible."

According to official documents, which I dug up both at home and in the Podolsk archives, Leonid left Kuibyshev in the late spring of 1942, not in the fall as Stepan originally claimed. These papers contradict Mikoyan's report that the young Khrushchev may have shot a man in that interim Soviet capital in September.

In fact, from a September 24 (rather offhand) letter to Lyuba, I also learned that by the fall of that year, Leonid had already completed four months of retraining to become a fighter pilot in Sasovo:

> Lyuba, Apologies for a long silence. What's new? How is Yulia? Please send her picture if you can. How is Tolya? I am far from the front now, but will be there in a few days. If you please send me a coat and boots, handkerchiefs and socks as soon as possible. Also smokes and matches. Please don't wait long to mail these. When I leave this place I won't be able to get it for some time. I am still not at the front because I was retraining for several months, but now it is pretty much done. I will likely be fighting with another aviation unit. Kiss Yulia and Tolya. With regards, Leonid.

In 2004, my mother asked her friend Mikhail Shvydkoi, then the Russian Minister of Culture, to procure further information from the military prosecutor's 1999 investigation. The letter she received from the Office of the Public Prosecutor of the Russian Federation offered a clear refutation of the bottle story or any other crimes for that matter: "There is no proof or evidence," the letter read, "that Senior lieutenant L. N. Khrushchev had ever been under any criminal investigation or prosecution."[139]

When I showed this letter to Stepan and pointed out the various contradictions in his accounts, the old pilot was dumbfounded. As for who had actually told him about Khrushchev's eight-year penal battalion sentence, Stepan couldn't remember: "It seems I've known this forever." I left his apartment feeling confident that Shcherbakov's assessment of both the "gang" and the "bottle" incident was correct: "When a story is told often enough, it becomes mythology," Shcherbakov said. "And then mythology becomes real."

As I continued my inquiry, it became obvious that the mythology regarding Leonid's treason was congealing into an alternate reality. Though the prosecutor's office had made it clear that Senior Lieutenant Khrushchev had committed no crimes, the rumors raged on. Getting more and more frustrated, I turned to cousin Nikita. He was a bit of a family archivist, and after some twenty years, I was finally ready to have his take on the now widely cited accusations by Molotov as primary source of Leonid's betrayal. Perhaps it was just the double speak. Still, why do they completely contradict what Stalin's faithful comrade had told us?

One summer in the mid-2000s, my cousin and I met in a park in central Moscow. We sat on a green bench, and for about an hour, he shared his thoughts. "Regardless of how we feel about Molotov's politics," Nikita said, "he was grand. An 'Old Bolshevik,' he fully believed in communism. He meant what he said to you because his faith was so strong that he didn't need to dirty our name to support his ideals. But others today need his Stalinist patriarch status to justify their disagreements with Grandfather. So they put words in Molotov's mouth according to what they think he might have felt. He wouldn't be pleased. Remember you wondered all these years ago, why I liked him. Because he was honest in his views, and he disliked the KGB."

This was our last long conversation. Another few years, and I would have never had solved my Molotov mystery—my cousin died in 2007 of heart disease.

In some ways, Nikita made me realize that Russia's new villains may be even worse than the old ones. With news of Leonid's "betrayal" reaching the wider world, I also found it ironic that it was Westerners, not Russians, who further disseminated the lies. Whoever had started the *versiya* in the first place must have been pleased; many would quickly dismiss the autobiographies of Stalinist generals, but when supposedly balanced and objective foreign writers bolster rumors about Khrushchev, deliberate misinformation suddenly becomes accepted fact. Some were well meaning and ethical such as Taubman, whose book is, by and large, an excellent account of my grandfather's life. But the same can't be said for others such as the British writer, Simon Sebag Montefiore, who often showed willful disregard for both facts and journalistic ethics in his captivating biography of Stalin's comrades, *The Court of the Red Tsar*. Not only did Montefiore, repeat the fibs about Khrushchev denouncing Stalin because of Leonid's alleged treachery, but he attributed them to my mother, something which is not only false but laughably absurd.[140] This includes a new twist on the story of Lyuba's arrest in 1943: "Rumors spread that [Leonid] had turned traitor—which, in Stalin's system, cast doubt on his widow."[141] Never mind that "treason" has become a common assertion only in the Putin decades, incidentally providing Lyuba with yet another opportunity to avoid responsibility for her actions.

There was, however, one piece of the puzzle that wasn't surreal so much as it was confounding: the testimony of Senior Lieutenant Ivan Zamorin, the flight leader, who last saw Leonid before his crash. Two days after the mission on which the young Khrushchev disappeared, Zamorin filed his initial report, which was formally signed by the 18th Regiment Commander Major Golubov and stored in the Podolsk archive:

> Two aircrafts—a leader piloted by Zamorin and a wing mate piloted by Khrushchev—were attacked by two FockeWulfs-190. The battle unfolded as follows: Zamorin attacked one FW-190. From a 50–70 meter distance he opened fire and knocked down the enemy. Khrushchev came to his right. When Zamorin destroyed the enemy aircraft, he noticed that Khrushchev was pursued by another Focker...Zamorin started a retaliatory barrage. The German pilot, in a disadvantage, rolled over Khrushchev...Zamorin pursued the German... Khrushchev abruptly went down at a 65–70 degree angle. When Zamorin returned after pursuit, Khrushchev was

nowhere in sight. Zamorin believed that his plane couldn't have been brought down as the fascist bombs exploded far away...It is possible that pulling the control stick the pilot fell into a tailspin.

The inconclusive nature of Zamorin's letter can be cited as the reason why Dultsev, the cameraman, wrote to the elder Khrushchev as late as July 1944, expressing his faith that one day they would see Leonid again. But as in most Leonid-related matters, there are other disputes. Not only is the battle itself called into question—some say it happened, some say it did not—but the search after the crash has been debated as well.[142]

In a personal letter that my grandfather received in April of 1943, Commander of the First Aviation Army Lieutenant General Khudyakov wrote: "A thorough search [of Leonid's plane] from the air brought no results. For a month after your son's disappearance, we hoped for his safe return to duty. But the conditions under which he went missing and the intervening time period lead us to grief and conclusion that your son Leonid Nikitich died a heroic death."

Yet every pilot I spoke to said that sending reconnaissance planes into the Nazi-occupied area would have been an unjustifiable risk. A more likely scenario is that the authorities in question *said* they looked for the young Khrushchev but in fact lied to cover their backs; refusing to search for the Politburo's member son, despite the danger involved in such a mission, could have been seen as treason.

The army certainly made a concerted effort to appear vigilant. A second version of Zamorin's story, officially sent up the chain of command, was included in Khudyakov's April letter to Khrushchev senior. It forcefully claimed that the lead man was steadfastly looking after his ward, saw him under attack, and turned his plane toward a FockeWulf to help Leonid out. Upon returning from pursuing the German, Zamorin, no longer seeing his wingman, assumed Leonid had safely returned to the airfield.

The third account came sixteen years later on November 23, 1960, when Khrushchev was now the all-powerful Soviet premier. The memo came from Guard Colonel Zamorin himself and reads in part, "When an enemy plane went after me, and I caught machine-gun fire, I had to sharply swerve away from further hits, and lost sight of Khrushchev...I returned to our base, and have no idea of what happened to my partner."

In that same year, Khrushchev ordered Commander of the Air Defense, Marshal Vladimir Sudets to renew the search for his son's remains. They found nothing conclusive.

I didn't know what to make of Zamorin's several accounts, but none of them indicate that treason was involved. Still I wondered, why did the lead man's recollections keep shifting?

From the get-go, my mother's legal battles seemed like something out of Franz Kafka's *The Trial* (1915), a harrowing narrative about a man who is arrested by phantom powers and indicted even though his crimes are never explained.

One of the first things Mother needed to solidify her case was Leonid's death certificate. But in order to procure it, she first had to find his original birth record, which had been lost amid the many upheavals of the twentieth century. Dogged and determined, Mother managed to locate a 1917 church registrar from Donetsk, Ukraine, with Leonid's birth entry.[143] After numerous phone calls, a cramped two-hour flight to Donetsk, and an afternoon in the local municipal office, she triumphantly returned home with the desired page from a ledger stating that Leonid Khrushchev was born November 10, 1917.

Back in Moscow the authorities raised (or created) other challenges: in the church registry Leonid's surname was listed as Khrushchov, the Ukrainian spelling, not Khrushchyov as it's spelled in Russian. Another problem, they claimed, was that the records identify Leonid's father as *M*ikita, again the Ukrainian version, rather than *N*ikita, as the name known in Russian.

The judge felt these spelling issues created doubt as to whether or not the records my mother acquired were in fact Leonid's. She requested experts from the Russian State Academy of Science's Institute of the Russian Language to confirm that the discrepancy between names was merely a linguistic issue. After hearing expert testimony that this was indeed the case, the judge ruled against it anyway on a minor technicality. Although the Academy of Science is part of the federal government, it is an independent agency and as such does not carry the Russian official coat of arms, the double-headed eagle, on its seal. The judge deemed the institute's expertise inadmissible for the lack of that official seal. She did agree to hear testimony about Leonid's life from relatives and friends who knew him personally, "in the hope," my mother explained, "that no one is still alive."

Despite contributing to the bottle rumor—more for show than out of malice—Stepan Mikoyan remained our good friend. In the fall of 2006, he tottered into the courthouse, joining Aunt Rada as a witness. Thanks to their statements, the judge accepted the proof that the Donetsk birth certificate was Leonid Khrushchev's and not some other Ukrainian Khrushchov. Leonid was officially recognized as the former premier's son. Since he was born, the court now agreed, he also should be considered dead, and it issued a long-awaited statement that the senior lieutenant died in a battle on March 11, 1943.

Mother now had this death certificate on record—a piece of irrefutable proof that Khrushchev's son couldn't have worked for the Nazis after his last flight—to go along with the military's 1999 and 2004 documents. All served as further ammunition against the accusations, which had no corroborating documents or actual witnesses. Armed with these records, Mother went after Yazov's *Blows of Fate*, and other pro-Stalin books including the encyclopedia *Stalin's Era*, charging the authors with defamation and libel under Russian Civil Code Article 152, "The Defense of Honor, Dignity and Official Reputation of Citizens."

In the meantime, the Russian television industry with its enormous profits and large audiences began pushing the treason allegations too. In 2005, Channel One, the most watched Kremlin-affiliated network in Russia and many other former Soviet states, produced an absurd pro-Stalin documentary miniseries called *Star of an Era*. On the surface, the show was about the famous actress Valentina Serova and her husband, the iconic Soviet poet and war reporter, Konstantin Simonov.[144]

A celebrity like Simonov deserves a biopic made about his life. Once an admirer of Stalin, he later became an avid supporter of Khrushchev's Thaw and a vocal opponent of later attempts to refurbish Stalin's image. So vocal in fact that both his and Serova's relatives refused to allow the producer, Yury Kara, to use the celebrities' real names. In the eight-part *Star* series, Simonov appears as some "poet Semenov" and Serova becomes "actress Sedova."[145]

My mother hoped that the court would make a similar ruling and block Kara from using Leonid Khrushchev's name in his show. To no avail. The young Khrushchev and Simonov never met in real life, yet Kara partially dedicated two episodes to Leonid's alleged Nazi defection, Soviet recapture, and death sentence. He even showed Nikita howling and beating up his son for treason. In Kara's "documentary," Khrushchev became the epitome of hysteria, "fittingly" the father of the son (name unchanged), whose treason is presented as an indisputable fact. The producer's only source for the episodes: the source-less *Stalin's Era* encyclopedia.

Mother's other legal battles proved to be equally fruitless. Despite Kuznetsov's confidence and bravado, he lost every motion. Moreover, in 2007 a Russian court accused him of his own treason for investigating the Kursk case, and he was forced to flee to the United States where he received asylum. With Kuznetsov exiled to New York City, the Kursk families' lawsuit quietly disappeared from public view, as did all his other cases, which, from the Russian government's perspective, was surely the point. Things had changed in the ten years since the flamboyant lawyer first stepped into the limelight. This was Putin's Russia now. The country was playing by the same set of arbitrary rules, but the winner's circle had changed hands.

Seeing the writing on the wall in 2006, my mother hired a new lawyer, Vitaly Galkin. A recent law school graduate, he was earnest, pedantic, and always in a formal dark suit. He was the perfect model of a lawyer in the drab Putin era, Kuznetsov's complete opposite. Galkin, however, was similarly convinced that the burden of proof should fall on the accusers, especially because he explained, "Since 2004, when Kuznetsov first tried to use law against the Eksmo-published encyclopedia *Stalin's Era* and other books, your family has supplied the courts with indisputable evidence against the younger Khrushchev's guilt. Therefore, any subsequent mentioning of his treason should cease to exist."

Feeling that Kuznetsov's antigovernment reputation must have impeded our case, in 2007 our new lawyer refiled a motion against the encyclopedia's publishing house in one of Moscow's district courts. His argument was that a "'factual' publication cannot hide behind fictional interpretations." He then also submitted our litigation to another district court against Telefilm and Channel One for producing and distributing *Star of an Era*.

To strengthen the case in the court of public opinion, my mother arranged for the newspaper *Izvestiya* to publish Leonid's death certificate. The document appeared along with Alexander Shcherbakov's article "Black Spots in Clear Skies,"[146] which slammed the military and security "epaulettes" for maligning Leonid's name. The publication also ran commentary by Vladimir Lukin, the Russian Human Rights Commissioner, who denounced the slander by explaining the death certificate as a legal record that no one can dispute, not even the president.

Yet a month later, the Moscow paper *Argumenty i Fakty* (Arguments and Facts) published another one of Dobryukha's "exposés"—"Why Nikita Sergeevich Denounced Stalin"— repeating the old rumors and lies about Leonid's bottle-shooting, treason, Nikita hugging Stalin's knees, and so on.[147]

With every new publication, my mother felt more and more distraught. Her skin disease wasn't going away, and she was becoming a hypochondriac, treating an occasional palpitation or sleepless night as symptoms of some grave illness. Completely consumed by my family's past and our legal challenges, I started writing articles, trying to rebut the rumors about the Khrushchevs. Clearing Leonid's and Nikita's names was becoming an increasingly herculean task—for each unfounded accusation we addressed, two more popped up like the heads of the Hydra. But Galkin, earnest and optimistic as ever, maintained his faith that we could not lose.

Despite the lawyer's assurances, the situation only got worse. "As historical figures," one judge ruled, "the Khrushchevs should allow for creative interpretation of their life stories," because "by law, mentioning a famous person in the art product does not require the consent of the heirs."[148] In other words, it was legal to fictionalize public or political figures in a work presented as nonfiction, such as journalism. Kafkaesque indeed.[149]

Another judge compared our family to the House of Stuart, the royals who once ruled Great Britain and Scotland. The Stuart dynasty lasted from the fourteenth to the eighteenth century, while Grandfather was in power for less than eleven years in what is regarded as a modern society, (arguably) with legal institutions, civic norms, and privacy laws. "No wonder I have a kingly skin decease," my mother attempted to poke fun at the verdict.

But seriously, when I shared our ordeal with a lawyer friend in New York, she simply laughed:

> It's so primitive how they abuse the law. First, all these accounts are hearsay. Moreover, the "documentarians" have

committed libel (which is defamation, but particularly for written, broadcast or otherwise published words) because they have made up "facts" to support their conclusions. The Stuart dynasty has nothing to do with "Leonid's estate," that is his *immediate* descendants, who have been *directly* damaged or hurt by these unsupported accusations that he committed treason. This would have made for a solid lawsuit in the US legal system.

For the past six years, our attorney has filed twenty-five motions for "degrading the honor, dignity, and good name of Leonid" in various Moscow courthouses. All have been rejected or ignored. Failing to get justice in Russia, in 2008 Galkin took Leonid's litigation to the European Court of Human Rights in Strasbourg, France. Kuznetsov has likewise filed a case with the Strasbourg Court over his own persecution. In other words, nothing has changed. We are still waiting.

⋘⋙

"Too bad I'm not in America," my mother quipped one night when I was visiting her in Moscow in late 2008. Barack Obama had just been elected president, and as a newly minted American citizen, I felt proud having voted for him. Again Mother and I were sitting next to each other and watching television. Only now instead of a Soviet state program, we were watching Jon Stewart on CNN International ridiculing the Birther Movement for its bogus claims about President Obama's foreign origins. "Just as American conservatives can't deal with having a black man in the White House, inventing a ludicrous rumor, the Stalinists can't forgive Grandfather for his secret speech," my mother said. "But you are lucky to live in a country where ludicrous rumors are ultimately dismissed, becoming nothing more than a punch line."

My mother was at least partially right. Yet despite irrefutable evidence to the contrary, a certain percentage of Americans continue to believe that Obama was not born in the United

States.[150] But if they came to live in Russia, they would see how much worse it can be.

"With us, ideology is inseparable from law," my mother continued. "Just as with the old dictatorship, our legal institutions are still based on the whim of the authorities."

"In no small part," I replied, "because Grandfather didn't speak the full truth. He didn't rehabilitate Bukharin or Trotsky when he could. His didn't close the gulags completely."

I uttered the words and immediately regretted them, expecting for her to respond with her usual defense of the Thaw. She believes that her father's legacy is ultimately a positive one, that the bravery of Khrushchev's secret speech, coming on the heels of Stalinism, outweighs any of his mistakes. I don't disagree, but I also think the more our family is open about Grandfather's mistakes, the more trustworthy we are in touting the merits of his rule.

To my surprise, this time Mother didn't attempt a rebuttal. She didn't so much as shift her weight on the couch. Instead, with sadness in her eyes, she quoted Grandfather's own assessment of the country he once ruled: "Russia is like a tub full of dough. You make a dent, push your hand all the way to the bottom, pull it out, and there, right before your eyes, the hole disappears, and again, it is a tub full of dough."

"THE DEVIL TOOK HIM"

On November 7, 1964, three weeks after my grandfather's abrupt dismissal from office, the family gathered to celebrate the Bolshevik Revolution at Khrushchev's grand Politburo mansion in Moscow's famed Lenin Hills. For as long as Grandfather was in power, this holiday party had been an exclusive event. Guests had included a who's who of the Soviet upper crust—foreign diplomats, Soviet functionaries, and members of the *intelligentsia*. This time the party was a smaller, more somber affair; roughly a dozen people came to the premier's two-story, yellow villa, where the family lived while Khrushchev served as the Soviet head of state. As the guests gathered around an enormous wooden table in a stately dining room, a sense of futility hung in the air like an invisible fog; they could see the rows of boxes, some already packed and filled with various personal belongings.

After everyone had arrived, Nikita stood at the head of the table and made a toast. He tried to appear firm, upbeat. He didn't want political misfortune to ruin his favorite holiday. My mother, then twenty-four years old, sat next to him, and as he struggled through his impromptu speech, she could feel her heart breaking. "I raise this glass to the greatest day of the Bolshevik victory," Khrushchev said. "This is an important day for me too because while fighting for the workers' freedom from exploitation at the Red Army front, I received word that I was the father of a son, Leonid! It was the best day of my life. Leonya—my boy, I imagined, would carry a revolutionary torch after me. And then he died, so carelessly…"

This was the first time my mother had ever heard about her biological father from Nikita, the man who had raised her—the only real father she'd ever known. As Khrushchev continued with his toast, my mother began to cry. He looked at her and tried to soothe her, tenderly placing his hand on her shoulder. "Don't cry," he said. "I wanted to bury him, but I ran out of time. I hope you will never be ashamed of me. There were mistakes, but those who don't make mistakes, they don't do anything, they don't try. Leonya too made mistakes, silly mistakes, and he had so much potential. We miss him in this room today."

My mother's tears continued to flow, and Grandfather sighed, holding back his own. He was now dealing with two great losses. In his eyes, the birth of the Soviet state was indistinguishable from the birth of his first son; his loss of power was synonymous with the tragedy of losing his child.

⚬⚬⚬

Almost seventy years after Leonid's death, in November of 2011, I thought of this story, which my mother had recently told me, as I sat in the passenger seat of my sister Ksenia's black Peugeot. It was 7:00 a.m. and pitch-black outside as she drove us toward Zhizdra, a small town some four hours west of the Russian capital. We wanted to visit the area where Leonid's plane was last seen to talk to residents of the town and to meet people who knew something about what had happened on the day of his disappearance. Snowflakes drifted down from the sky, and the road was open and quiet as we sat in the car, listening to the engine rumble through the darkness.

Our trip was a special one and not just because we were on a mission to learn more about Leonid's past. Growing up, Ksenia and I had always been close. We were very different—I liked books, while she preferred dolls and fairytales; I've always favored subtle colors, while for years she wore nothing but pink. We even look different—she is a tall blonde, while I am a short brunette. What brought us together, however, was hardship—not only our father's untimely death, but also our mother's unrelenting pressure to be perfect, to make sure that we always acted like Khrushchevs.

Over the past fifteen years, Ksenia and I have drifted apart. I left for America, and she got married, had children. I now live in New York, and she lives in our country house in Peredelkino, so we rarely have time to see each other. Going to Zhizdra was an opportunity to reconnect. Driving together was our chance to be just us again, to act silly, to be sisters, to speak to one another without finishing a sentence and yet effortlessly understand everything.

Earlier that fall, when I suggested going to Zhizdra, Ksenia wasn't sure she could get away. A long journey to the provinces on the eve of winter traversing bad Russian roads seemed like more than she could handle, but she eventually caved and went to Zhizdra out of love; she didn't want me to face the truth alone.

As we drove further away from the capital, the roads became bumpy and full of pits and potholes—a clear sign, we joked, that Putin had restored Russia's glory. Over the decade and a half he's been in power—first as president, then as prime minister, and then as president again—the Kremlin's attention has centered around oil and defense; provinces that are devoid of natural resources have been left to fend for themselves. As a result, in the last thirteen years, eleven thousand Russian villages and almost three hundred towns have been abandoned and now stand overgrown with weeds and shrubbery. During the winter months, these western provinces are blanketed by darkness. Light only lasts for roughly six hours a day, giving the whole region an air of doom and gloom.[151]

This sense of decay is tolerated because most Russians don't care for provincial life. Stalin's collective farming policies of the 1930s took away the peasantry's pride in working the land, and over the last century, the provinces have become increasingly neglected. Tired of rural poverty and the dullness of daily life, those living in the countryside today are largely looking to escape to the two main epicenters of politics and culture, Moscow and St. Petersburg.

As we drove, I told Ksenia how surprised I was that Zhizdra and its post-war history hadn't factored into all the allegations swirling around Leonid's fate. With the Russian elite *completely* ignoring the provinces as if they are part of a different country, our family didn't even think that Zhizdra might give us the needed answers. Having lived in America for more than twenty years, I now have a different worldview than other Russians, so that summer a few months before the trip, I decided to look at some local publications to see whether I could acquire some new perspective. Simply Googling "Khrushchev Zhizdra" proved immensely rewarding. Two sites, *Zhizdra News* and *Zhizdra's Guestbook*, immediately popped up, and I soon discovered a bevy of complaints each year cropping up around the anniversary of Leonid's death when Moscow newspapers and television programs regularly rehash the bogus stories about his "treachery."

One article that I found on *Zhizdra News* meticulously argued that Leonid was a hero, using local townspeople and their recollections as evidence: "Khrushchev's military card at TsAMO [Central Archive of Ministry of Defense] of the Russian Federation states that Leonid Khrushchev died March 11, 1943. And myths even in a movie or a documentary form do not debunk the facts."[152]

As I read—it was rare to see common sense written about Leonid and in the rural areas of all places!—I could feel my heart pounding. I seemed to be on the verge of a great discovery. Scrolling through the pages online, I was startled to see a photograph of the city's mass grave topped with a silver-painted figure of a warrior. Underneath the monument, which appeared to be some odd combination of a pilot and a partisan, four gray marble plaques listed the names of twenty-two privates, sergeants, and lieutenants; one of them is Senior Lieutenant L.N. Khrushchev.

I couldn't believe it. By then, I had little doubt that the allegations against Leonid were nothing more than a smear, but here was more concrete evidence. It had been right in front of our noses, and yet no one in my family had even thought to look for it. I immediately called my mother to ask her why. She was as shocked as I was and said that Grandfather must have known about the honor bestowed upon his son. He had ordered a search for Leonid's body while he was in power but had never found it. After 1964, Khrushchev was forced out of office, the former premier's name was stripped from the record, and since he almost never talked about his son, the monument's existence had been forgotten, neglected like everything else in the Russian countryside.

"It took your Americanism," my mother complemented me across the ocean, "your desire to follow the evidence, not accept what's convenient—to really uncover the truth." She said, she "was just too close to the tragedy, afraid to doubt what she had been told."

When we hung up, I found a phone number to the mayor's office in Zhizdra. An unusually polite young bureaucrat named Nikolai offered me even greater hope; he said that the monument was built in 1949—while Stalin was still in power. Nikolai knew all about the treason nonsense, had been incensed by the false allegations, and offered me the cell phone number of a local peasant who was famous for witnessing the young Khrushchev's plane crash. Nikolai spoke so passionately about Leonid that I was completely taken aback. "War is the most important thing that we had ever experienced," he said. "We would know our traitors, and the young Khrushchev wasn't one of them."

The Zhizdra monument was not the only piece of evidence hiding in plain sight. There had been other things my mother had missed along the way because she felt that with everything our family had gone through nothing short of finding Leonid's remains could prove his innocence. But I, in my American incarnation, believed that every small piece of information counts. So even before going to Zhizdra, I doublechecked all the familiar sources in hope to find some new evidence to help refute the rumors. For one I decided to reread one of Uncle Sergei's monographs on his father. Originally Sergei was a rocket scientist (the most valued profession in the space race era of the 1950s and 1960s), but in 1991 upon moving to the United States, he quit this profession and became a Soviet scholar at Brown University. He felt he needed to write books to explain and justify his father's policies, and in the 2000s, he put together a complete version of Khrushchev's memoirs, three giant volumes that contain perhaps every word that the former premier ever said to his son in private.

Reading Sergei's book, I was reminded that in 1981, ten years after my grandfather had passed and with Brezhnev then in power, Leonid's flight leader Zamorin had apparently sent yet another version of his wingman's last day to Defense Minister Marshal Dmitry Ustinov:

> Our regiment command was eager to take my version at "face value." They shared in severe liability for the pilot's death—the Politburo member's son! Afraid, I made a deal with my conscience, and falsified the facts, omitting in my report that when FW-190 attacked my plane by going under, Khrushchev, flying to the right, tried to save me. He threw his plane to intercept the firing Focker. Leonid knew

what he was facing. The FockeWulf shot his plane with an armor-piercing blow. His plane literally disintegrated before my eyes! It was impossible to find any traces of the disaster on the ground. The authorities didn't conduct an extensive search as the attack occurred over the German-occupied territory.[153]

The letter was cited by other sources as well and made perfect sense. Given Stalin's post-Stalingrad decision to keep children of high-level functionaries out of harm's way, it was safer for the Soviet military to categorize Leonid as missing in action than dead, even if he had died heroically while protecting another pilot. Zamorin was not, after all, a Politburo member's son.

What's more, Putin's own Ministry of Defense has officially accepted Zamorin's last account as evidence of Leonid's innocence. The ministry features this information on its public website.[154] It seems that in contrast to the old Stalinist guard for whom ideology is more important than the truth, many members of the current military would rather recognize their deceased officer as a hero than slander him as a traitor.

Wanting to know more, I turned to Major General Alexander Kirilin, director of the Department in Memory of the Fallen at the Russian Ministry of Defense.[155] Kirilin pointed out yet another sham of the gossip about Leonid: the man who had allegedly captured him was Pavel Sudoplatov, the former head of foreign military intelligence, an infamous mastermind behind the assassination of Trotsky in 1940. Sudoplatov had repeatedly refuted the Leonid-capture allegations, most forcefully in his otherwise very pro-Stalin memoir *Special-Ops*: "[I am] compelled to comment on a rumor—the fate of Leonid Khrushchev, lieutenant and pilot, who went missing in the spring 1943. A number of journalists and veterans of the security forces attributed to me a mythical operation to capture Khrushchev from behind German lines on charges of high treason. Nothing of the sort ever took place."[156]

By late morning, the sky had curdled to a dull shade of gray and more snowflakes clung to the battered highway. As we continued west, Ksenia and I began to see a series of bizarre billboards along the sides of the road: "Beware Paranormal Activity Zones! Twenty People Die in the Car Crashes Just in One Week!" This was another twist that my online exploration had revealed: we were not the only ones looking for Leonid's plane. For years, members of a group of extraterrestrial investigators known as Kosmopoisk (Spacesearch) had been combing these forests in search of aliens and flying saucers. They got fascinated by a number of paranormal claims that villagers have registered over the years: cars going up hills with no one behind the wheel, people vanishing into the trees, the appearance of strange voices, sounds, and lights.[157]

In May of 1998, while trekking through the mysterious woodlands of Smolensk, Bryansk, and Kaluga for UFOs, Kosmopoisk members stumbled upon a decomposed Yak-7B fighter. Although sightings of downed 1940s warplanes are not uncommon in the area, the probe created a sensation due to the personal interest of Vadim Chernobrov, the head of the UFO organization. Chernobrov, who by then was aware of the KGB's rumors about Leonid, became intrigued by the local myths and was eager to treat the disappearance of the young Khrushchev as a cosmic puzzle.

In September of 2011, I learned of Chernobrov's curious quest and called him. "Khrushchev's granddaughter?" he said. "I've been hoping you'd call." A chill went down my spine. The Kosmopoisk chief explained he was "eager to solve the Khrushchev mystery— this legend of the earth," as he described it, to be the first to provide "scientific answers" to Leonid's mysterious fate. In 1998, he apparently had reached out to Uncle Yury to help him unravel the truth behind his father's death. Yet the result of their search was open to doubt. Pavel Ivanov, the eminent Russian geneticist who had successfully identified the remains of seven members of Czar Nicholas's family murdered in Yekaterinburg in 1918, also looked into the issue but couldn't find a genetic match to Yury's DNA. Yury died in 2003, but Vadim explained that even without him, Kosmopoisk was still trying to find Leonid's plane. The last expedition took place in 2004, and although they found a similar aircraft, there was not enough evidence to conclusively link it to Leonid. Chernobrov also complained that since Putin's presidency, "it had become difficult to search. From an explicit authorities' support in 1998—you're doing God's work—to the deliberate stalling in the 2000s, you know who you're looking for, the *nomenklatura* son, a drunkard and a brawler?"

As Ksenia and I passed more alien billboards along the highway, I joked about my conversation with the Kosmopoisk man. We would not be meeting with him in Zhizdra, but he had also told me about the old villager who became a local celebrity because he claimed to have information on Leonid's death. It was the second time I heard of the villager and was curious of what he would say. I was also skeptical since Chernobrov, his good intentions notwithstanding, seemed so thoroughly caught up in paranormal nonsense.

"Perhaps there is something to this cosmic idea though," my sister said suddenly. "The question you always ask, 'What did Grandfather know about Leonid that made him so unforgiving even after his son's death?' If Leonid wasn't a traitor, why was Grandfather so angry? Was it his bad choice of female companions? The 'gang' rumor? The 'bottle-shooting'?"

"Must be all of it: Leonid's 'silly mistakes,'" I replied. That "fathers and sons" conflict? The talented young Khrushchev could have been a Soviet hero, could have made his father proud, but instead he had wasted it all away. Stepan Mikoyan once quipped, "If Leonid remained a bomber, he might have been alive today." Was Grandfather angry about that? His son was a great bomber. Why shake things up? And when he became a fighter pilot, it was only to die, to be lost, ingloriously, disappointing his father once again.

Grandfather wanted nothing more than to have Leonid follow in his footsteps, but he didn't want him to inherit his impetuous spirit. Khrushchev himself paid high price for the erratic behavior. In 1957, he announced a twenty-year goal of overtaking the United States in agriculture, a herculean effort that the rigid planned economy couldn't withstand. Then in 1959, after visiting the United States, he was so excited about corn's feeding capacity that he senselessly encouraged its growth even in the Siberian cold. The wheat farmer in Petrovo Dalnee who told Grandfather "to go to hell" with his instructions in front of cousin Nikita and me some forty years ago actually had a point. The premier's habit of constantly trying new policies with conflicting results must have been stressful to the country.

"In some cosmic sense," my sister added, "both their legacies remain in limbo."

As she spoke, we watched another billboard pass by. As if spooked by her own willingness to accept the existence of the paranormal, Ksenia fell silent. Some fifteen minutes later, we entered the Zhizdra area, and our strange journey became even more surreal.

—⁓⁓—

"The Devil took him," the old man said, his grave voice resonating with absolute authority. It was 11:30 a.m., and Ksenia and I were shivering in our fur-lined coats as we greeted the old peasant, who was chain-smoking *samokrutkis* (hand-rolled cigarettes) on a cold bench near his *izba*, a traditional Russian log cabin. His name was Pavel Uboryatov, and he was eighty years old. He had a farmer's stringy muscles and calloused, knotty fingers, which he frequently ran through his thin, white hair as if his hands were tilling his thoughts, plowing the spaces between his wispy tresses.

Sitting outside of Pavel's home in Vaskovo, a tiny village near Zhizdra, was like stepping into Ivan Turgenev's novella *Notes of a Hunter* (1852); I felt as if we were surrounded by woods that stretched for hundreds of miles. Most of the homes in the area were crumbling, but Pavel's seemed remarkably sturdy. "I rebuilt it myself. Bears scratch the cabin with their claws," he said, taking a long puff. "My whole life was spent here, my parents and grandparents were peasants for at least a few centuries before. This certainly defines our character."

That character was strengthened during the Great Patriotic War, when residents of Zhizdra suffered immensely. By the time the Red Army liberated the town in August 1943, many of the houses had been flattened by bombs or meticulously destroyed by the Nazis, street by street. During roughly two years of Nazi occupation, one-third of all the residents were killed, captured, or deported to Germany, so out of Zhizdra's thirty thousand inhabitants, only three thousand remained after the guns fell silent. All that was left of the town's center were piles of rubbish and red brick dust. As legend has it, the nearby village of Zikeevo was set to become the new city center, but Stalin, in a display of statesmanship, rejected this transition. His customary thick blue pencil, which signed so many death sentences, saved this town with a nimble one-liner: "War shouldn't wipe our cities off the face of the earth."[158]

Russians are often obsessed with their martial history. And why not? During World War II we lost more people than any other nation, including Germany. Here in Zhizdra, where heavy guerrilla fighting took place and numerous mass graves reside, many are still affected by these battles generations later.

After the Germans surrendered in 1945, the people of Zhizdra rebuilt their town; construction went hand in hand with the heavy plaudits given to veterans, the heroes of the Soviet Western Front. In the vicinity of Pavel's ten-hut village, the area has four mass graves, most marked with generic black plaques: "Here are buried unknown partisans and soldiers of the Soviet Army, who died heroic and courageous deaths for the motherland in 1942–1943."[159] The plaque, which lists Leonid's name, is located in the city's main park behind a dilapidated statue of Lenin. Its dedication reads: "To the fighters of the 413 Gunner Regiment who died for the liberation of Zhizdra." Not all the men memorialized were part of this regiment—Senior Lieutenant Khrushchev wasn't, and only a few bodies actually lie beneath the soil. But Nikolai, the Zhizdra clerk, explained: "The locals would proudly tell you that these are the names of brave men, who have given their lives for us."

Perhaps these memorials stand tall in this tiny town and its environs because the memory of suffering is all these people have to be proud of, all they had left after the war's devastation and the state's subsequent neglect. It wasn't just Zhizdra that had to be rebuilt in 1945 but also villages around it. Places like Pavel's Vaskovo that have endured the legacy of both communist collective farming and post-Soviet despair. Vaskovo still has some signs of life, but the few people who remain there today reckon with muddy roads, sporadic electricity, a lack of hot water, and modern sanitation. Pavel's life fits this picture of decay: his wife died years ago, his children moved away to larger cities to find work, to build families. Only Pavel chose to stay behind. He lives sparsely, utterly alone in the forest, his ancestral birthplace, with nothing to keep him company but ghosts.

After trading a few pleasantries in the cold, he welcomed us inside his small Turgenev-like house and seated us at an aged pine table in the center of the room, next to the old Russian clay stove on which he sleeps, allowing him to stay warm in the winter and cool in the summer. Sitting at the table, we sampled some stale crackers and sipped on tea, which Pavel heated in an antiquated copper *samovar*. Our contribution to this simple feast was a box of popular chocolate-covered marshmallow puffs that Ksenia and I had brought from Moscow.

As Pavel savored this treat, he told us about the glory of great Russia, a force of good that he believes cannot be defeated. "With the help of these magic woods, spiritual Russian land has always repelled the enemy," he said. "Our partisans, the forest brothers, together with the Red Army ruined the Germans' ambition. We stood against the evil that always comes from the West. From the fourteenth century—first it was those Teutonic Knights, then the Nazis, now America wants to take over. Here, we are grateful to Putin for standing up against foreign imperialism."[160]

He looked at me sharply as he made his point, though I hadn't told him I live in New York.

For five hundred years, the people who live near Kaluga, Smolensk, and Bryansk have said that the surrounding woods are haunted. The blood spilt there over the centuries has made it the stuff of legends, *a la* Robin Hood's Sherwood Forest. In the 1400s, when Russia began positioning itself as an empire, its czars—eager to replace collapsing Byzantium as the heads of the Orthodox Church—ensured that the territory became the final line of defense against the invading Polish and Lithuanian armies.

In the 1600s, Catholic Poland briefly took over the area, and three centuries later, these "cursed" woods, as if in revenge, witnessed the infamous Katyn massacre. At the start of World War II, the Soviets detained tens of thousands of Polish officers and Catholic clergy in Kozelsk some fifty miles northeast of Zhizdra, then shot them in Katyn, just twelve miles west of Smolensk, one of the regional capitals.[161]

It's perhaps because of this history of violence that many in these woods have continued to believe that evil resides here, that it refuses to retreat. Stalin, always brilliant in deciphering the mood of the nation, ruthlessly exploited this superstition for propaganda purposes, especially during the Great Patriotic War. Speaking like a Soviet prophet, Stalin warned his countrymen of their potential spiritual desolation—a dark force from which the USSR needed to protect itself. "Brothers and sisters," he said. "The enemy is out to restore the rule of landlords, to restore czarism, to destroy national culture and the national state existence of the... free people of the Soviet Union, to Germanize them, to convert them into the slaves of German princes and barons."[162]

If Russia is *holy* by definition, then anything foreign is evil, insidious. This sentiment was perhaps most popularly expressed in what had become a hymn in defense of the motherland, composed on Stalin's orders to confront the Nazi invasion:

> Arise, enormous country
> Arise to the mortal combat
> Against the dark fascist forces
> Against their cursed hordes.
> Our noble wrath seethes like waves.
> Patriotic war is on, The Holy War.[163]

My nanny Masha was from Korolkov, a small town in the nearby Orel region, which is now nothing more than an abandoned patch of forest. For as long as I can remember, she associated her birthplace with the Germans and a mysterious evil they brought with them, viewing everything foreign with suspicion.

Even the names of the towns in this vast countryside— places like Chertovo Gorodnishche (Devil's Township), and Chertovskaya (Devilish) River—reflect the local superstitions. Masha, whose favorite writer was Turgenev—"a poet of peasant life," she said—used to tell me about Vedmin Tupik (Witches Point), a place where witches gathered. Years of Soviet agnosticism in the capital never altered her faith in magic, and the villagers, whose remote provincial life has hardly changed since the time of Peter the Great, are steadfastly wedded to their beliefs as well.

In his superb book *The Agony of the Russian Idea*, the historian Tim McDaniel explained why Marx's dialectic materialism— Western and rational—couldn't break our traditional ways of thinking. Russia was a deeply religious feudal serfdom only decades before the Bolsheviks announced egalitarianism. After the bloody 1917 revolution, the country forged ahead in hopes of creating a utopia of equality and social justice, but the change came so quickly that for much of the twentieth century, Russia couldn't escape its own dysfunction. It was not Marxian development, but "the uneasy combination of despotic state power, rapid modernization,"[164] along with hostility toward the West that formed the modern Russian character, McDaniel writes. In the end the USSR wasn't built upon "Western rationalism or atheism…it too quickly succumbed to Russian traditions of despotism and obscurantism…Behind Stalin's collectivization of agriculture laid not Marxism 'but the social and moral-psychological tradition of serfdom.'"

⸺⬥⬥⬥⸺

While we sat at the table, picking at crackers, Pavel explained that in these rural communities, Leonid's death had become the stuff of legends and fairy tales, a Russian version of *Where the Wild Things Are*. Pavel says he was just eleven years old in 1943 when he personally saw a black German fighter plane flying behind a swift Soviet aircraft, hitting it twice with gunfire:

> No one jumped with a parachute. We saw the crash, ran to the scene through the snow, and found three fingers of a pilot, a screw shaft engine with the Yak numbers, and some half-burnt documents. We couldn't dig long into the wreckage. It was getting dark, and suddenly the Germans arrived on a motorcycle. In their uniform with the Hitler crosses, they inspected the fresh crater with huge flashlights, but I hid the documents and the fingers under my belt.

Similar legends were once common in other villages nearby, but most of the alleged eyewitnesses are now dead, Pavel said.

As he spoke, his voice brimmed with satisfaction that he was the only one left to tell the story:

> My cousin Anna also insisted she found Leonid Khrushchev's plane in her own village Yasenki, where the Germans seized the pilot's documents. But it isn't true; my friends and I buried those fingers behind the house and hid the documents in the basement. My mother handed them over to the Soviet officers after the liberation. They praised us but, seeing Khrushchev's name on the papers, strictly ordered us to keep silent about what we saw. I told my history teacher on Victory Day and when my mother found out what I had done, she whipped me with nettle so I wouldn't disclose state secrets.

Pavel was spitting out his words at a rapid clip, clearly excited to tell someone of his discovery after all these years; our family name obviously made it even more satisfying for him. Pavel swore he had been reporting details of Leonid's death for decades, even writing letters to the Kremlin in the 1950s. "Do you know if the documents ever reached your grandfather?" Pavel asked. "Did Nikita Sergeevich ever get them?"

I wish I knew. After considerable research, it's still unclear whether or not Grandfather received these letters—with Khrushchev in power, many Russians claimed knowledge of his son's character and life—but in 1960, he did entrust Marshal Vladimir Sudets, Commander of Soviet Air Force, to find Leonid's grave.

Pavel recalls that Sudets's subordinates visited his village a few times in the summer of 1960 but ultimately abandoned the search:

> First they were searching in too many places and listened to too many people, my cousin, and so on. Besides, I told them, Khrushchev's son was taken by the devil, and it was the witches' meddling. That's why they can't confirm the

identity of the plane or find the body. The postwar mass grave with the senior lieutenant's name didn't satisfy the visitors. "Nikita Sergeevich wants to bury his son," said the Moscow emissaries.

In the mid-2000s, when I was just getting interested in my family's story and long before I met Pavel, my mother took me to chat with Galina Sudets, the marshal's daughter. We drove to her *dacha* one summer Sunday for some tea and melon in the Sudets's lush garden not far away from our own country house in Peredelkino. The strong scent of cantaloupe and the overwhelming greenery around us made it hard for me to concentrate, and my mother laughingly recalled Big Yulia's comment from years back, "A city boy, Leonya too disliked trees."

Galina kindly ushered us inside the house, and when we finally settled into her dark, spacious living room, it was a very long conversation. Galina's brief marriage to my mother's half-brother left her with a daughter, Ekaterina, my cousin by blood although I never met her. Ekaterina so despised all things Khrushchev that she went by her mother's name—Sudets—and refused to be in touch with her father. Yet Galina and my mother managed to remain friends, so my former half-aunt was excited to share what she knew. For three solid hours, she poured out her memories, telling me that her father had mentioned the local claims about the documents taken to Moscow in 1943 but that he had never uncovered these papers and didn't know if they existed. And so by 1960, she said, the marshal was not about to jump on a murky tale about recovered fingers. A communist agnostic, he did not believe in the Devil's tricks. Instead, Sudets reported to Khrushchev that finding planes in the area's thick woods, deep swamps, and high vegetation was very difficult. If they had not been able to find the plane when the town was liberated some five months after the crash, it would have been far more challenging to locate it in the dense forest nearly two decades later.

Sipping tea in Uboryatov's warm hut, I found myself surrendering to the mood of the moment. "What about other missing pilots in the area?" I said. "Were they taken by the devil as well?" My sister turned to me and stared, her eyes wide with fear and disbelief. As if stunned by her own prediction of the strange and the supernatural that we'd encountered during our trip, Ksenia's face had been frozen in an anxious smile from the moment she met Pavel.

The old man responded matter-of-factly. "They were," he said. "Until Khrushchev became a czar, all were warriors who perished defending us from the invasion of our holy land. We found many bodies since then, but people were coming here, asking for just the one, the leader's son."

He paused before adding, "Nikita shouldn't have gone to America. Stalin never did." Pavel insisted he had nothing against Khrushchev but later admitted thinking that the premier's 1959 peace-making visit to the US had betrayed Russia—and God. "The confusion over the poor lad's fate," he said, "is a result of God's refusal to give him peace because of his atheist father."

My head began to spin. I had set out to find out what had exactly happened to Leonid. We had gathered more evidence disproving the allegations, but we still didn't have a body. We still didn't have a plane. And we would never truly know if Pavel had seen Leonid crash in the woods in 1943. What we did know for sure, however, was that deep in the Kaluga woods, far away from Moscow, Grandfather could still do no right.

Later that afternoon, Ksenia and I finally reached Zhizdra's city park. We wanted to see the plaque—the closest thing we could find to Leonid's actual grave. The park was cold, dreary, and covered with snow. Lenin's statue loomed behind us, his hand stretching out toward the now defunct communist future, which

Grandfather once so wholeheartedly predicted would surpass capitalism by 1980. Black crows rested on bare branches, and gray clouds floated across an empty sky. As dusk prepared to settle, we placed red Soviet era carnations on the monument. In visiting this mass grave, we wanted to acquire a sense of closure, a way to put the past behind us, and to say good-bye to Leonid, the grandfather we never knew. Instead we felt nothing but sadness. The knowledge that the body is lost has kept the ambiguity alive, perhaps not in our heads but certainly in our hearts.

Despite our best efforts, the young Khrushchev's unsettled life has never received a settling conclusion. A grave without a burial must be heartbreaking for any parent. Under normal circumstances, parents can cry, confide in friends, consult psychiatrists. But in the home of a communist apparatchik, where public image always trumped private needs, a true recognition of grief was taboo. There were no tears, no time for healing. As Rada once recalled, "It was painful to never mention Leonya, or to watch Mother, your grandmother, silently overcoming another war death, of her favorite nephew Vasya."

As we left the forest later that evening, I couldn't stop thinking about Grandfather's sad admission some five decades earlier: "I wanted to bury him." Khrushchev loved the war poet Alexander Tvardovsky, and his favorite lines were from Tvardovsky's post-Victory "Requiem" for the fallen soldiers:

> I was killed near Rzhev in a nameless bog...In a violent
>   air raid
> I didn't hear that explosion; I didn't see that flash
> Into an abyss from a cliff, no start, no end
> And in this whole world to the end of its days
> Neither patches, nor badges from my tunic you'll find...
> I am where the blind roots seek for food in the dark...
> Where for a wake even my mother can't come...
> In the summer of forty-two I was buried without a grave
> Everything that would have come later was taken by
>   death.[165]

When I was seven, I often listened to Grandfather recite this poem. Even before I knew anything about Leonid's fate, the line "Neither patches, nor badges from my tunic you'll find" always made me sad.

Knowing what I know now, it breaks my heart.

Lyuba at the geological expedition, Kushmurun, Kazakhstan 1949

My mother, Yulia (right), and aunt Rada at
Moscow State University, 1958

My mother and Grandfather Nikita examining
corn fields in Russia, 1959

My father, Lev Petrov (second right), translating to the Americans at the construction site of the first Soviet exhibition in New York City, 1959

Grandfather, still the Soviet Premier, with Anastas
and Stepan Mikoyan, in Livadia 1963

Nina and Maria Budenny, Marshal Budenny's daughter and wife, with
my mother at the Budenny country house near Peredelkino, 1963

Grandfather Nikita, Anastas Mikoyan and I in a stroller, 1964

My mother and father, Moscow 1966

I am on Grandfather's lap with Grandmother, Petrovo Dalnee 1967

Grandfather, Mother, my sister Ksenia, and I
in Petrovo Dalnee, January 1967

Grandfather Nikita concerned with the affairs of
the Soviet state, Moldova, May 1959

Grandfather, a pensioner, with the locals in Petrovo Dalnee 1968

Grandfather at the head of the table next to my mother; on the left
end Lyuba is sitting next to Grandmother Nina, Peredelkino 1969

My father Lev Petrov and I in the last year of his life, Peredelkino 1969

Grandfather Nikita, my mother, and Victor Gontar (Big Yulia's husband) [back right] in Petrovo Dalnee for Grandfather's last 77th birthday

Grandfather, mother and I on his 77th birthday

Grandfather's funeral at Moscow's Novodevichie cemetery,
September 13, 1971. Grandmother in the center, Big Yulia
behind her, Lena next, and my mother on the right

Sea of people at Grandfather's funeral. Our nanny Maria
"Masha" Vertikova is with the flowers on the left

My mother Yulia and I visiting Grandmother Nina in Zhukovka 1983

My mother and others are at Grandfather's grave on
Novodevichie cemetery for his birthday on April 17, 1986

Uncle Sergei Khrushchev, Rada, my mother and I at Grandfather's centennial celebrated by the Gorbachev Foundation, Moscow 1994

Mikhail Gorbachev and I, Columbia University, New York City 2002

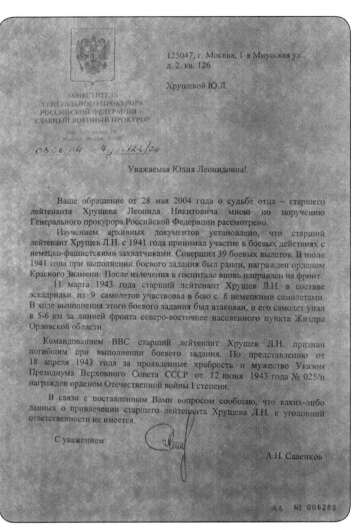

125047, г. Москва, 1-я Миусская ул.,
д. 2, кв. 126

Хрущевой Ю.Л.

ЗАМЕСТИТЕЛЬ
ГЕНЕРАЛЬНОГО ПРОКУРОРА
РОССИЙСКОЙ ФЕДЕРАЦИИ –
ГЛАВНЫЙ ВОЕННЫЙ ПРОКУРОР

Москва, Россия, К-160

03.06.04 № 4ус-122/04

Уважаемая Юлия Леонидовна!

Ваше обращение от 28 мая 2004 года о судьбе отца – старшего лейтенанта Хрущева Леонида Никитовича мною по поручению Генерального прокурора Российской Федерации рассмотрено.

Изучением архивных документов установлено, что старший лейтенант Хрущев Л.Н. с 1941 года принимал участие в боевых действиях с немецко-фашистскими захватчиками. Совершил 39 боевых вылетов. В июле 1941 года при выполнении боевого задания был ранен, награжден орденом Красного Знамени. После излечения в госпитале вновь направлен на фронт.

11 марта 1943 года старший лейтенант Хрущев Л.Н. в составе эскадрильи из 9 самолетов участвовал в бою с 8 немецкими самолетами. В ходе выполнения этого боевого задания был атакован, и его самолет упал в 5-6 км за линией фронта северо-восточнее населенного пункта Жиздра Орловской области.

Командованием ВВС старший лейтенант Хрущев Л.Н. признан погибшим при выполнении боевого задания. По представлению от 18 апреля 1943 года за проявленные храбрость и мужество Указом Президиума Верховного Совета СССР от 12 июня 1943 года № 025/н награжден орденом Отечественной войны I степени.

В связи с поставленным Вами вопросом сообщаю, что каких-либо данных о привлечении старшего лейтенанта Хрущева Л.Н. к уголовной ответственности не имеется.

С уважением

А.Н. Савенков

АА № 006280

Letter from Russian Prosecutor to Mother confirming
the absence of Leonid's criminal record

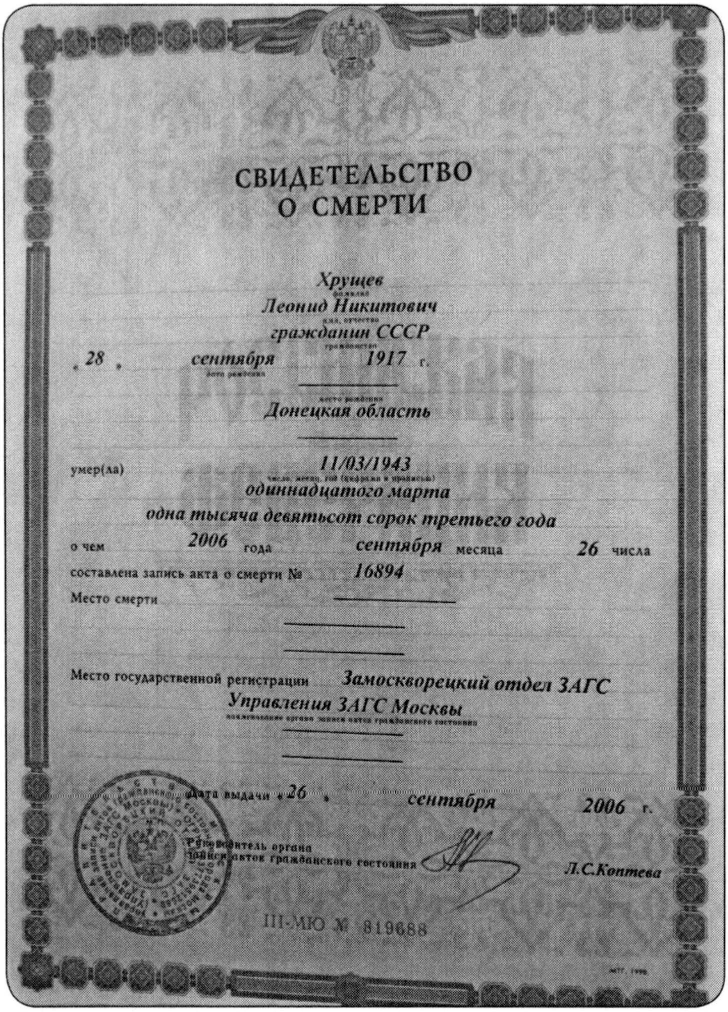

СВИДЕТЕЛЬСТВО
О СМЕРТИ

Хрущев
Леонид Никитович
гражданин СССР
«*28*» *сентября* *1917* г.

Донецкая область

умер(ла) *11/03/1943*
одиннадцатого марта
одна тысяча девятьсот сорок третьего года
о чем *2006* года *сентября* месяца *26* числа
составлена запись акта о смерти № *16894*
Место смерти

Место государственной регистрации *Замоскворецкий отдел ЗАГС Управления ЗАГС Москвы*

Дата выдачи «*26*» *сентября* *2006* г.

Руководитель органа записи актов гражданского состояния *Л.С.Коптева*

III-МЮ № 819688

Leonid Khrushchev's death certificate issued in 2006

Lyuba in Kiev 2009

My sister, Ksenia Khrushcheva, at Leonid's mass grave in Zhizdra 2011

Mass grave's plaque with Leonid's name at the bottom

My mother at the Moscow demonstration
against Vladimir Putin, May 2012

Stalin display at a bookstore on central Arbat Street in Moscow 2012

EPILOGUE: THE GULAG OF THE RUSSIAN MIND

It was a cold and dreary day on October 14, 1964, when the Communist Party's Central Committee told my grandfather that his days as the top Kremlin official were over. No longer one of the most powerful men in the world, the seventy-year-old ex-premier stepped out of his large black car at the gates of his home and found my mother pacing back and forth in the dusk. She wanted to speak to him first, before anyone else, and as he made a few steps, their eyes met.

"Let's walk," he said, and they slowly made their way along the white marble path through the garden. When they got to the back of the house, he stopped short and turned to her.

"That's it," he said. "I'm now a pensioner," he said it almost clinically, like a bureaucrat announcing the latest statistics in agricultural production. My mother, in tears, threw her arms around him, hugging him silently just as she had some twenty years prior. As they embraced, she once again felt like that little girl in Kuibyshev clinging to him because she thought her parents were gone because he was all she had left. Only this time, much as her father's ouster saddened her, she was heartened that he was still alive. Few Soviet leaders had been so fortunate.

"It's okay," Khrushchev said, forcing a joke. "I will have time to read now, to keep up with your intellectual friends." She smiled and then began crying again.

For the next hour, as they walked around the house in the cold, my grandfather recited the poems of Nikolai Nekrasov, his favorite writer. One by one, in a low almost expressionless voice, he read aloud until dusk turned to darkness until the stars poked out through the tapestry of night and there was nothing left but blackness and the low din of his voice:

> All is ever dreary and dismal,
> Pastures, fields, and meadows…
> Here's a drunken peasant driving
> His collapsing nag
> Into far-off blueish mists…
> It makes one weep!

Khrushchev would never have wept, at least not openly. But inside, he was crushed. He knew the Thaw was being destroyed, and he must have thought about his legacy, about the country he was leaving behind.

As Stalin's immediate successor, my grandfather tried to break away from despotism, but he was often bogged down by it, sucked back into the abyss. In considering his legacy, it is hard to ignore his contribution to Russia's national "schizophrenia"—a constant balancing act between liberal reforms and autocracy. For three decades, Khrushchev had been the dictator's faithful ally, and like many high level members of the communist party, he prosecuted enemies of the state and pushed for collectivization and the centralization of power. He was an enthusiastic participant in many of the state's infamous show trials, including that of Bukharin, his favorite revolutionary.

Khrushchev's own reign began with bringing Stalinesque charges against Beria, accusing him of being a Western spy, as if the former NKVD chief didn't have real crimes for which to try him. Khrushchev went back and forth on policies: in 1956, he manifested himself as both a reformer who launched the secret speech and a despot who in typical Soviet fashion sent tanks to Hungary to suppress an uprising, which, ironically, was inspired by his words.[166] In doing so, he fell prey to Russia's great weakness—our most honorable aims often justify the most brutal means of achieving them.

My grandfather's impetuous spirit, which I enjoyed so much as a little girl, frequently translated into rash political action while he was in power. Known in America for his (much mythologized) promise to "bury" the United States,[167] at home Khrushchev was criticized for his stormy relations with the Soviet *intelligentsia* such as Andrei Sakharov, who refused to participate in the USSR's nuclear program, or Ernst Neizvestny and other artists with whom the premier clashed at Moscow's Manezh Gallery over avant-garde art versus communist-appropriate "socialist-realism."[168]

For all his mistakes, though, Grandfather never entirely fell victim to the gulag of the Russian mind, a mental prison that compels our leaders to paper over historical injustices rather than addressing them candidly—all in order to protect our outdated image of national greatness, of imperial grandeur based on Russia's enormous size of almost seven million square miles and nine time zones that stretch from Germany to Japan. Khrushchev once famously told my mother's friend, the writer Mikhail Shatrov, "My hands are covered in blood up to the elbows. But I did what others did. I participated in repression because I was convinced that only the total annihilation of the enemy could ensure the shining future of international communism."

He wasn't excusing himself, but rather, as historian Roy Medvedev explained to me, "was openly admitting his mistakes. He reconsidered his policies, he apologized to everyone he affected. By acknowledging past errors, Russia too can find a way out of its repetitive pendulum swings—from dictatorship to democracy and back again."

Unlike many other Russian leaders, Khrushchev had a heart and was a human being, a rare breed among the Soviet apparatchiks of the post-Stalin era. Even if he relentlessly criticized Leonid, like his son, he also craved freedom: he wanted to free the party from the guards and the gulags.

My mother says Khrushchev hated being guarded by government agents behind the Kremlin walls. He always fought against the traditional separation between the Russian elite and the masses, and he often longed for the unscripted exchanges with the *narod*, the people. While still in power, Grandfather used to take his lunch hour to walk around, "to touch the pulse of the nation, just to sit on a bench in the park next to his Kremlin office, and to watch people pass him by, to chat with the workers about their lives and their needs," in Mother's words.

I thought of this habit of his a few years back when on a rainy July day Ksenia and I took one of our now customary trips to explore the family's past. First we drove to Zhukovka, where Grandmother and Molotov once lived as neighbors. Only now the gray Soviet cottages had been replaced with huge luxury homes and well-armed policemen guarding the country's financial elite. We begged the guards to let us in to check on Grandmother's house, but they just laughed in our faces. "Khrushchev who?" one of them asked.

Turned away, we drove ten miles down the road to Grandfather's former government estate in the village of Usovo west of Moscow. Today Putin lives there, and since he took over this palatial *dacha* a dozen years ago, the locals have rarely seen the former KGB apparatchik. What they have seen are the twenty-foot tall fences, the guards armed with machine guns, and occasionally, if they're lucky, they catch a glimpse of the elongated shadow of Putin's black limousine with dark-tinted windows.

As we walked through the village streets, we met a *babushka* named Anna who lived in a blue wooden house, which was fit for a fairy tale. Like most Russians in the provinces, she was kind and hospitable. When we told her who we were, she invited us in for tea and gooseberry jam and talked excitedly about Grandfather:

> He was not like other leaders. After a busy Kremlin day, he still often made neighborly visits with Rada and the grandkids. Nikita was a simple guy. He loved the animals and always asked if his kids could see our cattle. Our goat was a bit restive and once tried to escape. Khrushchev caught the goat himself. Everyone in Usovo adored him. Sometimes men would return from work, from the farm, and the nation's leader was right there greeting them and shaking their hands. The peasants were shy. They would always say: "Nikita Sergeevich, our hands are dirty!" But he would always respond: "Your hands aren't dirty. These are real working hands."

That openness that he indiscriminately showed to Russian farmers in his free time or on the job to the Ukrainian peasants during *Holodomor*…that humility is why Grandfather would have loved Gorbachev's glasnost and perestroika. He would have also admired the man himself; Gorbachev was an embodiment of Khrushchev's dream of the liberating changes that the Thaw generation would contribute to Soviet politics.

But Putin, the product of yet another pendulum swing in Russia, would have left him despondent. Khrushchev was an imperfect reformer, yet he aspired to make our country a less isolated nation. For all his disapproval of Leonid, my grandfather respected the sacrifices his son made during the Great Patriotic War. He never expected fairness from the KGB, but he couldn't have imaged that forty years later, Putin and his cohorts would use Leonid's death as a crass political tool to debase the Thaw and resurrect the "glories" of Stalinism. Half a century after the dictator's death, it would seem improbably Stalinesque.

My grandmother too could never have foreseen what would become of Leonid's legacy but for very different reasons. On the same day that the party replaced Khrushchev, Nina was on vacation with Brezhnev's wife, Victoria, in Czechoslovakia. They were staying at a resort called Karlovy Vary, enjoying the water, taking long walks, and having a pleasant time away from the pressures of supporting their husbands. But on October 14, Victoria had stepped away for a moment, and as my grandmother was sipping on tea in the *nomenklatura* rest home's spacious lobby, a clerk told her that she had a phone call from Mikhail Zimyanin, the Soviet Ambassador to Czechoslovakia. Nikita was no longer in charge, he said, and the country won't have to tolerate his idiotic politics any more. A moment of excruciating silence passed as Zimyanin realized that out of habit he asked for Comrade Khrushcheva, not Comrade Brezhneva, that he had been on the phone with the wrong person. A staunch communist until her dying day, Grandmother didn't flinch. It was the party's decision she always said, and the party knew best. She hung up the phone. When Victoria returned, my grandmother looked at her and smiled. "Now you will be inviting me to the Kremlin dinners and state receptions," she said.

And that's how Nina was. Unlike her husband, the Soviet Union's reluctant czar, she believed that the party was God. I remember in the late summer of 1969, my mother took me for a ride to see my grandparents in Petrovo Dalnee. She was rushing to pick up Ginsburg's *Into the Whirlwind* and Solzhenitsyn's *First Circle*. Censored by the Soviet state, the two books had been published abroad, and Roy Medvedev had lent them to my grandparents a week prior. Now his "customers" all over Moscow were waiting for their *samizdat* fix.

We were in a hurry, so we met Grandfather outside in front of the house. He loved the books and was almost giddy with excitement. "I was so right," he said, referring to the secret speech.

Then he lowered his voice. "Don't be upset though. Your mother didn't like them." Soon Grandmother stepped onto the porch and walked toward us carrying the forbidden books as if they gave off some foul odor—like garbage or a dead mouse.

"I didn't finish reading," she said, handing my mother the books.

"Roy will let you keep them for a bit longer," my mother replied.

"No," Grandmother said, waving her off. "This is all a lie. If this were true, how come we are still alive?"

When my grandfather denounced Stalin, Grandmother accepted his every word, not because he was her husband but because he was the leader of the party and thus the absolute authority in her life. If the party said something, it was true, and so she didn't dispute the anti-Stalin views Nikita espoused. Yet when confronted with a fictional recreation of the gulag's brutality, Grandmother, a propagandist by trade, saw the two novels as little more than malicious attempts to debase the Soviet state. Years later, I asked her about those books, and she was still firm in her disdain: "We had to make sacrifices for Bolshevism, not splash our troubles on the page and for the whole world to see." Khrushchev's own memoirs were already in the works, and my mother said that Nina was dead afraid that even if it was not critical of the Brezhnev USSR, too many people were involved in the project, which by its sheer novelty could hurt or upset the party.

Nina passed away in 1984. She didn't live to see the demise of her grandiose delusions. She never lived to see Leonid being used to denounce her husband and his reforms. But if she had, I can't help but wonder if she would have found some creative way to accept the party line, that grand and ubiquitous lie; if she, like my grandfather's rival Molotov would have blamed the collapse of the Soviet Union on the "reformers," namely Khrushchev, her husband, for unleashing that beast called democracy. For her whole life, Grandmother viewed the Bolshevik Revolution as pure unmitigated good and capitalism as pure unmitigated evil. She spent her last days still trapped within its illusions: her letters to friends were always signed, "With communist hello, Comrade Nina Kukharchuk." Rejecting those illusions would have been admitting that she too had failed, that the cause to which she used to propagate so vigorously ultimately did not make our country a better place.

—◁▥◊▥▷—

If my grandmother Nina represents one side of the gulag of the Russian mind—that the guards can do no wrong—Lyuba's life serves as another, an even more disturbing example of our country's delusional state. For her, the guards are benevolent and kind. In Lyuba's world, the gulag can be used to her advantage, and every parade portrays her as an important person who achieved great things.

Even the physical gulag failed to dampen this woman's spirit. In 1949, upon her release from the Mordovia labor camp, the NKVD authorities exiled her to Kushmurun, a small town in Kazakhstan, where she immediately married Isai Grigerman, a geologist and a political exile. She keenly joined in his (or rather returned to her old) line of work, mineral excavation.

As Lyuba tells it, even the local NKVD was impressed with "my trustworthy communist disposition." Right away they asked her to become an informant, and she agreed after a bit of back and forth. Today, she says she never reported on anyone. It might be mere coincidence that Vera Grigerman, Isai's sister, was arrested in 1952 for using the word "junk" to describe Soviet life. She disappeared into the dungeons of the NKVD, never to be heard from again. Yet on one occasion, which I tape recorded in the summer of 2004, Lyuba let it slip that after Vera's arrest, she was "increasingly pressured to report on *even more* anti-Soviet instances." Indeed, it would have been impossible for an informant to avoid the NKVD denunciation quotas for five years without risking going back to gulag for lack of vigilance.

In March 1954, Lyuba—"exhausted by the pressure," she says—decided to quit spying altogether. *Convenient*, I thought. Stalin had been dead for a year, and people were leaving the camps even before the official rehabilitation began two years later. She, however, insists, "I didn't know the changes were coming. I was inspired by a book I read at the time, Nikolai Shpanov's *The Arsonists*." A national best-seller glorifying international intelligence, the novel featured a female character, who refused to work for the Nazis and bravely dared her captors to shoot her. "I felt exactly like that woman," Lyuba says.

Her war-time affair with the Frenchman made espionage seem romantic, and Lyuba was finally able to live out her fantasies. She recalls how, expecting fireworks, she firmly told her handler that she was quitting the NKVD no matter the consequences. But the officer, indifferently, simply told her to submit a request for rehabilitation.

Just like that, Stalinism was over.

For millions of ex-inmates all over the colossal USSR life was to begin anew—even an unhurried cup of coffee in the morning for many would become a difficult challenge. Svetlana Alliluyeva wrote about her aunt Alliluyeva-Redens: freed from the gulag, Stalin's sister-in-law was indifferent to everything in her regular existence, from her children to her favorites foods. Most former prisoners describe the same feeling of apathy.[169]

But Lyuba was different. Upon release as she put it, "I immediately resumed the life I was supposed to live." She never became sad or pensive. She had assiduously kept up on Moscow's and Kiev's latest trends in fashion, theater, and gossip. She seemed unable to lament or to cry. She betrayed no remorse. The hard life must have caused her to purposely block out anything that didn't reinforce her vision of herself as a virtuous woman who overcame all obstacles.

Orphaned by her mother's death and given to God by her father at early age, Lyuba didn't receive enough attention as a child. To make it bearable, she began to imagine herself as perfect and universally beloved. A psychiatrist friend in New York City says she may have narcissistic personality disorder, which was gradually amplified by the demands of the Russian state to uphold an image of strength, no matter what.

With the gulag years now an excuse of any and all Lyuba's past missteps, she began to write letters to Grandmother Nina in hopes of seeing my mother and reclaiming her parental rights. Because her relationship with Leonid was essentially over by the time she voluntarily gave up her daughter in 1942, she had lost all claims to her child. But as the young Khrushchev's widow, she could demand to see Little Yulia and so get access to the first family of the Soviet Union, which is perhaps why she continued to lie about her marriage to Leonid. Against my grandfather's objections, Grandmother allowed Lyuba be a part of my mother's life. Nina, after all, was the one who made the rules for our family, even if Khrushchev set the rules for the country.

One early September morning in 1956, Grandmother sat my mother down and said decisively, to avoid any arguments: "Lyuba was in the gulag. She shed lots of tears. You need to see her. She will explain everything. She is staying at Arisha's." My mother, then sixteen, looked at Nina numbly. For years, she assumed that Lyuba had passed away along with Leonid in 1943 since her name was unspoken around the house. Now, Lyuba was suddenly alive.

That same day my mystified mother went to Arisha's apartment on Karmanitsky Street. She had only touched the doorbell when a youthful forty-four-year-old woman in a form-fitting white dress burst through the door and enthusiastically hugged her, screaming: "Daughter! She looks exactly like Leonya! I've missed her so much!" Words were rolling off the woman's tongue at a rapid clip, and my mother says it was uncomfortable to be hugged by a stranger who oddly kept referring to her in the third person.

Soon they were flipping through a large photo album. There were pictures of Lyuba in her pilot fatigues, of Leonid holding my mother as a baby and Lyuba sitting on a bench with a young man in a foreign military uniform.

"Who is that?" my mother asked, interrupting Lyuba's excitement.

"Oh, a friend, a Frenchman," Lyuba paused uncomfortably.

Twirling her blonde braids, Yulia was trying to comprehend what it meant to have two mothers, laying claim to her existence. She had so many questions that afternoon but found it impossible to get through her birth mother's energetic façade. From then on, a well-rehearsed version of Lyuba's faultless past had turned into a staple of their relationship. And even if she became a permanent part of my mother's life and later mine, there was never any closeness; Lyuba insisted on being recognized as *the mother* (and *the grandmother*, although I have never called her that).

But what failed completely was her attempt to reconnect with Khrushchev, whom she wrote two letters asking for some post-gulag privileges and accommodations. Nikita never responded personally but did help with an apartment, and Lyuba eventually settled in Kiev, the city where she was born.

Their first meeting since the war came in June 1969 at our family's *dacha* in Peredelkino for my sister's fifth birthday. Grandfather entered the garden on foot from the back door, leaving his KGB handlers in a car outside the fence. He walked toward the house along a path under the apple trees when Lyuba intercepted him. She must have wanted to gauge his reaction in private, to prevent gruff treatment in front of the guests.

"Hello, Lyuba," he said coldly and passed her by. He never spoke to her again.

As far as Grandfather was concerned, she didn't only betray his son; she betrayed the motherland. It was bad enough that Leonid was an inadequate communist. But how could he forgive Lyuba for an affair with a French national, for deserting her children in the middle of the war? And yet since he never openly challenged her narrative that the gulag interrupted the family's bliss, now, some forty years after Khrushchev's death, in all of Lyuba's stories, Nikita loved her. The family loved her. Even though the truth, I think, was that my grandmother Nina forced Lyuba back into our lives to compensate for Lyuba's older son Tolya's misfortunes.[170] After Leonid's "wife" was arrested in 1943, the boy ended up in an orphanage, and for that, Grandmother must have felt, she owed Lyuba a bit of motherhood.

Today, Lyuba is one hundred, but she still thinks of herself as that heroine she invented as a child, a Soviet Rosie the Riveter of in a stylish leather jacket and her hair tied in a red kerchief. When she marked her centennial on December 25, 2012, she sat in an armchair watching people crowd into her Kiev apartment for yet another parade of her life. There were relatives, a few elderly neighbors, and though I was in New York at the time, I too was a "guest" by way of Skype. For two hours, I watched her take her bow. Lyuba's mind, sharp as ever, zeroed in on one core message: Her familial importance as Leonid's beloved widow and Nikita Khrushchev's favorite daughter-in-law. "It was a city-wide celebration," she later told my mother over the phone.

Afterward, Mother sneered, "Lyuba is like those Stalinist generals with Leonid's 'treason.' Everyone knows it's untrue, but they push the story anyway."

In Lyuba's life, there is no secret speech or glasnost. A product and a victim of communism, her personal lies mirror those of the Kremlin, which held grand parades, as the people suffered and starved. But the ultimate joke is on my propagandist grandmother: In expecting Soviet citizens to act flawlessly, the system only reinforced their flaws, a fate both Leonid and Lyuba could not escape.

But while Leonid was a communist nonconformist, the rarest breed in the 1930s, Lyuba is the ultimate product of Soviet conformity, the perfect embodiment of what the USSR wanted of its citizens—someone who always surrenders to the demands of the regime. There was no slogan that she didn't approve of, no heroic profession for which she didn't strive. Once a devout communist and atheist, she now believes in capitalism and church—just as the state prescribes.

A typical Russian, she also believes in czars, not peasants, and hates rulers who seem ordinary—Khrushchev with his energetic fists, Gorbachev with his readiness to amend the mistakes of the Soviet past. "Real" Russians are strong and unapologetic, which is perhaps why she loves power, why she is partial to leaders who project absolute authority: Stalin who instilled "order" (her time in the gulag notwithstanding), Putin who has "might," and Yeltsin, Yeltsin, mostly because he was "an attractive man."

⸻⸙⸻

My mother too is the product of the gulag, not its physical brutality but its mind-set. All countries suffer from delusions, but Russia thrives on a unique, paradoxical form of tyranny. The people seem to live their lives perpetually fluctuating between two extremes—total oppression during dictatorship on one end and disorderly remission during reform on the other—which ultimately makes compromise impossible and hampers the country's ability to move forward.

In an effort to preserve her father's legacy, "communism with the human face" as it was called during the Thaw, my mother eagerly fought against Stalinism. But she too remains trapped between two opposing worldviews; in her life these are of her two "mothers"—Nina's delusion of universal dictatorship of proletariat and Lyuba's illusion of personal achievements.

In my mother's life, one normalizing factor was Nikita. She was a granddaughter turned daughter, an orphan who needed more love and care. She knew he was sorry that Lyuba ended up being a social climber rather than the upright Soviet he thought she was. She knew that perhaps he even felt guilty about how harsh he was with Leonid.

Despite Grandfather's love, though, my mother never stopped feeling like that tiny toddler in Kuibyshev, both belonging and not belonging, waiting for her birth parents to come home, always afraid to be pushed to the side. That's why she often believes today that nothing will ever work out, so it's better to remain in the dark, to close her eyes and ears to anything that might upset her. Why she never read Khrushchev's memoir or any of Sergei's books. For her, the truth is simply too unsettling.

A lot of this is personal, of course. But it also reflects the mind-set of many Russian people who are accustomed to their leaders making decisions for them. For as much as my mother yearned for liberation, like many intellectuals in the 1960s, she didn't welcome the fall of the Soviet Union. She mourns a time when freedom didn't exist, when everything was soaked in meaning. When they could complain from their kitchens but never go out into the street justifying their lethargy by fear of the gulag. But in truth, because of all they've endured, it is change that Russians fear the most, especially a change of power. We tolerate the worst aspects of despotism and have an equal distrust of individualism and freedoms. The latest poll shows that Russians prefer state capitalism to its *laissez-faire* version, moreover they demand more control and oversight from the Kremlin: censorship to uphold moral standards and limit to human rights to maintain order.[171] As the old saying goes, the devil you know is better than the devil you don't.

Still, my mother didn't entirely give up efforts to confront the regime. She took charge by defending the family honor through courts. And when Russian legal system failed her—inspired by my trip to Zhizdra—she overcame her usual complacency and traveled to Strasbourg in the fall of 2012 to see if she could get European justice for Leonid once and for all.

The sun was warm that morning as she walked through the train station, the light shining through the clear glass vestibule. My mother's eyes darted in all directions as she followed the throng of morning commuters, periodically stopping to adjust her paisley pashmina around her beige suede jacket or pat down her hair, styled in an elegant bob.

She had heard there were strikes over the weekend in Strasbourg, but on that day, the city was calm. A good sign, she thought, as she hailed a cab and, in broken French, asked the driver to take her to the edge of the city to the Palais des Droits de L'Homme. Soon they arrived at the embankment near the European Court of Human Rights, a tall round glass building with a pair of welcoming automatic doors. There were no lines at the entrance, no overly intrusive searches or guards barking unreasonable demands. The whole scene exuded transparency, modernity, and legal order—the complete opposite of a typical Russian office building. Everything seemed to be falling into place, and somewhere deep inside her, she heard a soft jingle of confidence rising up in her gut. She tried to dampen the sound of those optimistic notes but couldn't help feeling consumed by the prospect of hope. For five years, my mother had been waiting for a decision from the European Court. Nothing had come, so she finally made an appointment to talk to someone about her case. In her head, she knew that it was a lost cause, that they would never force the Russian government to crack down on Leonid's libelers. But in her heart…in her heart, it was a different matter entirely.

That sense of optimism carried my mother up the elevator. The doors popped open on the sixth floor; a young female clerk in an efficient dark-blue suit greeted her, "Mrs. Khrushcheva?"

My mother nodded, repressing a smile.

"Your file 32680-07, *Khrushcheva v. Russia*, is ready for consultation."

They sat at the conference table right there next to the lifts, and right away her optimism dissolved. "There is no decision on a formal inquiry," the clerk said in English. "Not even on hearing your case yet. You should have checked through your lawyer."

"I needed to come," my mother replied a low voice, her accent sounding like Greta Garbo's in *Ninotchka*. "I need to know one day this matter will be resolved."

"But with the all cases coming from Russia, your case…" The friendly clerk didn't want to be discouraging. She said reassuringly, "One day…" and took the file back.

My mother returned to the train station on foot, crossing the river on Pont de la Rose Blanche and wandering for two hours through the clean Alsatian streets. The trees had lost most of their foliage, but while Moscow had already seen its first snow, winter in Strasbourg seemed distant like a dream you forget the minute you wake up. When she finally reached the station, she felt exhausted, utterly depressed. The afternoon sun now hid behind a veil of clouds, and the vestibule was silent and cold. The information board was blinking green, which meant a train was leaving for Paris, so she scurried toward the track.

That night, Mother called me, full of reproach. It was I, she said, who had pushed her to fight on: "I knew it wouldn't lead to anything. We'll never get justice." Then she paused and muttered, perhaps out of guilt, "Just promise me that you'll finish your book."

Her voice was calm, but I could sense a tinge of bitterness and defeat on her tongue. There was more of it, I knew, in the words caught in her throat. This is how I imagine Grandfather must have sounded the day of his ouster, how he must have felt when he learned that Leonid, his first son, was gone. For our family, all losses are political, all losses are intertwined. All loses are expressed in what's left unsaid.

⫷⫸

Sometimes while sitting in my East Village apartment, safely ensconced from the chaos of the city, I think about changing my last name back to Petrova. Sometimes I even think of returning to Russia. Not for the idyllic white birches, as my memories of playing in the pumpkin patches around Grandpa's pensioner *dacha* have forever destroyed my appreciation for nature, but because I think Nabokov was right when he said that in some ways, the immigrant is always "longing for home," that we all have, to some extent, a myopic sense of nostalgia for the past, for the place where we're from. I normally shake those thoughts away the moment they pop into my head, knowing that I'm far more content in New York than I would ever be in Moscow, even if it means that I'll forever live across the ocean from my family. It is just a nine-hour flight away, and as long as the option to return exists, I'm happy to remain right where I am.

But several years ago, I came close to understanding what it would mean to never return. It was the summer of 2007, and Russia was in the throes of Putin's second term in office. Oil prices had skyrocketed, and Putin was using the windfall to pump billions into military spending, seemingly restoring the power and influence of the Russian state, turning Russia into a great power in terms of energy production. Never mind that scant investment had been made to upgrade the country's crumbling infrastructure, to maintain and improve the oil and gas fields, and to modernize education and new technology—what mattered was selling the reserves and being rich *now*, not finding more for later.

Yet for many, the former KGB man was a beloved figure, someone to be admired for having returned the country to its rightful place on the world stage. As it was once had been around Stalin, a cult of personality had developed around Putin too. There were mugs and calendars; his face was tattooed on people's chests and embroidered on decorative rugs. And this cult of personality grew to such an extent that the techno pop duo *Poyushchie Vmeste* (Singing Together) became an instant sensation after they released their hit, "I Want Someone Like Putin."

> Someone like Putin, full of strength;
> Someone like Putin, who doesn't drink;
> Someone like Putin, who doesn't hurt me.[172]

To some in Russia and the United States, the song was hilarious, a pitch-perfect parody of the absurdities of dictatorship. But it was also a prime example of Putin's political genius that tapped into a deep-seated insecurity of a large nation that had suddenly become insignificant. More than a decade after the collapse of the Soviet Union, being perceived as powerful was more important to Russians than actually being powerful. Putin didn't need to modernize the country so that it could compete with other global powers; he just needed to puff out his chest enough—appropriately symbolized by his now world-famous bare-chested posing—so people would think that Russia had once again become first rate. Always ready to pretend he bravely serves the nation, Putin has been navigating submarines, flying airplanes, and riding tractors—all dutifully broadcast on state-controlled TV to show off the president's man-of-the-people persona. These silly PR stunts went hand in hand with the Kremlin's heavy investment in historical propaganda, which is how the rumors about Leonid's "treason" and his father's "shame" came to resurface.

Watching the drama unfold from abroad, Putin's playbook seemed like a bad version of Nikolai Gogol's play *The Inspector General* (1836), a mordant and hilarious story about a pompous but trivial official named Khlestakov who fools everyone into thinking he's important. In August of 2007, I published an article in the *International Herald Tribune* that made the comparison between Gogol's character and Putin, writing that Russia was still a nation where, "individual needs are neglected, the state's needs are overstated, and everyone is condemned to a life of cheating and stealing, consoling themselves that, while there is no justice, they are at least part of a great country."[173]

Almost immediately, my mailbox was flooded with more than five hundred hateful e-mails. Someone by the handle of *Sibiryak* (from Siberia, implying an image of strength) warned me against promoting the West's domination of Russia.

Several days later, a once liberal-politician-turned-Putin-flunky called me in New York, delivering a stern warning from the Kremlin. "The boss felt very let down by you," he said. "He thought you would have the right perspective. You of all people should know how hard it is to rule this country." Both flattered and terrified that Putin read my article, I explained—admittedly with trepidation—that I understood how difficult it is to run the country and that I hoped Putin would make steps toward progress, not more backward. I told the flunky about the hate mail I had received and asked whether there would be further repercussions. I never got an answer. He simply hung up.

Around the same time I had to renew my passport at the Russian consulate on Manhattan's Upper East Side. It was supposed to be ready in a month, but time passed, and I had heard nothing. In December, an official letter finally came. "To obtain information about the status of your document please make an appointment with the deputy political attaché Mr. V. P. Ivanov."

Mr. Ivanov: no first name, no patronymic, just the initials. Like most Russian citizens, I know when my government is upset with me. My passport delay and my anti-Putin stance were undoubtedly connected. Of course Putin's Russia in 2007 is not the same as Stalin's Soviet Union in 1937, but at that moment, I realized what it must have been like seventy years ago when people knew that the state was always watching. *What if I never get my passport?* I thought. *What if I get arrested?*

On a cold morning before Christmas, I went to the consulate. Dressed impeccably in a pink shirt and matching tie, Mr. Ivanov, a well-polished man in his early thirties, greeted me at the entrance. He still never told me his first name. We walked through some winding corridors until we arrived at his office, where he offered me a seat, opened a drawer, and pulled out a folder. My folder. I couldn't believe I even had one. Inside I was trembling.

"Nina Lvovna!" he said. "We have been following your writing."

As I sank down into the chair, I felt like I was watching myself from afar, as if I had suddenly been transformed into a character in a Solzhenitsyn novel.

"We are impressed with your analysis," he said. "However, you understand that your critical views could be interpreted as an incitement of hatred against Russia's leadership."

Seriously, am I that important? I thought to myself. My mind flashed back to what had happened to my grandfather and his memoirs. *How could my little articles be an incitement of hatred?* But I, of course, said nothing.

"We are not going to ask you to sign anything," Mr. Ivanov told me, which meant I didn't need to go on record and promise never to write a critical word about Putin again. "But we hope you will think of how your words about your country resonate."

"Yes, thank you," I replied.

He reached into my folder, pulled out my new red passport, and handed it to me, his face bearing the expectation that from then on I would act like an obedient Russian citizen. But how could I? How could I sit back silently while Putin and his *siloviks*—the new military industrial complex—used the country as their personal playground and all the while Leonid and my grandfather are being defamed?

The travesty of the situation hit me several years later during my annual trip to Moscow. Whenever I'm in town, I always take the metro, the only surviving and well-functioning relic of the Soviet past. On Stalin's orders, my grandfather oversaw its construction, and the trains still run perfectly every two minutes as they did before the USSR collapsed.

This time my visit was specifically to the mosaic-and-marble-covered vestibule in Kurskaya station, the latest talk of the town. Refurbished to its 1950 appearance, it bore a new gold engraving from the war version of the Soviet national anthem—*Stalin brought us up to be loyal to the nation, inspired us to labor and great deeds.* I was too young to witness the Thaw, but I also never saw

Stalin's name on public monuments. Brezhnev had rolled back Khrushchev's reforms, instilling a form of latent Stalinism, but it was only under Putin that Stalin's name had been fully rehabilitated.[174]

If that wasn't bad enough, the return of the Stalin worship has also marked the return of show trials, adding yet another layer of farce to the Russian legal system. First there was the trial of Mikhail Khodorkovsky, an oil oligarch who began criticizing Putin in 2003 and soon found himself serving eleven years behind bars in a gulag in northern Russia for theft and embezzlement. A decade later, and the Khodorkovsky trial seems almost normal, commonplace. In 2012, three members of the feminist punk band Pussy Riot were arrested for performing an anti-Putin song in Moscow's main cathedral of Christ the Savior. And in July 2013, Aleksei Navalny, an anticorruption lawyer, blogger, and budding politician, joined the growing list of the supposed criminals whose only crime seems to be their opposition to Putin's power. Navalny allegedly defrauded a state-run provincial timber company, an accusation, which I'm sure has a lot to do with him leading a series of massive protests around Russia's most recent president elections. Navalny is lucky though. He's alive. The same can't be said for Sergei Magnitsky, another lawyer and whistleblower who spoke out against official corruption before he was starved to death in prison and posthumously convicted of tax evasion, a move that harkened back—in an ironic reversal—to Khrushchev's and Gorbachev's posthumous acquittals of many victims of the Great Purges.[175]

Stalin's show trials were held to demonstrate the USSR's "impartiality." The same legal jargon is used today to protect Putin and his associates from accountability. His cohorts are unyielding in their disdain for the opposition, saying that life behind bars is "the path for all who are connected to the West and work against Russia."[176]

But acting as a modern czar, who rules in the name of traditional values and repulsed by Western decadence, Putin and his propaganda aim to portray him compassionate and benevolent. In December 2013 Khodorkovsky and Pussy Riot were pardoned and released, even if the Kremlin's real motivation had nothing to do with any conventional concept of law and order, much less with a move toward democracy. By freeing his opponents, the Russian president simply sought to appease foreign critics before the winter Olympics in a resort town of Sochi the following February.

When I hear these news, I can't help but wonder: *If Grandfather had gone further with his reforms, would the USSR have lasted as long as it did? If Grandmother hadn't believed in the Soviet system so unquestionably, would the system have remained so resistant to democracy? If Lyuba hadn't accepted everything that the authorities told her, would Russia still have pretended to be a great nation? If my mother wasn't so afraid to speak up when she could and not just in her "dissident" kitchen, would we have a former KGB man leading the country today?*

The answer became perfectly clear when I learnt that, Nadezhda Tolokonnikova, one of the Pussy Riot members, would be serving a two-year sentence for hooliganism in the exact same penal colony where Lyuba was imprisoned some seventy years ago. In contemporary Europe, there is no space for political crimes, but just imagine recent European prisoners like the singers Cheb Mami from Algeria or Seth Gueko of France—jailed for violence, not songs—serving out their sentence in a cell in Auschwitz. It's preposterous. Some institution should simply disappear for their notorious associations alone, but Russia never went through its own version of the Nuremberg trials, despite the promises of the secret speech. Grandfather denounced Stalin and the gulag system, but the prisons still remain, both physically and in the minds of the Russian people.

In Khrushchev's defense, my mother often reminds me of what he used to say: "I touched the surface of this tub full of dough, others will come and finish the job." And she's right. Some six decades after the Thaw, it is too late for my mother's generation to take responsibility for the despotism we have come to tolerate, even if to her credit she now goes to every anti-Putin demonstration that is held in Moscow. But it has also been more than twenty years since the collapse of the USSR, which makes my generation, those in the forties and fifties—more so—the twenty and thirty somethings, responsible for any change we may see in the future.

The good news is that the new show trials have revealed a shift: neither Navalny, nor Khodorkovsky, nor Pussy Riot has admitted any guilt; instead, have continued to speak out from gulag prison cells and courtrooms challenging the gulag in our minds. The bad news is that the Russian mind is still rife with political duality.

Today we object to "Putin's Party of crooks and thieves," a line coined by Navalny. We finally began to resent the "stolen" 2011 parliamentary and 2012 presidential elections, but let's be honest, they were stolen before, and then we remained silent.

We said nothing when Yeltsin simply "nominated" Putin as his replacement in 1999; Putin did the same in 2008 with his protégé Dmitry Medvedev, now the prime minister.

We are guilty of complacently allowing the Kremlin men to obtain the riches under the pretense of serving the state. In 2000, we complained about Yeltsin's corruption and his personal fortune of some meager fifteen million dollars. How did we let Putin amass seventy billion dollars in personal wealth all the while his annual Kremlin salary is just 5, 7 million rubles ($173,000)?[177]

Russians who have acquired a middle class lifestyle under Putin's oil bonanza and just a few years ago used to praise their strong leader suddenly feel betrayed by the czar's failed promises to instill post-Yeltsin justice, order, and control.[178] The public is now demanding more accountability from the Kremlin. A reasonable demand, yes, but this demand is plagued by an absurdity. Nearly half of the country also approves of Father Stalin for his egalitarianism and ability to uphold discipline, two fronts on which the current president seems to have failed.[179] The irony, of course, is that it was Putin who had tried to resurrect Stalin; it was under his watch that the dictator's reputation was refurbished.

Which is why I will remain a Khrushchev till my end of days. Russia's pendulum swings are far from over. One day Putin will be gone, and another liberal reformer will rise and follow the examples set by the Thaw and perestroika. Yet there is no guarantee that the cycle of despotism won't soon continue, and the legacy of both my grandfather and Leonid will be besmirched again.

I am not a dissident, and unlike some others who speak out against Putin, I enjoy my freedom for now. But I have become allergic to my family's ideology of silence, a form of small-scale tyranny. Some thirty years after my encounter with Molotov, learning the full truth about Leonid has helped me see him in a different light. Not only is he the protagonist in this story, he is the character I now admire the most. For all his flaws, he ignored the straightjacket of communism even if it meant the possibility of death. In this sense, he became the Soviet Union's first dissident. He died heroically in battle and spoke the truth no matter the consequence, something that is rare in the history of our people. If Putin had his way, heroes like Leonid would become less common every day.

FAMILY GLOSSARY

- Nikita Sergeevich Khrushchev (1894–1971)—my great-grandfather (in the book, Grandfather), first secretary of the Communist Party of the Soviet Union (CPSU) 1953–64, chairman of the Council of Ministers (premier) 1958–64. In 1964, he was dismissed for "volunteerism in leadership," "erratic policies," and for "undermining the teachings of communism." His earlier posts included First Secretary of the Moscow City (1934 and 1949–53) and regional (1935–37 and 1949–53) Communist Party (CP) Committee, first secretary of CP of Ukraine 1938–41 and 1943–49, political commissar at various fronts during World War II (in Russia known as the Great Patriotic War 1941–45) 1941–43, and second secretary of the Moscow CP Committee 1932–34.
- Ksenia Ivanovna Khudyakova (1872–1945)—Nikita Khrushchev's mother, a peasant from Kalinovka, a Russian village in Kursk region on the border with Ukraine.
- Irina "Arisha" Sergeevna Khrushcheva (1896–1959)—Nikita's younger sister, the daughter of Ksenia Ivanovna

and Sergei Nikanorovich Khrushchev (1870–1937). Irina was married to Abram Mironovich Kobyak, an engineer. They had two daughters, Irma (1920–1996) and Rona (1924–?).

- Efrosinia "Frosya" Ivanovna Pisareva (1896–1919)—Khrushchev's first wife, died of typhus during the Russian Civil War.

- Nina Petrovna Kukharchuk (1900–1984)—my stepgreat-grandmother (in the book, Grandmother), Khrushchev's (common law) wife and a Communist Party propagandist in her early career. Although never officially married, the Khrushchevs were together from 1922 until Nikita's death in 1971. They had three children: Rada (b. 1929), Sergei (b. 1935), and Elena "Lena" (1937–1975).

- Yulia "Big Yulia" Nikitichna Khrushcheva (1915–1973)—Nikita Khrushchev's and Efrosinia Pisareva's eldest daughter, married to the director of the Kiev Opera Theater, Victor Petrovich Gontar (1902–1986). She spent most of her life in Kiev, Ukraine.

- Leonid "Leonya" Nikitich Khrushchev (1917–1943)—second child of Nikita and Efrosinia, a military pilot, killed in a battle over central Russia in World War II, in Russian—the Great Patriotic War.

- Lyubov "Lyuba" Illarionovna Sizykh (b. 1912)—thought to be Leonid's wife from 1939 to 1943 until, she accidentally revealed in 2011 that they had never officially married. She's a low-level communist party official, geologist, and pilot. Arrested in 1943, Lyuba spent ten years in the gulag. From her earlier marriage to Efim Belonenko, she had a son, Anatoly "Tolya" Lezhnenko (1933–2000), a military engineer. Now age one hundred, she lives in Kiev. In the text of *The Lost Khrushchev*, she is at times referred to as the "wife," the "widow," or the "daughter-in-law."

- Yulia "Little Yulia" Leonidovna Khrushcheva (b. 1940)—daughter of Leonid and Lyuba; my mother, on whose recollections of *The Lost Khrushchev* draws its strongest support. When Leonid died and Lyuba was imprisoned, Yulia, Nikita's granddaughter, was adopted by her grandfather and Nina Kukharchuk as their fourth daughter. Yulia worked as a journalist and then as literary director of Moscow's Vakhtangov Theater for almost thirty years. In this book, her relations with Nikita and Nina are referred to as father and mother respectively—although the Khrushchevs were her grandparents, she was raised as their daughter and considers them parents. In describing my own relations with the older Khrushchevs, I refer to them as grandfather and grandmother.
- Lev Sergeevich Petrov (1922–1970)—my father, the Great Patriotic War veteran, and a journalist who spent several years working for the Soviet News Press Agency (APN) in Europe, Canada, and the United States. He graduated from the Military Institute of Foreign Languages (VIIYaK) and, like most of its alumni, had "unofficial" Soviet espionage credentials.
- Ksenia Lvovna Khrushcheva (b. 1964)—my younger sister. Graduated from the Moscow University Philology Department, she then received a PhD in sociology and has spent most of her career in the human rights field as a researcher and program officer for western foundations and NGOs. She is now a New York–based Open Society Foundations representative in Moscow.
- Maria "Masha" Ivanovna Vertikova (1930–1992)—was our family nanny and housekeeper from 1964 for almost thirty years.
- Yury Leonidovich Khrushchev (1935–2003)—Leonid's son with Esfir Ettinger, the woman Leonid dated briefly in the mid-1930s. Like his father, Yury became a military

pilot. He was, also briefly, married to Galina Sudets, and they had a daughter Ekaterina.

- Rada Nikitichna Adzhubei (Khrushcheva)—Nikita's and Nina's eldest daughter; educated as a journalist, she spent most of her career working as an editor at *Nauka i Zhizn* (Science and Life), a Soviet-published academic science journal. Rada was married to Aleksei Ivanovich Adzhubei (1924–1993), a journalist of record, editor of *Komsomolskaya Pravda* (The Komsomol Truth) and, later, *Izvestiya* (Information) newspapers. Adzhubei served as the unofficial "soft power" political advisor to Nikita Khrushchev. They had three children, Nikita (1953–2007), Aleksei (b. 1956), and Ivan (b. 1960).
- Sergei Nikitich Khrushchev—Nikita's and Nina's son; originally a rocket scientist, upon moving to the United States in 1991, Sergei became a historian of the Soviet Union at Brown University, authoring numerous books about his father.
- Nikita Sergeevich Khrushchev (1960–2007)—Sergei's eldest son. Nikita studied psychology at Moscow State University and later worked as a technology researcher and reporter for the Russian newspaper *Moskovskie Novosti* (Moscow News).

POLITICAL GLOSSARY

- Viktor Semeonovich Abakumov (1908–1954)—minister of Internal Affairs (MVD) 1946–51, chairman of SMERSH (an abbreviation of *smert shpionam*, death to spies), Special Counterintelligence Section of the People's Commissariat for Internal Affairs (NKVD) 1941–46.
- Lavrenty Pavlovich Beria (1899–1953)—deputy prime minister/supervisor of the Organs of State Security (OGB, later KGB, Committee for State Security) 1946–53, People's Commissar for the NKVD 1938–45, first secretary of CP of the Republic of Georgia 1934–38.
- Vasily Konstantinovich Blyukher (1889–1938)—marshal of the USSR and one of the most outstanding revolutionary Red Army commanders. Blyukher was among the prominent victims of the Great Purges—a 1936-38 campaign of prosecution of Iosif Stalin's political opponents, all of whom were broadly branded as enemies of the state—before the Great Patriotic War.
- Leonid Iliych Brezhnev (1906–1982)—first (as of 1966, general) secretary of CPSU 1964–82, chairman of the

Presidium of the Supreme Soviet 1960–64, first secretary of CP of the Republic of Kazakhstan 1955–56, first secretary of CP of the Republic of Moldova 1954; his political career began in the 1930s in an industrial city of Dnepropetrovsk in Ukraine.

- Lev Davydovich Bronshtein, a.k.a. Trotsky (1879–1940)—Bolshevik Revolutionary, People's Commissar for the Military and Navy Affairs 1919–25, People's Commissar for Foreign Affairs 1917–18. Trotsky was exiled from the USSR in 1929 for heading the so-called Left Opposition, which opposed centralization of power under Stalin. His teachings developed into an ideology known as Trotskyism, which argued for the establishment of a vanguard party of the workers. Trotskyism critically disagreed with Stalinism, an argument for developing socialism in one separately taken country. Trotskyism saw this as a betrayal of Internationalism and a neglect of the proletarian mass democracy versus absolute power that was promoted under Stalin.

- Semeon Mikhailovich Budenny (1883–1973)—one of the first military marshals of the USSR and the creator of the Red Cavalry 1918–19. Budenny was an officer of the Russian Army before the Revolution.

- Nikolai Ivanovich Bukharin (1888–1938)—Bolshevik Revolutionary, chairman of the Communist International (ComIntern) 1926–29, editor-in-chief of newspapers *Pravda* (Truth) 1918–29, and *Izvestiya* 1934–36. Bukharin perished during the Great Purges.

- Nikolai Alexandrovich Bulganin (1895–1975)—prime minister of the Republic of Russia 1937, Minister of Defense 1953–55, chairman of the Council of Ministers (premier) of the USSR 1955–58.

- Victor Mikhailovich Chebrikov (1923–1999)—chairman of the KGB 1982–88.

- Felix Edmundovich Dzerzhinsky (1877–1926)—Polish and Russian Bolshevik Revolutionary, known as Iron Felix for his brutal tactics in promoting Bolshevism; creator of Soviet state security, first as ChK (Emergency Committee) 1917–22 and then as GPU (State Political Directorate) 1922–26. Both organizations were precursors to KGB.
- Iosif Vissarionovich Dzhugashvili, a.k.a. Stalin, pseudonym from the Russian word *stal*, steel (1878–1953)—Bolshevik Revolutionary, general secretary of CPSU 1922–52, chairman of the Council of Ministers (premier) 1941–53, People's Commissar for Defense of the USSR during the Great Patriotic War 1941–46; the Generalissimus as of 1945. In the USSR, Stalin was known as father of nation; in the Western narrative, he is often referred to as the great dictator.
- Mikhail Sergeevich Gorbachev (b. 1931)—general secretary of CPSU 1985–1991, president of the Soviet Union 1990.
- Lazar Moiseevich Kaganovich (1893–1991)—chairman of State Committee for Labor and Wages 1952–57, for Material-Technical Supply 1948–52, for Building Materials 1944–47, People's Commissar for transport 1943–44, for oil industry 1939–40, for heavy industry 1937–39, for railways 1935–1937, first secretary of the Moscow CP Committee 1930–1935, first secretary of CP of Ukraine 1925–28 and 1947, propaganda commissar of the Red Army 1918.
- Mikhail Ivanovich Kalinin (1875–1946)—Bolshevik Revolutionary and a staunch supporter of Stalin's power; chairman of the Presidium of the Supreme Soviet of the USSR 1922–46. Kalinin was a nominal head of state.
- Andrei Gennadievich Kirilenko (1906–1990)—first secretary of the Dnepropetrovsk Regional CP Committee

1965–1977; like Brezhnev, he was a Dnepropetrovsk native, and although he didn't officially hold high political positions, Kirilenko was Brezhnev's chief lieutenant through the 1970s.

- Stanislav Vikentievich Kosior (1889–1939)—general (as of 1934—first) secretary of CP of Ukraine 1928–38. When in 1938 Stalin appointed Khrushchev to replace Kosior, Polish by birth and accused of sabotage and treason as a result, Stalin quipped, "Better a Russian to run Ukraine than a Pole."
- Dmitry Anatolievich Medvedev (b. 1965)—prime minister of the Russian Federation (RF) 2012–present, president of RF 2008–2012, first deputy prime minister of RF 2005–2008.
- Anastas Ivanovich Mikoyan (1895–1978)—Old Bolshevik, chairman of the Presidium of the Supreme Soviet 1964–65, first deputy premier 1955–64, Minister of Trade 1938–55, and People's Commissar for External and Internal Trade 1926–38.
- Vladimir Vladimirovich Putin (b. 1952)—president of RF 2012–present, prime minister of RF 2008–12, president of RF 2000–08, prime minister of RF 1999, chairman of the Federal Security Service (FSB, successor to the KGB) 1998; as the KGB colonel of counterintelligence, Putin was stationed in Dresden, East Germany, 1985–90.
- Alexander Alexandrovich Shcherbakov (1901–1945)—Chairman of the Political Department of the Red Army during the Great Patriotic War, together with writer Maksim Gorky, is a founder of the Soviet Writer Union 1932.
- Vyacheslav Mikhailovich Skryabin, a.k.a. Molotov (1890–1986)—pseudonym from the Russian word *molot*, hammer; Old Bolshevik, minister of Foreign Affairs 1939–1949 and 1953–56, chairman of the Council of

People's Commissars 1930–41, secretary-in-charge of CP 1921–22.

- Vladimir Alexandrovich Sudets (1904–1981)—marshal of Soviet Aviation, commander of the Soviet Reconnaissance Aviation 1955–62, commander of Defense Aviation of USSR 1962–66.
- Pavel Anatolievich Sudoplatov (1907–1996)—director of NKVD's special operations, responsible for the death of Lev Trotsky, then in hiding in Mexico in 1940. Beria's close associate Sudoplatov was arrested in 1953. Accused, among other things, of crimes against humanity, he was sentenced to fifteen years in prison, released in 1968, and fully rehabilitated only in 1992 after the fall of communism.
- Semeon Konstantinovich Timoshenko (1895–1970)— People's Commissar for Defense of the USSR 1940–1941.
- Mikhail Nikolaevich Tukhachevsky (1893–1937)—marshal of the USSR, one of the leaders of the Red Army during the Russian post-1917 Civil War, a protégé of Trotsky and a victim of Stalin's Great Purges.
- Vladimir Iliych Ulyanov, a.k.a. Lenin (1870–1924)— pseudonym after the Lena River in Siberia, place of exile throughout Russian history, Bolshevik Revolutionary, chairman of the Council of People's Commissars 1917– 24, leader of international communism since 1903.
- Dmitry Timofeevich Yazov (b. 1923)—Minister of Defense of the USSR 1987–91, one of the coup d' état leaders against Gorbachev in 1991.
- Boris Nikolaevich Yeltsin (1931–2007)—president of RF 1991–99, president of Russia (Republic within the USSR) 1991, Chairman of the Russian Supreme Soviet 1990.

SELECT BIBLIOGRAPHY

BOOKS

Adler, Nanci D. *Victims of Soviet Terror. The Story of the Memorial Movement.* Greenwood Publishing, 1993.

Adzhubei, Aleksei. *Te desyat let* [Those Ten Years]. Moscow: Sovetskaya Rossiya, 1989.

Alliluyeva, Svetlana. *Twenty Letters to a Friend.* Harper & Row, 1967.

Andreev, Nikolai. *Tragicheskie sudby* [Tragic Fates]. Moscow: Olma Press, 2001.

Applebaum, Ann. *Gulag: A History.* Doubleday, 2003.

Ariztov, A., and I.N. Shevchuk, V.G. Khlopov, eds. *Reabilitatsiya: kak eto bylo 1953-1956* [Rehabilitation As It Was]. Moscow: Demokratiya, 2000.

Bacon, Edwin, and Mark Sandle. *Brezhnev Reconsidered.* Palgrave Macmillan, 2002.

Beria, Sergo. *Moi otets—Lavrenty Beria* [My Father Lavrenty Beria]. Moscow: Sovremennik, 1994. In English published as Beria, Sergo. *Beria: Inside Stalin's Kremlin.* Translated by Brian Pearce. London: Gerald Duckworth & Co., 2001.

Brackman, Roman. *The Secret File of Joseph Stalin: A Hidden Life.* Frank Cass, 2000.

Carey, John M., and Matthew Soberg Shugart. *Executive Decree Authority.* Cambridge University Press, 1998.

Cathala, Jean. *Sans Fleur ni Fusil* [With Neither Flowers Nor Guns]. A. Michel, 1981.

Chamberlin, William Henry. *The Ukraine: A Submerged Nation.* New York: Macmillan, 1944.

Chernobrov, V.A. *Entsiklopedia zagadochnykh mest Kaluzhskoi oblasti* [Encyclopedia of Mysterious Places in the Kaluga Region]. Kosmopoisk, 2008.

Chuev, Felix. *Molotov: Poluderzhavny vlastelin* [Molotov: A Semi-Czar]. Moscow: Olma Press, 2000.

Cienciala, Anna M., Natalia S. Lebedeva, and Wojciech Materski, eds. *Katyn: A Crime Without Punishment.* Yale University Press, 2008.

Cohen, Stephen. *Bukharin and the Bolshevik Revolution: A Political Biography, 1888-1938.* Oxford University Press, 1980.

Dedkov, Igor. *Dnevnik 1953-1994* [Diary 1953-1994]. Moscow: Progress-Pleyada, 2005.

Djilas, Milovan. *Conversations with Stalin.* Translated by Michael B. Petrovich. New York: Harcourt, Brace & World, Inc., 1962.

Dokuchaev, Mikhail. *Moskva. Kreml. Okhrana* [Moscow. Kremlin. Security Guard]. Moscow: Business Press, 1995.

Erickson, John. *Hitler Versus Stalin.* Carlton Books, 2002.

Filipov, A.V. *Noveishaya Istoriya Rossii 1945-2006: Kniga dlya uchitelya* [Modern Russian History: Teacher's Manual]. Moscow: Prosveshchenie, 2007.

Ginzburg, Eugenia. *Journey Into the Whirlwind.* Translated by Stevenson, Paul, and Max Hayward. Harcourt, 1967.

Goldman, Wendy. *Women, the State and Revolution: Soviet Family Policy and Social Life, 1917-1936.* Cambridge: Cambridge University Press, 1993.

Gorbachev, Mikhail. *Gorbachev: On My Country and the World.* Translated by George Shriver. New York: Columbia University Press, 2000.

Hellbeck, Jochen. *Revolution on My Mind: Writing a Diary Under Stalin.* Cambridge and London: Harvard University Press, 2006.

Hill, Fiona, and Clifford G. Gaddy. *Mr. Putin: Operative in the Kremlin.* Washington, DC: Brookings Institution Press, 2013.

Ibarruri, Dolores. *Pasionaria: la lucha y la vida* [Struggle and Life]. Planeta, 1985.

Kennedy, David M., ed. *The Library of Congress World War II Companion.* Simon&Schuster, 2007.

Khalansky, Sergei. *Kreshchenye adom* [Baptized by Hell]. Magadan: Diky Sever, 2003.

Khrushchev, Nikita. *Memoirs of Nikita Khrushchev: Volume 1, Commissar, 1918-1945.* Edited by Sergei Khrushchev. Pennsylvania State University Press, 2005.

_____. *Memoirs: Volume 2, Reformer, 1945-1964.* Edited by Sergei Khrushchev. Pennsylvania State University Press, 2006.

_____. *Memoirs: Volume 3, Statesman, 1953-1964.* Edited by Sergei Khrushchev. Pennsylvania State University Press, 2007.

Khrushchev Remembers. With an Introduction, Commentary and Notes by Edward Crankshaw. Translated and edited by Strobe Talbott. Little Brown and Co., 1970.

Khrushchev Remembers: The Last Testament. Introductions by Edward Crankshaw and Jerrold Schecter. Translated and edited by Strobe Talbott. Little Brown and Co., 1974.

Khrushchev, Sergei. *Khrushchev on Khrushchev.* Little, Brown & Co, 1990.

_____. *Khrushchev.* Moscow: Vagrius, 2001.

Koop, Volker. *In Hitlers Hand: Sonder- und Ehrenhäftlinge der SS* [In Hitler's Hands: Special and Honorable Detainees of SS]. Böhlau Köln, 2010.

Krasikov, Sergei. *Vozle vozhdei* [Near the Leaders]. Moscow: Sovremennik, 1997.

Lenin, V.I. *Collected Works in 80 Volumes*. Moscow: Progress Publishers, 1972.

Lotman, Yury. *Kultura i vzryv* [Culture and Explosion]. Moscow: Gnozis, 1992.

Lowen, Alexander. *Narcissism: Denial of the True Self*. New York: Touchstone, 2004.

McDaniel, Tim. *The Agony of the Russian Idea*. Princeton University Press, 1996.

Medvedev, Roy. *Let History Judge: The Origin and Consequences of Stalinism*. New York: Alfred A. Knopf, 1972.

Medvedev, Roy, with Zhores Medvedev. *Khrushchev: The Years in Power*. Columbia University Press, 1976.

Medvedev [Roy] o Putine [Medvedev about Putin: Twelve Frank Interviews about the Most Popular Russian Politician of the 21st Century]. Moscow: Tribuna, 2011.

Mikoyan, A.I. *Tak bylo* [As it Was]. Moscow: Vagrius, 1999.

Mikoyan, Stepan. *Memoirs of Military Test-Flying and Life with the Kremlin's Elite*. Airlife Publishing, 1999. In Russian published as Mikoyan, S.A. *My—Deti voiny* [We, Children of the War]. Moscow: Eksmo, 2006.

Montefiore, Simon Sebag. *Stalin: The Court of the Red Tsar*. Alfred A. Knopf, 2004.

_____. *Young Stalin*. Alfred A. Knopf, 2007.

Moskoff, William. *The Bread of Affliction: The Food Supply in the USSR During World War II*. Cambridge University Press, 2002.

Pipes, Richard. *A Concise History of the Russian Revolution*. New York: Vintage, 1996.

_____. *Communism: A History*. New York: Modern Library, 2001.

Pistrak, Lazar. *The Grand Tactician: Khrushchev's Rise to Power*. London: Thames Hudson, 1961.

Prudnikova, Elena. *Stalin: Vtoroe ubiistvo* [Stalin: The Second Murder]. St. Petersburg: Neva, 2003.

Pstygo, Ivan. *Na boevom kurse* [On the Battle Course: Military Memoir]. Moscow: Voenizdat, 1989.

Roberts, Geoffrey. *Stalin's Wars: From World War to Cold War, 1939-1953.* Yale University Press, 2007.

Rybakov, Anatoli (*sic*). *Children of the Arbat.* Translated by Harold Shukman. Little, Brown and Company, 1988.

Sakharov, A.D. *Vospominaniya* [Memoirs]. Moscow, 1996.

Schecter, Jerrold L., and Leona P. Schecter. *Sacred Secrets: How Soviet Intelligence Operations Changed American History.* Potomac Books, 2003.

Scholl, Susanne. *Reise nach Karaganda* [*Journey After Karaganda*]. Wien Molden, 2006.

Solzhenitsyn, Alexander. *The Gulag Archipelago 1918-1956: An Experiment in Literary Investigation Volume 1-2.* Translated by Thomas P. Whitney. Harper & Row, 1973, 1975.

_____. *Cancer Ward.* Random House, 2011.

_____. *First Circle.* Random House, 2011.

Stadnyuk, I.F. *Voina* [The War]. Moscow: Voenizdat, 1987.

Stalin, J.V. *Problems of Leninism.* Peking: Foreign Language Press, 1976.

Sudoplatov, Pavel. *Spetsoperatsii: Lubyanka i Kreml, 1930-1950* [Special-Ops: Lubyanka and the Kremlin, 1930-1950]. Moscow: Olma-Press, 2003.

Sukhodeev, Vladimir, ed. *Epokha Stalina: Sobytiya i Lyudi* [Stalin's Era: People and Events. An Encyclopedia]. Moscow: Eksmo, 2004.

Sukhotin, Yakov L. *Syn Stalina: Zhizn i gibel Yakova Dzhugashvili* [Stalin's Son: Life and Death of Yakov Dzhugashvili]. Leningrad: Lenizdat, 1990.

Taubman, William. *Khrushchev: The Man and His Era.* New York: W.W. Norton & Co., 2003.

Tertz, Abram (Andrei Sinyavsky). *A Voice from the Chorus.* Translated by Fitzlyon, Kyril, and Max Hayward. New York: Farrar, Straus, and Giroux, 1976.

Torchinov, V.A., and a.m. Leontyuk. *Vokrug Stalina* [Around Stalin]. Saint Petersburg, 2000.

Trotsky, Leon. *Literature and Revolution.* Edited by William Keach. Chicago: Haymarket Books, 2005.

Tvardovsky, Alexander. *Rossiya—Rodina moya* [Poems: Russia is My Motherland]. Moscow: Khudozhestvennaya Literatura, 1967.

Tucker, Robert. *Stalin as Revolutionary: 1879-1929.* W.W. Norton & Co., 1973.

_____. *Stalin in Power: The Revolution from Above, 1928-1941.* W.W. Norton & Co., 1992.

Vasilieva, Larissa. *Kremlin Wives: The Secret Lives of the Women Behind the Kremlin Walls—From Lenin to Gorbachev.* Arcade Publishing, 1994.

Ulam, Adam. *Stalin: The Man and His Era.* Beacon Press, 1973.

Yazov, Dmitry. *Udary Sudby: Vospominaniya soldata i marshala* [Blows of Fate: Memoirs of a Soldier and a Marshal]. Moscow: Kniga i Biznem, 2000.

Zenkovich, Nikolai. *Tainy ushedshego veka* [Mysteries of the Century Passed]. Moscow: Olma-Press, 2004.

Zinoviev, Alexander. *The Radiant Future.* Translated by Gordon Clough. New York: Random House, 1980.

ARTICLES AND REPORTS

Albats, Eugenia. "Chisto konkretny kandidat" [A True and Real Candidate]. *The New Times*, February 27, 2012.

"An Interview with Mikhail Gorbachev." *Time*, September 9, 1985.

Arkhipov, Andrei. "Rech Khrushcheva na XX sezde KPSS do sikh por zasekrechena" [Khrushchev's Speech at the XX Congress of the CPSU is Still a Secret]. *Otchizna*, March 11, 2006.

Arutunyan, Anna. "Thousands protest sentence for Putin critic." *USA Today*, July 18, 2013.

Ascherson, Neal. "Oo, Oo!" *London Review of Books* 25/16. (August 21, 2003):15-16.

Barinov, Aleksei. "Bard Stalinskoi epokhi" [The Bard of the Stalin Era]. *Argumenty i Fakty*, August 8, 2003.

Bigg, Claire. "Russia: Putin Delivers Annual State-Of-The-Nation Address." RFERL, April 26, 2007.

Bondorenko, Stanislav. "Interview with Rada Khrushcheva." *Khronograph.ru*, February 6, 2004.

"Born in the U.S.A. The truth about Obama's birth certificate." *FactCheck.org*, August 21, 2008.

Bush, Jason. "Oil: What's Russia Really Sitting On?" *Business Week*, November 22, 2004.

Chamberlin, William Henry. "The Issue of U.S. Prestige." *The Wall Street Journal*, November 1, 1960.

Davies, Emily. "Vladimir Putin's spokesman earns double the President's salary." *Daily Mail*, April 13, 2013.

Defrance, Corine. "Raymond Schmittlein (1904–1974): médiateur entre la France et la Lituanie" [Schmittlein: Mediator between France and Lithuania]. *Cahiers Lituaniens*, 2008.

Drabkin, A. "Interview with Nikolai Tsibikov," *I Remember: Soviet WWII-veteran Memoirs*, February 4, 2011.

Dudin, Valentin, and Nikolai Poroskov. "Vypolnyaya prikaz my ne ostanavlivalis ne pered chem" [Following Orders We Didn't Halt Before Anything: Interview with Ivan Pstygo]. *Vremya Novostei*, May 7, 2004.

Gudkov, Lev. "Vremya i istroiya v soznanii rossiyan" [Time and History in the Russian Consciousness]. *Vestnik Obshchestvennogo Mneniya*, No 2 104 (April-June 2010).

Holmes, Stephen. "Simulations of Power in Putin's Russia." Carnegie Endowment for International Peace, Washington, D.C., October 1, 2001.

Ignatov, Andrei. "Porazheniya Krasnoi Armii v pervye mesyatsy Velikoi Otechestvennoi Voiny" [Red Army's Reversals During the First Months of the Great Patriotic War]. *Istoriya* 32 (2002).

Isachenkov, Vladimir. "Russian sub had nukes during December fire." AP, February 13, 2012.

Konradova, Nataliya. "Moskovskie shkolniki obsuzhdayut SSSR" [Moscow Schoolchildren Discuss the USSR]. *Snob*, April 12, 2011.

Levada, Yury, and Victor Sheinis. "1953-1964: Pochemu togda ne poluchilos" [Why it Didn't Work Out Then]. *Moskovskie Novosti*, May 1, 1988.

Lisnichenko, Irina. "Lyubov Sizykh: Posle moego aresta moya doch ostalas v semie Khrushchevykh i Nikitu Sergeevicha nazyvala papoi" [Lyubov Sizykh: After My Arrest My Daughter Remained in the Khrushchevs's Family and Called Nikita Sergeevich Father]. *Fakty i Kommentarii*, September 25, 2009.

Loginov, V. "Moi Stalin" [My Stalin]. *Shpion* 2 (1993).

Kachanov, A.M. "Geroi" [Hero]. *Duel*, July 27, 1999.

Kalashnikov, M. "Na frontakh otechestvennoi voiny" [At the Patriotic War Front]. *Pravda*, July 26, 1941.

Khrushcheva, Nina L. "Russia's New Inspector General." *International Herald Tribune*, August 10, 2007.

Khrushcheva, Nina. "Cultural Contradiction of Post-Communism: Why Liberal Reforms Did Not Succeed in Russia." New York: Council of Foreign Relations Paper, 2000.

_____. "Za chto stalinisty mstyat Khrushchevu" [Why the Stalinists Seek Revenge on Khrushchev]. *Nezavisimaya Gazeta*, April 4, 1998.

"Kinematografisty publichno izvinilis za 'Vnuka Gagarina'" [Cinematographers Publically Apologized for *Gagarin's Grandson*]. *Lenta.ru*, October 23, 2007.

Kolesnik, A. "Leonid Khrushchev." *Argumenty i Fakty* 46, November 18-24, 1989.

Konchalovsky, Andron. "Uzhasnis sam sebe" [Get Horrified with Yourself]. *Kommersant Vlast*, February 27, 2012.

Kulish, Nicholas. "Polish President Dies in Jet Crash in Russia." *The New York Times*, April 10, 2010.

Nad (Dobryukha), Nikolai. "Predatel ili geroi" [Traitor or Hero]. *Versiya*, June 20-26, 2000.

_____. "'Khrushchev polzal za nim na kolenyakh...' Pochemu Nikita Sergeevich razoblachil Stalina?" [Khrushchev Crawled After Him on His Knees. Why Nikita Sergeevich Denounced Stalin?]. *Argumenty i Fakty*, November 21, 2007.

_____. "U predatelei ne bylo shansa vyzhit" [Traitors Had no Chance to Survive]. *Komsomolskaya Pravda*, January 16, 2013.

_____. "Poslednie dni Khrushcheva" [Khrushchev's Last Days]. *Komsomolskaya Pravda*, January 23, 2013.

Nysten-Haarala, Soili. "Russian Property Rights in Transition," Interim Report IR-01-006. International Institute for Applied Systems Analysis, Laxenburg, Austria, 2001.

Orlova, Anna. "Skandal vokrug seriala 'Zvezda epokhi'" [Scandal Around Series *Star of an Era*]. *Moskovsky Komsomolets*, April 26, 2005.

Pestov, B.E. "Pogib? Propal bez vesti? Zhiv?.." [Died? Disappeared Without a Trace? Alive?]. *Voenno-istorichesky Zhurnal* 4 (1990).

Pobol, Nikolai, and Pavel Polyan. "Stalin i Khrushchev" [Stalin and Khrushchev]. *Novaya Gazeta*, February 2, 2009.

Poroskov, Nikolai. "Geroi i mify" [Heroes and Myths] *Vremya Novostei*. May 22, 2009.

"Putin's Russia 'now a mafia state.'" BBC, February 29, 2012.

Pyanov, Volodymyr. "Khrushchev—A Magnate's Son?" Translated by Marta D. Olynyk. *Literaturna Ukraina,* July 20, 2006.

Savodnik, Peter. "The trial of Leonid K." *The National,* May 8, 2009.

Shapiro, Henry. "Nikita's Favorite Son-in-law May Have Peddled His Notes." *The Pittsburgh Press,* January 3, 1971.

Shcherbakov, Alexander, and Vladimir Lukin, "Chernye pyatna na chistom nebe" [Black Spots in the Clear Skies]. *Izvestia,* October 11, 2007.

Shevtsova, Lilia. "Yeltsin and the Evolution of Electoral Monarchy in Russia." *Current History,* October 2000.

"Skolko stoila pobeda? Velikaya Otechestvennaya Voina v tsifrakh" [The Cost of Victory? Great Patriotic War in Figures]. Ria Novosti, March 23, 2005.

Sokolov, Boris. "Kak pobedila Rossiya" [How Russia Won]. *Novaya Gazeta,* April 24, 2010.

Solodar. Ts. "Leonid Khrushchev i ego ekipazh" [Khrushchev and his Team]. *Komsomolskaya Pravda* (n.d.).

Songarova, Tatiana. "Kak zakalyalas stal Lyubov Sizykh" [How Lyubov Sizykh's Steel was Tempered]. *Kamuflyazh,* March 2003, 21-23.

"Stalin: Terror po pervoi kategorii" [Terror in the First Order]. *Moskovsky Komsomolets,* August 5, 2007.

"Stalina podderzhivayut 50 % Rossiyan" [Stalin is Supported by 50 % of Russians]. *NIKA-Media.ru,* May 22, 2013.

Sukhomlinov, Andrei. "Bez vesti propavshy" [Without a Trace]. *Sovershenno Sekretno,* March 2000.

Sukhotin, Yakov. "Za chto Stalin kaznil syna Khrushcheva?" [Why did Stalin Execute Khrushchev's Son?]. *Duel,* July 27, 1999.

Taubman, William. "Did He Bang it?: Nikita Khrushchev And the Shoe." *The New York Times,* July 26, 2003.

Teplyakov, Yury. "Stalin's War Against His Own Troops: The Tragic Fate of Soviet Prisoners of War in German Captivity." *Moscow News* 19 (1990).

Udilov, Vadim. "Za chto Khrushchev otomstil Stalinu" [Why Khrushchev Sought Revenge on Stalin]. *Nezavisimaya Gazeta*, February 17, 1998.

Uvarova, T.B. "Zhenshchiny, gosudarstvo i revolyutsiya" [Women, State and Revolution]. *Sotsiologicheskie issledovaniya* 8-9 (1994).

Weitz, Richard. "Reforming Russia's Military Industrial Complex." *Project Syndicate*, May 30, 2007.

Welles, Benjamin. "Khrushchev Bangs His Shoe on Desk." *The New York Times*, October 13, 1960.

"What's News." *The Wall Street Journal*, October 13, 1960.

Wheelwrigth, Julie. "Poisoned Honey: the Myth of Women in Espionage." *Queen's Quarterly* 100/2 (Summer 1993).

Yablokov, Anatoly. "Vinovnym naznachen Beria" [Beria is Now Guilty]. *Novaya Gazeta*, April 22, 2009.

"Yeltsin i ego 'Semiya'" [Yeltsin and his "Family"]. *Compromat.ru*, May 16, 2001.

Zholi, Elena. "Stepan Mikoyan: Stalin neset otvetstvennost za ochen mnogie oshibki, privedshie k gromadnym chelovecheskim zhertvam" [Stalin is Responsible for Many Mistakes that Led to Great Human Losses]. *Komsomolskaya Pravda*, May 6, 2010.

Zorkaya, N. ed. *Obshchestvennoe mnenie: Ezhegodnik* [Public Opinion 2011: An Annual Review]. Moscow: Yury Levada Analytical Center Publication, 2012.

WEBSITES

Associated Press (AP). http://www.ap.org

British Broadcasting Corporation (BBC). http://www.bbc.co.uk

Compromat.ru. http://www.compromat.ru

Ekho Moskvy [Moscow's Echo]. http://www.echo.msk.ru

FactCheck.org. http://www.factcheck.org

Gostevaya kniga Zhizdry [Zhizdra's Guest Book]. http://a.mod-site.net/gb/u/ZHIZD-1/p/35.html

History Today. http://www.historytoday.com

I Remember: Soviet WWII-veteran Memoirs. http://iremember.ru/

Khronograph-Narod. http://hronograph.narod.ru

Lenta.ru. http://lenta.ru/news/2007/10/23/vnuk/

Levada-Center. http://www.levada.ru/

Lozh i pravda o Leonide Khrushcheve [Lies and Truth about Leonid Khrushchev]. http://trizna.ru/forum/viewtopic.php?f=27&t=42477&start=80

Marxists Internet Archive. http://www.marxists.org/

NIKA-Media. http://nika-media.ru/

PBS. http://www.pbs.org

Pobeda Vitebsk [Victory Vitebsk]. http://www.pobeda.witebsk.by/sky/epizode/hruschev/

Project Syndicate. http://www.project-syndicate.org

Radio Free Europe Radio Liberty (RFERL) http://www.rferl.org

Ria Novosti. http://en.rian.ru

Russian Ministry of Defense. http://encyclopedia.mil.ru/warriors_calendar.htm?month=3&day=11&value(dayMonth)=0311&cond(dayMonth)==

Soviet-History. http://soviet-history.com/

The Washington Post. http://www.washingtonpost.com

World War II Memorial. http://www.obd-memorial.ru/

Zhizdra News. http://www.zhizdra.ru/news/

ARCHIVAL SOURCES AND OFFICIAL DOCUMENTS

"Arresty i nakazaniya s 1921 po 1953 god" [Arrests and prosecutions from 1921 to 1953]. Note of the Special Section of the Ministry of Internal Affairs of the USSR about the arrests and prosecutions by VChK, OGPU, NKVD in 1921-1953. December 11, 1953. http://soviet-history.com/doc/prison/1953_12_11_spravka_mvd.php.

Leonid Khrushchev's personal file from the Third United School of Civilian Pilots and Aviation Technicians of the USSR Air Fleet, May-September 1937. Family archive.

Leonid Khrushchev's military file. Copy issued by the General Prosecutor of the Russian Federation, September 17, 1960. Podolsk Central Archive of the Ministry of Defense of the USSR (TsAMO), File 290, Description 32631c, Case 4, 44-47.

"Pismo Chlenu Voennogo Soveta Voronezhskogo Fronta General Leitenantu Khrushchevu ot komnadueshchego 1 Aviatsionnoi Armii General Maiora Khudyakova" [Letter to Member of the Military Council of the Voronezh Front Lieutenant general Khrushchev from Commander of the First Aviation Army Major general Khudyakov] (n.d.). TsAMO, File 290, Description 32631c, Case 4, 44-47.

"Pismo ot zamestitelya prokurora Rossiiskoi Federatsii A.N. Savenkova to Y.L. Khrushcheva" [Letter from Deputy Prosecutor of the Russian Federation-Chief Military Prosecutor A.N. Savenkov to Y.L. Khrushcheva]. June 6, 2004. No 7ya-122/04. Family archive.

"Poteri 303-i armii Mart 10-20, 1943" [Losses of the 303d Army from March 10-20, 1943]. TsAMO, File 58, Description 18001, Case 1404.

"Otkaz v rassmotrenii ugolovnogo dela Yuriya Khrushcheva ot Zamyshlyaevoi V.V., Prokurora po nadzoru za soblyudeniem federalnoi bezopasnosti" [Ruling of Refusal of Criminal Investigation to Yury Khrushchev from V.V. Zamyshlyaeva, Prosecutor of the Department of Overseeing of Execution of Laws of Federal Security]. October 23, 2000. Family Archive.

"Spravka po reabilitatsii Lyubovi Illarionovny Sizykh" [Lyubov Sizykh's Note of Rehabilitation]. Copy issued by the General Prosecutor of the Russian Federation, September 28, 1992, No 13/3-4472-92. Family archive.

"Voennaya kharakteristika na leitenanta 134 Skorostnogo Bombardirovochnogo Polka Leonida Nikitovicha Khrushcheva" [Military Evaluation of the 134th Bomber Regiment Pilot Lieutenant Leonid Khrushchev]. January 9, 1942, TsAMO, File 292, Description 32634, Case 4, 11.

LETTERS FROM THE FAMILY ARCHIVE

Adzhubei (Khrushcheva), Rada to Lyuba Sizykh, April 13, 1943.

Dultsev, Leonid to Nikita Khrushchev, July 17, 1944.

Elinov, Vladimir to Leonid Khrushchev, September 8, 1941.

Golovanov, Vladimir to Leonid Khrushchev, August 17 and September 9, 1941.

Ivanov, Feodor to Leonid Khrushchev, August 4 and September 1, 1941.

Ivanov, George to Leonid Khrushchev, August 4 and 15, 1941.

Khrushchev, Leonid to Lyuba Sizykh, September 24, 1942.

Novikov, Nikolai to Leonid Khrushchev, August 5 and September 8, 1941; January 13, February 12, March 29, May 8, August 3 and October 12, 1942.

Solodenko, V. to Leonid Khrushchev, September 8, 1941.

DIARIES AND RECOLLECTIONS

Alfeeva, Galina. "Zapiski dlya Rady" [Notes to Rada]. October 30, 1993, Kiev, Ukraine. Family archive.

Brezhnev, Aleksei (no relations to Leonid Brezhnev). "Zametki dlya Nikity Khrushcheva, 1961" [Notes to Nikita Sergeevich Khrushchev]. Family archive.

Fomin, Viktor. "Lichnye memuary Viktora Andreevicha Fomina o Leonide Khrushcheve i ego voennoi sluzhbe v 3 eskadrile 134 Polka s 1939 po 1941 god" [Personal memoirs by Victor Fomin of Leonid Khrushchev and his military service in the Third Squadron of the 134th Regiment 1939-1941]. February 5, 1998. Family archive.

Gontar, Victor. Diaries 1955-1980. Family archive.

Ivanov, Feodor. "Zametki Polkovniku S. Kovalevu, redaktoru 'Krasnoi Zvezdy'" [Notes to Colonel S. Kovalev, deputy editor of newspaper *Krasnaya Zvezda (Red Star)*]. March 7, 1964. Family archive.

Pavlov, Ivan. "Vospominaniya o Leonide Khrushcheve: Predatel ili geroi?" [Memoirs of Leonid Khrushchev: Traitor or Hero?]. *Pobeda.Witebsk.by*, June 9, 2010.

CONVERSATIONS AND INTERVIEWS

Adzhubei (Khrushcheva), Rada. Multiple interviews from 1994 to 2013, Moscow.

Budennaya, Maria. Multiple interviews from 1993 to 2002, Moscow.

Budennaya, Nina. Multiple interviews from 2003 to 2013, Moscow.

Chernobrov, Vadim. October and November, 2011, Moscow.

Ginzburg, Eugenia. Multiple conversation from 1974 to 1977, Peredelkino.

Gorbachev, Mikhail. Multiple interviews from 1994 to 2008, New York City and Moscow.

Khrushchev (cousin), Nikita. Multiple conversations till 2006, Moscow.

Khrushchev, Sergei. Multiple conversations. Moscow and Providence, RI.

Khutsiev, Marlen. August 2010, Moscow.

Kobyak, Irma. August 1994 and October 1995, Moscow.

Kolchinskaya, Asya. Multiple conversations from 1994 to 1996, Moscow.

Loginov, Vladlen. Multiple conversations from 1994 to 2010, Moscow.

Lukin, Vladimir. Multiple conversations from 2002 to 2006, Moscow and New York City.

Malinovskaya, Raisa. Multiple interviews from 1994 to 1995, Moscow.

Medvedev, Roy. Multiple interviews from 1975 to 2013, Moscow, Peredelkino.

Mikoyan, Stepan. Multiple interviews from 2004 to 2007, Moscow.

Molotov, Vyacheslav. April 1981, Zhukovka.

Neizvestny, Ernst. June 1998, October 2004, New York City.

Primakov, Eugeny. Multiple conversations from 2002 to 2004. Moscow, New York City.

Rybakov, Anatoly. Multiple conversations from 1988 to 1998. Peredelkino, New York City.

Schecter, Jerrold. June 2013, by telephone, Washington, D.C.

Shatrov, Mikhail. Multiple conversations from 1994 to 2005, Moscow, New York City.

Shcherbakov, Alexander. Multiple interviews from 2004 to 2011, Moscow.

Sizykh, Lyubov. Multiple interviews from 1994 to 2013, Kiev, Moscow.

Smelyanksy, Anatoly. June 2010, Moscow.

Sudets, Galina. June 2006, Perkhushkovo outside Moscow.

Talbott, Strobe. June 2013, by telephone, Washington, D.C.

Uboryatov, Pavel. November 2011, Vaskovo outside Zhizdra.

NOTE ON TRANSLATIONS AND TRANSLITERATION

B ibliographical references and Russian words cited in this book follow a modified version of the Library of Congress system of transliteration ("ya" instead of "ia," for example). Soft signs are omitted from Russian words, and names are given in their transliteration from the Russian rather than in standard English form ("Iosif Stalin" rather than "Joseph Stalin," for example.) The only exception is made for Boris Yeltsin; although his last name should be spelled as Eltsin, he is too well known as Yeltsin so the change of spelling might be confusing. Unless otherwise indicated, translations from the Russian, French, and German are my own.

INDEX

ENDNOTES

1. Though Leonid is my biological grandfather, in this book, when I speak of grandmother and grandfather, I refer to Nina Kukharchuk and Nikita Khrushchev, the grandparents I grew up with. My mother considers the Khrushchevs her actual parents, and thus refers to them as Mother and Father.

2. In homage to my father, I always use my middle initial—L—for Lvovna, my Russian patronymic. Most names in Russia are gender specific and all full names consist of three parts: birth name, father's name, and family name. For example, Nikita (first name) Sergeevich (son of Sergei; Sergeevna would be for a daughter of Sergei); Khrushchev (Khrushcheva for a woman).

3. My grandfather was certainly a Soviet autocrat, although even the uncompromising American historian, William Taubman, in his Pulitzer Prize winning biography of Khrushchev explained that the dictator's future successor never "initiated or controlled carnage... Khrushchev wasn't a member of Stalin's inner circle until the end of the [1940s] decade."

William Taubman, *Khrushchev: The Man and His Era* (New York: W. W. Norton & Co., 2003), 74.

4. See, Nanci D. Adler, *Victims of Soviet Terror. The Story of the Memorial Movement* (Westport: Greenwood Publishing, 1993); Alexander Solzhenitsyn, *The Gulag Archipelago 1918-1956: An Experiment in Literary Investigation Volume 2* (New York: Harper & Row, 1975), 10.

5. Just in 1954-56 the number of "politicals" dropped from 467,000 to 114,000, a 75 percent decrease, bringing the total amount of incarcerated to less than a million. A. Ariztov and Shevchuk I.N., Khlopov V.G., ed., *Reabilitatsiya: kak eto bylo 1953-1956* (Moscow: Demokratiya, 2000), 104.

6. Actually an acronym, GULag: *Glavnoye Upravleniye ispravityelno-trudovykh Lagerei i kolony* (Chief Administration of Corrective Labor Camps and Colonies); it stands for the government agency that ran labor camps from 1930 to 1956, which consisted of about 200 major sites with numerous branches across the USSR. Over 25 years, a total of 20 million people went through those camps; at least one million died in detention. In 1960 my grandfather officially dissolved the Gulag system, however, some individual camps exist even today. See, Sergei Khalansky, *Kreshchenye adom* (Magadan: Diky Sever, 2003).

7. Igor Dedkov, *Dnevnik 1953-1994* (Moscow: Progress-Pleyada, 2005), 65.

8. Cited in Felix Chuev, *Molotov: Poluderzhavny vlastelin* (Moscow: Olma Press, 2000), 422-23, 433.

9. Stalin's daughter Svetlana never denounced her father's legacy, but chose to go by her mother's surname, Alliluyeva. Upon immigrating to the United States in 1967, she further distanced herself from her Soviet past becoming Lana Peters until her death in 2011, even though her marriage to the American architect William Wesley Peters only lasted a few years.

10. "An Interview with Mikhail Gorbachev," *Time*, September 9, 1985.

11. See, Yury Levada, Victor Sheinis, "1953-1964: Pochemu togda ne poluchilos" *Moskovskie Novosti*, May 1, 1988.

12. By then we had moved from the posh Kutuzovsky Avenue into a smaller place in the non-elite Novoslobodsky area.

13. When Boris Yeltsin left the Kremlin in 2000, his and his family's secret fortune was estimated at least at $15 million. See, "Yeltsin i ego 'Semiya,'" *Compromat.ru*, May 16, 2001.

14. Lev Gudkov, "Vremya i istroiya v soznanii rossiyan," *Vestnik Obshchestvennogo Mneniya*, No 2 (104) April-June 2010, 30.

15. This and the following quote are from N. Zorkaya, ed., *Obshchestvennoe mnenie: Ezhegodnik*, (Moscow: Yury Levada Analytical Center Publication, 2012), 101.

16. This and the following quote are from Dmitry Yazov, *Udary Sudby: Vospominaniya soldata i marshala* (Moscow: Kniga i Biznem, 2000), 43-44.

17. After Hitler's invasion of the Soviet Union in June 1941, with the Nazis quickly advancing towards Moscow, Kuibyshev (Samara before the Bolshevik Revolution and after the fall of the USSR), a large city on the Volga River 450 miles southeast of the capital, became the new center hosting the evacuated institutions of Soviet power—ministries, facilities critical for Soviet defense and military along with families of government officials.

18. As a child, Sergei suffered from bone tuberculosis.

19. Most Russians love the countryside. For regular people, the Soviet state's universal allowance of *shest sotok* (six hundredth), 650 square feet, was a palace getaway. And indeed, the *dacha* culture in Russia dates back to the lavish 17th century country estates of aristocrats during the reign of Peter the Great, and to their peasants—the serfs—whom they permitted a tiny patch of land to privately grow their own cabbage and potatoes.

20. Two main factions within Russian Social-Democratic Workers' Party, the *Mensheviks* (the minority) and the *Bolsheviks* (the majority), were involved in the anti-czar movement in the early 20th century. Vladimir Lenin, heading the Bolsheviks, argued for advancing socialism by an all-sweeping revolution fighting the White czarist guard. The Mensheviks insisted on a gradual approach to change and were against Lenin's centralized party model, which only involved workers. They wanted to work with the bourgeoisie to create a capitalist democracy in Russia. But the Bolsheviks, with Lenin's stance on immediate peace in World War I, his promise of bread and land to all in the Russian empire, succeeded in seizing power in October 1917 following what is known as the Bolshevik Revolution.

21. See, Richard Pipes, *A Concise History of the Russian Revolution* (New York: Vintage, 1996).

22. Cited in Jochen Hellbeck, *Revolution on My Mind: Writing a Diary Under Stalin* (Cambridge and London: Harvard University Press, 2006), 5-6.

23. Leon Trotsky, *Literature and Revolution*. Edited by William Keach (Chicago: Haymarket Books, 2005), 207.

24. The exact quote reads, "We know that an unskilled labourer or a cook cannot immediately get on with the job of state administration." See, V.I. Lenin, "Can the Bolsheviks Retain State Power?" in V.I. Lenin, *Collected Works in 80 Volumes: Volume 26* (Moscow: Progress Publishers, 1972), 87-136. Historically in the USSR this line has been used as I quote it; it became synonymous with the reasons behind the humble origins of the state leadership.

25. Alain Delon was then a very popular French actor, whose many films include *Eclipse* (dir. Michelangelo Antonioni, 1962), *The Leopard* (dir. Luchino Visconti, 1963) and *Nouvelle Vague* (dir. Jean-Luc Godard, 1990).

26. Later in life, Nina wrote roughly 100 pages about her life, describing, among other things, her upbringing and her experiences before she became the Soviet first lady. These notes were partially reproduced in her son-in-law Aleksei Adzhubei's book, *Te desyat let* (Moscow: Sovetskaya Rossiya, 1989), 38-50. They were also added as an appendix to Grandfather's three-volume complete memoirs, edited by Uncle Sergei. See, Nikita Khrushchev, *Memoirs: Volume 2, Reformer, 1945-1964* (Pennsylvania State University Press, 2006), 677-766.

27. T.B. Uvarova, "Zhenshchiny, gosudarstvo i revolyutsiya," *Sotsiologicheskie issledovaniya*, 1994, No 8-9, 206-209.

28. This and the following quote are from Wendy Goldman, *Women, the State and Revolution: Soviet Family Policy and Social Life, 1917-1936* (Cambridge: Cambridge University Press, 1993), 51, 54.

29. This was a common and ingenious form of punishment. At the time, most people in the USSR only had one pair of pants and no one would dare leave the house in just their underwear. Eleonora, Stepan Mikoyan's wife of 64 years (she passed away in 2009), once told me she hid Stepan's pants every time she found out he was going to the Bolshoi ballet performance. There, he would party and flirt with the dancers. This "visiting with the ballerinas" was a favorite *boys-will-be-boys* pastime, and "no Soviet wife should have been fine with that," Eleonora said.

30. There are rumors that Nikita's father was not the Kalinovka peasant, Sergei Khrushchev, but the painter Ivan Tereshchenko, the son of Nikolai, a local sugar magnate. Allegedly, Ivan fathered the boy with Ksenia, a village maiden, and then "to conceal the sins of his son, old Tereshchenko, married her off to a young fellow from a village in Podillia [Ukraine] named Khrushch and gave him some land in Kalinovka village in Kursk region on condition that he would adopt the

future child and not reveal this secret." (Volodymyr Pyanov, "Khrushchev—A Magnate's Son?" *Literaturna Ukraina*, July 20, 2006.) The Khrushchevs never had any land though. When I visited Kalinovka for Grandfather's centenary in 1994, the tiny hut they lived in was no more, but the spot was preserved, and it could only have belonged to a very poor family. Irina "Arisha," Khrushchev's younger sister, thought Nikita's paternity rumor might have started from their mother's own embellished accounts of her son's birth.

31. Despite the lack of formal family ties, in 1951 Nina helped Yury—a qualified student—get admitted to a prestigious military school, the Suvorov Academy in Kalinin. Upon graduating he became a pilot. Yury visited the Khrushchevs over the years, but was never fully accepted as a family member, except for developing strong relations with Uncle Sergei. Yury died after a car accident in 2003.

32. There was a stunning contrast between the meager individual living conditions—people habituated in communal apartments with 30 or more families on one floor, sharing a kitchen and a lavatory for all—and the magnificence of public works projects. Moscow subways, for example, were more than just utilitarian; they were underground masterpieces made of marble, granite, bronze and stained glass, constructed to remind citizens of the grandeur of the Soviet endeavor.

33. The following information and quotes (unless otherwise indicated) are taken from Leonid Khrushchev's personal file from the Third United School of Civilian Pilots and Aviation Mechanics of the USSR Air Fleet, May-September 1937. Family archive.

34. Trotsky's belief in "permanent revolution" around the world went against Stalin's theory of "socialism in one single country," the tenets of which included the promotion of supreme leadership, national self-sufficiency and pre-eminence. In the 1930s, the punishment for anyone suspected

of following Trotsky's teachings was potentially death or the gulag. When Khrushchev denounced Stalin in 1956, he put Stalinism in contrast with Vladimir Lenin's teachings: Dictatorship of proletariat as a process of direct democracy, which would bring socialism, and eventually communism, to the world poor.

35. Though the scandal was short lived, it became known around Moscow, and the rumor that my mother may be Rosa's daughter is persistent to this day: as recently as 2012, until I made a proper change, Leonid Khrushchev's profile on Wikipedia stated just that.

36. Taubman, *Khrushchev*. In his Khrushchev biography, Taubman alleges that Nikita was hurt by his son's fast-moving love interest from one to another because the father, too, lacked "stricter moral standards… of which he repeatedly fell short" (61). The author maintains that between Leonid's mother Efrosinia and his stepmother Nina, elder Khrushchev had another wife "Marusia, whose last name isn't known" (58). For one, why marrying Marusia, provided that there was a marriage, indicates the absence of moral standards. Secondly, the woman's fathom existence was strongly denied by Aunt Rada and other family members. Efrosinia's younger sister Anna Pisareva, an aviation engineer, talked a lot about the early Nikita years until her death in the 1980s. She never once mentioned some third wife. Nikita's garrulous mother, Ksenia, always ready to share personal details with anyone willing to listen, also never spoke of a Marusia. Taubman also says that Marusia was the reason that my grandparents "never officially registered their marriage until after his ouster in the late 1960s" (58). In fact, Nina and Nikita *never* registered their marriage for political reasons.

37. Nikita Khrushchev, *Memoirs of Nikita Khrushchev: Volume 1, Commissar, 1918-1945* (Pennsylvania State University Press, 2005), 145.

38. There was also Chairman of the All-Russian Central Executive Committee, Mikhail Kalinin, whose wife was forced under torture to confess to "counterrevolutionary Trotskyite activities" in 1938, and consequently spent almost ten years in a labor camp. Accused of right-wing deviationism (an alliance of the working class and peasantry versus the correct Bolshevik belief in the totality of dictatorship of proletariat) Kaganovich's brother Mikhail committed suicide in 1941 because Lazar failed to defend him. Budenny, whose revolutionary reputation at the time was inferior only to Lenin's or Stalin's, sacrificed his wife, the opera singer, Olga Budnitskaya, to the purges and married Olga's cousin, Maria, who was 33 years his junior.
39. Khrushchev, *Memoirs: Volume 1*, 107-108.
40. Richard Pipes, *Communism: A History* (New York: Modern Library, 2001), 64.
41. See, "Terror po pervoi kategorii," *Moskovsky Komsomolets*, August 5, 2007. According to Sergei Khrushchev, "Father himself never denied that he had to countersign orders prepared by the NKVD [People's Commissariat of Internal Affairs] for the arrest of people with whom he worked. That is how things were in those times. And just let anyone try not to countersign such a paper!" Sergei Khrushchev, "The History of the Creation and Publication of the Khrushchev Memoirs (1967–1999)" in Khrushchev, *Memoirs: Volume 1*, 720.
42. Taubman, *Khrushchev*, 103-104.
43. The photographer, Roy Schatt, described his friend Dean as a man who "was a disrupter of norms, a bender of rules, a disquieter of calm." Cited in "James Dean New York 1954," http://www.baranyartists.com/royschatt/roy_schatt_thumbnails.html.
44. Khrushchev, *Memoirs: Volume 1*, 138-139.
45. "All-Union Population Census for 1937"; http://www.marxists.org/.

46. Those drastic measures also appeared to be an attack on Ukrainian nationalism. Modern Russia derives from Kievan Russia, which emerged in 880, and the Ukrainians have claimed supremacy ever since. Fearing the possibility of the republic's independence, Stalin suppressed it through collectivization. In Russia today the cause of *Holodomor* is still debated. In 2006 the Ukrainian parliament declared the *Holodomor* an act of intentional genocide, but in April of 2010 the Kremlin backed President Viktor Yanukovich reversed Ukraine's policy on this issue.

47. See, William Henry Chamberlin, *The Ukraine: A Submerged Nation* (New York: Macmillan, 1944).

48. "All-Union Population Census."

49. To calm the outrage, in 1938, Ukraine's Polish-born leader, Stanislav Kosior—who only in 1935 received the Order of Lenin "for remarkable success in the field of agriculture"— was arrested for sabotage and treason. See, Roy Medvedev, *Let History Judge: The Origin and Consequences of Stalinism* (New York: Alfred A. Knopf, 1972).

50. Milovan Djilas, *Conversations with Stalin* (New York: Harcourt, Brace & World, Inc., 1962), 118, 122.

51. This and the following quotes are from Khrushchev, *Memoirs: Volume 1*, 162-163, 136, 63-64.

52. Ibid., 136.

53. In 1935, as the famine was in full swing Stalin delivered his famous "Stakhanovites" speech. Aleksei Stakhanov, a Russian miner who in August of that year claimed to have produced 102 tons of coal in five hours—14 times the normal output, originated a movement to prove Soviet economic superiority over capitalism. "The basis for the Stakhanov movement was…the radical improvement in the material welfare of the workers," Stalin declared. "Life has improved, comrades. Life has become more joyous. And when life is joyous, work goes well…Hence the heroes and heroines of labor." J.V. Stalin,

Problems of Leninism (Peking: Foreign Language Press, 1976), 775-794. The production statistics lagged in Ukraine, and Khrushchev, once a miner, too, was expected to make Stalin's call for the heroes of labor a reality.

54. This and the following quote are from Djilas, *Conversations with Stalin*, 122, 121.

55. This information is from Leonid Khrushchev's military file at Podolsk Central Archive of the Ministry of Defense of the USSR (TsAMO), File 290, Description 32631c, Case 4, 44-47.

56. I found this information in the notes of Victor Fomin, a plane mechanic, who serviced equipment in Leonid's bomber regiment. "Lichnye memuary Viktora Andreevicha Fomina," February 5, 1998. Family archive.

57. In his "Lichnye memuary" Fomin mistakenly claimed that Elinov never returned from the foray. Stepan Mikoyan made the same mistake: "One of the four-crew members had been killed while still in the air." (Stepan Mikoyan, *Memoirs of Military Test-Flying and Life with the Kremlin's Elite* (Airlife Publishing, 1999), 76.) In fact, Leonid's plane had a three-man crew. In August, Elinov, alive, wrote to Leonid detailing his terrible medical experiences. In subsequent letters, Leonid's friends mentioned Elinov's later promotion and transfer to another regiment.

58. Andrei Ignatov, "Porazheniya Krasnoi Armii v pervye mesyatsy Velikoi Otechestvennoi Voiny," *Istoriya*, No 32, 2002.

59. It is because of the massive losses in Soviet Russia—in five years the country lost more than any other nation, 26 million military personnel and another 17 million civilians—we refer to World War II as the Great Patriotic War. (See, Boris Sokolov, "Kak pobedila Rossiya," *Novaya Gazeta*, April 24, 2010.) We think of it as our own, as though we were the only ones who fought it, without 30 plus other countries. Even

today, Russians treat May 9, the anniversary of the Allied victory, as a sacred national moment. Others, particularly in the rural parts of the country, still call the conflict, quite logically, the German War.

60. See, Sokolov, "Kak pobedila Rossiya" and Ignatov, "Porazheniya Krasnoi Armii."

61. Russian State Archive of Socio-Political History (RGASPI), File 17, Description 167, Case 60, 26. Cited in Nikolai Pobol, Pavel Polyan, "Stalin i Khrushchev," *Novaya Gazeta*, February 2, 2009.

62. Tver was under partial Nazi occupation until December 1941 when the Soviets re-took control of it.

63. A copy of Ivanov's official letter to the newspaper's deputy editor Colonel S. Kovalev from March 7, 1964 made its way into and was preserved in our family archive.

64. Yury Teplyakov, "Stalin's War Against His Own Troops: The Tragic Fate of Soviet Prisoners of War in German Captivity," *Moscow News*, No 19, 1990.

65. "Skolko stoila pobeda? Velikaya Otechestvennaya Voina v tsifrakh," Ria Novosti, March 23, 2005.

66. Ts. Solodar, "Leonid Khrushchev i ego ekipazh," *Komsomolskaya Pravda* (n.d.).

67. M. Kalashnikov, "Na frontakh otechestvennoi voiny," *Pravda*, July 26, 1941.

68. Fomin, "Lichnye memuary." In the USSR, where the military industrial complex was a priority and where enjoying consumer goods was considered sinful, it was easier to find a person operating a tractor or a crop duster than one driving a personal vehicle, especially a luxurious one like Leonid's black Emka, the 1930s Soviet passenger car originally based on the Ford Model B.

69. See, William Moskoff, *The Bread of Affliction: The Food Supply in the USSR During World War II* (Cambridge University Press, 2002), 138-139.

70. Khrushchev arranged not only an apartment in Kuibyshev, but also Arisha's post-war residence in Moscow on central Karmanitsky Street. In the 1960s, while Khrushchev was still in power, Arisha's oldest daughter, Irma, moved into our posh apartment complex on Kutuzovsky Avenue, also with Grandfather's help.

71. S.A. Mikoyan, *My—Deti voiny* (Moscow: Eksmo, 2006), 99-100.

72. Cited in A. Kolesnik, "Leonid Khrushchev," *Argumenty i Fakty*, No 46, November 18-24, 1989.

73. On August 4, 1941 Ivanov wrote:

> My dear son Leonya! For your suffering we'll avenge the enemy so he remembers what it means to be a Stalin falcon. We, Stalin's Falcons, have steel blood and the fascists won't escape us. We will intermix their Aryan blood in our dark black soil, so they will never dare to battle us again. For each of ours, we will kill a thousand and more of theirs. As we were pounding them with you, I will be pounding them for you, our battle comrade, who stepped up in the front lines responding to the call of our leader, our commander, Father Stalin.

74. "Voennaya kharakteristika na Leonida Nikitovicha Khrushcheva," January 9, 1942. TsAMO, File 292, Description 32634, Case 4, 11.

75. "Pismo Chlenu Voennogo Soveta Voronezhskogo Fronta General Leitenantu Nikite Khrushchevu" (n.d.). TsAMO, File 290, Description 32631c, Case 4, 44-47.

76. See reference 53.

77. William Taubman once joked to me that he must have been Lyuba's "last conquest," as he found her "remarkably irrepressible." When he met Lyuba in the early 1990s, he was overwhelmed by this 80-year-old lady. Upon the completion of his Khrushchev biography, she insisted on reading the

pages related to her. She convinced an acquaintance in Kiev to translate those pages and was incensed with her portrayal, which she thought didn't do her justice, even though Taubman was complimentary to her character giving her ample space in the book.

In three pale green school notebooks in thirty meticulous points, Lyuba documented her indignation. "I read parts about myself, for a month I have been in a state of shock. God! Who told you these black lies about me?" Every other sentence in these notes is punctuated by an exclamation mark and is peppered with accusations that Taubman painted a "horrible," "dark and unfair" picture of her. Khrushchev's biographer later told me that he was "startled by the vehemence with which Lyuba demanded corrections." Her demands were absurd though: In one instance she was upset that the biographer stated that she "had a past" before meeting Leonid. She did have that past—at least one prior relation with Efim Belonenko, Tolya's father. Yet she was indignant, "Which past? I was only twenty-four. I had only the present." In 1938 Lyuba was actually twenty-six, and for someone who is so concerned with the truth, this is deliberately deceptive. She didn't want the difference in her and Leonid's ages to be known.

78. See, Irina Lisnichenko, "Lyubov Sizykh: Posle moego aresta moya doch ostalas v semie Khrushchevykh i Nikitu Sergeevicha nazyvala papoi," *Fakty i Kommentarii*, September 25, 2009.

79. Taubman, *Khrushchev*, 158.

80. Corine Defrance, "Raymond Schmittlein (1904–1974): médiateur entre la France et la Lituanie," *Cahiers Lituaniens*, 2008.

81. A brilliant man by all accounts, Schmittlein had written books, established the post-war university l'École balte des Beaux-Arts de Fribourg, and went on to become a politician

in northeast France in the 1950s. In 1961, as vice-president of the France-USSR Association, he met with Premier Khrushchev in Moscow. Was Khrushchev aware that the man he was meeting was the same with whom Lyuba cheated on Leonid twenty years earlier? Did Schmittlein himself mention that he met Leonid? None of these details are given in a brief description of his visit in the September 2, 1961 issue of a local French newspaper, *Courrier de Belfort.*

82. Jean Cathala, *Sans Fleur ni Fusil* (A. Michel, 1981), 302.

83. This version of events stands in contrast to Taubman's account (provided by Lyuba herself) that "Vera Chernetskaya... had persuaded [her] to study French." (Taubman, *Khrushchev,* 158.) The institute later became my father's alma mater and served as a training ground for Soviet spies, an esteemed profession during the Great Patriotic and then the Cold War.

84. Cited in Julie Wheelwright, "Poisoned Honey: the Myth of Women in Espionage," *Queen's Quarterly* 100/2 (Summer 1993), 291-309: 293.

85. "Spravka po reabilitatsii Lyubovi Illarionovny Sizykh," September 28, 1992, No 13/3-4472-92. Family archive.

86. During the war with Germany, these charges—contact with foreigners, along with espionage—were widespread. The Soviet Union was on the lookout for class enemies and capitalist adversaries, and the NKVD was vigilant like never before. In 1942, even when Stalin needed bodies to defend the country, the number of political prisoners in the Gulag camps still soared to 1.5 million, a jump from the one million imprisoned during the sweeping 1937 purges. One-third of them, that is as many as 500,000 people, were considered spies. See, "Arresty i nakazaniya s 1921 po 1953 god," *Soviet-History.com,* December 11, 1953.

87. Tatiana Songarova, "Kak zakalyalas stal Lyubov Sizykh," *Kamuflyazh,* March 2003, 21-23.

88. Reviewers raved about Taubman's depiction of the young Sizykh: "[He] has unearthed the story of Lyuba, the pretty widow of Khrushchev's son Leonid, who was arrested and sent to the camps for talking to foreign diplomats; her father-in-law pretended she had never existed." See, Neal Ascherson, "Oo, Oo!" *London Review of Books*, Vol. 25 No 16, August 21, 2003, 15-16.

89. Khrushchev, *Memoirs: Volume 2*, 690-691.

90. Eugenia Ginzburg, author of the critically acclaimed dissident memoir *Journey into the Whirlwind*, which described her own years as a victim of Stalinism, was my mother's friend, and in the late 1970s I was fortunate to have spoken to her many times at our *dacha* in Peredelkino, the famed writers retreat 15 miles southwest of Moscow. Ginzburg said that rape was all too common in the camps, although she herself was lucky. "I was touched inappropriately many times though," she said. "I even brought myself to write about this in *The Whirlwind*: "'Undress I said...' 'I won't!' 'Oh yes, you will...,' said the Nabob in sudden rage, and before I knew what was happening, he started to undress me by force. I felt his paws on my breast." Eugenia Ginzburg, *Journey Into the Whirlwind* (Harcourt, 1967), 218.

91. Susanne Scholl, a veteran Austrian TV journalist posted in Russia for 20 years, wrote a book about her own family in both Hitler's and Stalin's detention camps. She says it is common for concentration camp victims to deny the horrors they went through, finding it hard to accept the inhumanity of the past while living in the human present. Scholl's own mother lied about her experiences, and many former prisoners often refuse to acknowledge any bad memories. See, Susanne Scholl, *Reise nach Karaganda* (Wien Molden, 2006).

92. David M. Kennedy, ed. *The Library of Congress World War II Companion* (Simon&Schuster, 2007), 528. The battle of

Stalingrad was bloodiest combat of the Eastern Front; two million Soviets lost their lives.

93. See, Elena Zholi, "Stepan Mikoyan: Stalin neset otvetstvennost za ochen mnogie oshibki, privedshie k gromadnym chelovecheskim zhertvam," *Komsomolskaya Pravda*, May 6, 2010.

94. The boys' mother Ashkhen waited for years for Vladimir, barely out of high school, to miraculously return. Father Anastas Mikoyan has touchingly described the pain of that loss in his 1999 memoir *Tak bylo*. Although Vladimir, like Leonid, was an MIA, unlike Leonid he has never been the target of the treason accusations. Elder Mikoyan's legacy was never as controversial as Khrushchev's, even if Anastas was a much closer Stalin's associate before he became Nikita's comrade-in-arms.

95. This and the following three quotes are from Ivan Pavlov, "Predatel ili geroi?" *by from Pobeda Vitebsk*, June 9, 2010. Further citations from Pavlov are from this document without attribution.

96. I indirectly learned of these reports from Alexander Shcherbakov, another fighter pilot, and from Stepan Mikoyan, as they both had acquaintances who used to serve in the 18th Regiment.

97. Admittedly, it also led to the militarization of the space race and accelerated the Cold War. But this was a problem of politics more so than the science behind space exploration. In fact, Grandfather used to tell a funny story, which could have been a scene from *Dr. Strangelove*, to explain why the arms race was almost inevitable: US President Dwight Eisenhower once asked him: "Premier Khrushchev, you seem to be a reasonable man, why are there these escalations of weapons and so on?" Grandfather answered: "My generals run into my office every morning, saying, 'The Americans did this, the Americans invented that. We need to strengthen our

might.' And what about you, President Eisenhower? What's your excuse?" The US president responded: "Same thing, Premier Khrushchev."

98. "Khrushchev's daughter-in-law Lyuba Sedykh (*sic*), the wife of Khrushchev's older son, who had been condemned to a punishment battalion in Stalin's time and who died as a result." Alexander Solzhenitsyn, *The Gulag Archipelago 1918-1956: An Experiment in Literary Investigation Volume 1* (Harper & Row, 1973), 159.

99. S.A. Mikoyan, *My—Deti voiny*, 100. In the late 1980s, Larisa Vasilieva, an obscure Soviet poet turned Russian gossip writer, interviewed my aunt for a book called *Kremlin Wives* (Arcade Publishing, 1994). Trying to deflate other people's rumors about Leonid, Rada mentioned that she heard of the "bottle" story, although she didn't mention she heard it from Mikoyan. It appeared that she knew it from her childhood, and that's how Vasilieva wrote about it. From then on, Rada's interview has become one of the most popular references for Leonid's mishaps. Today, some continue to cite Rada's words as *evidence* that Leonid was a murderer, among other thing. See, Stanislav Bondorenko, "Interview with Rada Khrushcheva," *Khronograph.ru*, February 6, 2004.

100. This and the following quote are from Sergo Beria, *Moi otets—Lavrenty Beria* (Moscow: Sovremennik, 1994), 58. Despite these allegations, Beria does write that Leonid died a hero, "After becoming a pilot Leonid bravely fought the enemy and died in a battle…in the spring of 1943." (Ibid.)

101. Mikhail Dokuchaev, *Moskva. Kreml. Okhrana* (Moscow: Business Press, 1995).

102. Around the same time, another equally obscure Kremlin security officer, Sergei Krasikov, painted an even more ominous picture: "Stalin pushed broken Khrushchev's head to the floor and began beating on it with the pipe, ranting

and shouting." Sergei Krasikov, *Vozle vozhdei* (Moscow: Sovremennik, 1997) cited in Nikolai Andreev, *Tragicheskie Sudby* (Moscow: Olma Press, 2001), 121.

103. Andrei Sukhomlinov, "Bez vesti propavshy," *Sovershenno Sekretno*, March 2000.

104. Chuev, *Molotov*, 421-422. However, political analyst Vyacheslav Nikonov, Molotov's grandson, with whom I have cordial professional relations, shared his doubts that the compiler of these interviews, Chuev, accurately recorded his grandfather's words. According to Nikonov, in Chuev's version, Molotov seemed whiny and petty. Nevertheless, the younger Molotov, a strong Putin supporter and a politician with the government party United Russia, has publicly insisted that his grandfather told him that Leonid "was a traitor." (Cited in Peter Savodnik, "The trial of Leonid K," *The National*, May 8, 2009.) Not wanting to start a public feud between the grandchildren of political celebrities, I have never mustered up the courage to look Vyacheslav in the eye and ask him if this was indeed true.

105. Vadim Udilov, "Za chto Khrushchev otomstil Stalinu," *Nezavisimaya Gazeta*, February 17, 1998. Also cited in Yakov Sukhotin, "Za chto Stalin kaznil syna Khrushcheva?" *Duel*, July 27, 1999. Udilov also insisted that Leonid convinced his whole squadron to abandon their posts. No war record has ever indicated any defection from the 18th Fighter Regiment, let alone a scandalous mass desertion.

106. Valentin Dudin, Nikolai Poroskov, "Vypolnyaya prikaz my ne ostanavlivalis ne pered chem," *Vremya Novostei*, May 7, 2004.

107. Excerpts from the military journalist B.E. Pestov's interview with Ivan Pstygo cited in online forum *Lozh i pravda o Leonide Khrushcheve*, April 26, 2012.

108. TsAMO of the USSR, File 290, Description 32631c, Case 4, 44-47.

109. Nikolai Nad, "Predatel ili geroi," *Versiya*, June 20-26, 2000. Nad is the pen name of Nikolai Dobryukha. A prolific journalist who never misses an opportunity to glorify Stalin, Dobryukha, often writing as Nad, is the author of many bogus "investigations," including a derogatory expose about American rock music, which was part of a State Department project to sew dissent in the USSR.

110. "Otkaz v rassmotrenii ugolovnogo dela Yuriya Khrushcheva ot Zamyshlyaevoi V.V., Prokurora po Nadzoru za Soblyudeniem Federalnoi Bezopasnosti," October 23, 2000. Family Archive. The journalist in question is Ivan Stadnyuk, the author of the famous Stalinist multi-part novel, *The War* (1971-80).

111. Grandfather repeatedly told my mother about his infatuation with Bukharin: "I first heard him speak in 1919 in a theater in a small town, a short man in a leather coat. He made me very enthusiastic about communism." He also remembered how Bukharin dared to challenge Stalin's leadership by questioning the lack of Soviet transparency, triggering the dictator's devious response. On February 23, 1937 at the opening of the Plenum of the Central Communist Party Committee, Stalin saw Bukharin all alone. "What are you standing there for, Bukharchik?" he asked gently. "Come, you are one of us." A week later Bukharin was arrested, interrogated for months, and after confessing to leading a Trotskyite coup, he was executed the following year.

112. "Putin Awarded Yazov with the Order of Merit," Ria Novosti, November 17, 2004.

113. Vladimir Sukhodeev, ed. *Epokha Stalina: Sobytiya i Lyudi* (Moscow: Eksmo, 2004).

114. Russian authorities allegedly didn't attempt a serious rescue or accept other countries' offers of assistance. They also failed to acknowledge any responsibility for the deaths. In an interview with CNN's Larry King Putin famously

quipped: "The boat simply sunk." See, "Russian President Vladimir Putin Discusses Domestic and Foreign Affairs," CNN, September 8, 2000.

115. Six years prior, I had written a letter to the editor of *Nezavisimaya Gazeta* (Independent Newspaper) questioning the veracity of General Udilov's allegations against Leonid. (See, Nina Khrushcheva, "Za chto stalinisty mstyat Khrushchevu," *Nezavisimaya Gazeta*, April 4, 1998. This article was written in response to Udilov, "Za chto Khrushchev otomstil Stalinu.") That was my only involvement in the treason story before my mother's decision to start the legal battle.

116. See Jerrold L. Schecter, Leona P. Schecter, *Sacred Secrets: How Soviet Intelligence Operations Changed American History* (Potomac Books, 2003). In 1970, just before *Time, Inc.* announced it had acquired the memoir, the KGB forced Sergei to hand over the tapes and transcripts, saying that a foreign intelligence agency was trying to acquire them. By then, however, the leak had already occurred, which surprised my mother. Sergei assured her that after he gave all the materials to the KGB the agency would leave our family alone.

117. Following Khrushchev's death, the Brezhnev regime, which was upset about the memoir incident, sought to punish our family. "The Politburo started looking into Grandfather's affairs," Grandmother once told me. "The country was already very different, and the party quickly realized since we were never officially married I had no formal claim to widow's privileges—a pension, an apartment, health insurance." Eventually, Victoria Brezhneva, the new first lady, who used to be Grandmother's close friend, intervened on her behalf; our family's benefits were restored.

118. Henry Shapiro, "Nikita's Favorite Son-in-law May Have Peddled His Notes," *The Pittsburgh Press*, January 3, 1971.

119. Andrei Sakharov once wrote that Louis, officially a British *Evening News* reporter, "is both a Soviet citizen and an English newspaper correspondent (an inconceivable combination), active and long lasting KGB agent, who works on the most delicate and provocative assignments." See, A.D. Sakharov, *Vospominaniya* Moscow, 1996.

120. See, Schecter, *Sacred Secrets*, 235.

121. Sergei Khrushchev, *Khrushchev on Khrushchev* (Little, Brown & Co, 1990), 251.

122. Louis apparently told Schecter that our family loved the memoir; that Grandmother Nina had helped translate it into Russian for Nikita. However, according to my mother and Aunt Rada, Grandmother never spoke of the memoir. She thought it was a mistake to do it in the first place and was incensed when the text made it to the West and then got published, further tainting Khrushchev's Bolshevik reputation. For her, the memoir was the beginning of her husband's demise, which was brought about by my father's betrayal, and she was upset that my mother had married a man who, she felt, had been so disloyal to the Khrushchevs.

123. I live in the United States too, and do share in Uncle Sergei's "betrayal." But I am further removed from the Khrushchev orbit—a granddaughter, technically a great granddaughter, whom Grandfather knew only as a willful seven-year-old. Sergei, Nikita's only surviving son after Leonid's death, was his father's pride, a rocket scientist, who aided in preserving Khrushchev's final word to posterity. Grandfather would have vehemently objected to his son accepting fellowship at Brown University and becoming a US citizen shortly after.

124. Udilov, "Za chto Khrushchev otomstil Stalinu." There is no evidence that Yakov ever cooperated with the Nazis, yet the German propaganda leaflets of his alleged surrender flooded the USSR through the Nazi-occupied territories. "Don't shed blood for Stalin!" one such flyer read. "He

already escaped to Samara [Kuibyshev]! His son has surrendered! He saved himself by serving us, and you don't need to sacrifice yourself either!" (Cited in John Erickson, *Hitler Versus Stalin* (Carlton Books, 2002), 46.) The leaflets with Leonid's name don't exist, which is further proof that the KGB allegations are bogus.

125. See among other sources, John M. Carey, Matthew Soberg Shugart, *Executive Decree Authority* (Cambridge University Press, 1998); Soili Nysten-Haarala, "Russian Property Rights in Transition," Interim Report IR-01-006 (International Institute for Applied Systems Analysis, Laxenburg, Austria, 2001).

126. See, Lilia Shevtsova, "Yeltsin and the Evolution of Electoral Monarchy in Russia," *Current History*, October 2000; Nina Khrushcheva, "Cultural Contradiction of Post-Communism: Why Liberal Reforms Did Not Succeed in Russia" (New York: Council of Foreign Relations Paper, 2000). Our personal tragedy was that our nanny Masha was ruined by the Yeltsin anarchy. Once a feisty, independent 60-year-old woman who had spent her entire life taking care of my family, she struggled living on her own when Ksenia and I grew up. She took her own life in June 1992, leaving a note, which explained that without universal healthcare she didn't want to be a burden to others. My 1991 decision to study in the United States had also devastated her. In her mind, she couldn't imagine life outside of the Soviet borders. She thought I was "abandoning the motherland for that ungodly land" never to come back. I was devastated in return, blaming the Russian government for failing her along with many others.

127. Even after 13 years in power, in June 2013, Putin was still considered by many "an ideal or 'close to ideal' president of Russia…Overall, 64 percent…said that they approve of the president's dealings." "41% of Russians See Putin as Ideal Leader," *The Moscow Times*, June 10, 2013.

128. See, Jason Bush, "Oil: What's Russia Really Sitting On?" *Business Week*, November 22, 2004. The author suggests that Russia's oil reserve is at 200 billion barrels, 15 percent of the world's total, and also accounting for 40 percent of Russia's national GDP.

129. Richard Weitz, "Reforming Russia's Military Industrial Complex," *Project Syndicate*, May 30, 2007.

130. Chuev, *Molotov*, 433.

131. This and the following quote are from Elena Prudnikova, *Stalin: Vtoroe ubiistvo* (St. Petersburg: Neva, 2003), 7–9.

132. Andrei Arkhipov, "Rech Khruscheva na XX sezde KPSS do sikh por zasekrechena," *Otchizna*, March 11, 2006.

133. Richard Cavendish, "Lavrenti Beria Executed," *History Today*, Volume 53 No 12, 2003.

134. This and the following quote are from Taubman, *Khrushchev*, 157, 689.

135. Mikoyan, *Memoirs of Military Test-Flying*, 76.

136. Andreev, *Tragicheskie Sudby*, 120.

137. Nikolai Dobryukha, "'Khrushchev polzal za nim na kolenyakh…' Pochemu Nikita Sergeevich razoblachil Stalina?" *Argumenty i Fakty*, November 21, 2007.

138. Grandfather once described Shcherbakov Sr. as "malicious… [with] the poisonous, viperlike nature," and "a trained attack dog." (Khrushchev, *Memoirs: Volume 2*, 40-41). Of course, there were many instances in which Khrushchev himself served as Stalin's cheerleader as the *Holodomor* example certainly indicates.

139. "Pismo ot zamestitelya prokurora Rossiiskoi Federatsii A.N. Savenkova to Y.L. Khrushcheva," June 6, 2004. No 7ya-122/04. Family archive.

140. My mother did have dinner with Montefiore once in 2003 at the fancy Pushkin restaurant in Moscow. They talked about Khrushchev, of course, but this was not a professional interview. Montefiore didn't mention his work on Stalin

or any other books. He didn't take notes and he gave my mother the impression that it was just an informal, casual conversation by a journalist who was simply interested in history. They spoke in English (as Mr. Montefiore explained, he didn't know Russian), which was a struggle for my mother. When *The Court of the Red Tsar* came out a year later, Mother was astonished to find a chapter on Khrushchev and was even more stunned to discover herself as its main source. Montefiore refers to their casual dinner as a formal interview in which she apparently provided the author with a wealth of information on Nikita, his son, and the rest of the family. In the book, much of it just plain false or twisted beyond factual recognition. For example, Montefiore did not bother to check Lyuba's actual last name; all throughout the book he calls her Lyubov Kutuzova instead of Lyubov Sizykh.

141. Simon Sebag Montefiore, *Stalin: The Court of the Red Tsar* (Alfred A. Knopf, 2004), 453.

142. For example, Stepan Mikoyan's friend Ivan Zhuk, who served with Leonid and observed the combat, confirmed the crash, which "was obscured by the ongoing battle and haze." (Mikoyan, *My—Deti voiny*, 100.) A contradicting account came from Nikolai Tsibikov, another squadron pilot: "We went on the same mission over Bryansk on 11 March... After we returned and reported that everything was fine, we realized [Leonid] was gone. Then Golubov sent two search teams into the area. They flew very low but found nothing. Later I read that Leonid died in a dogfight. But I believe that there was no air combat." A. Drabkin, "Interview with Nikolai Tsibikov," *I Remember: Soviet WWII-veteran Memoirs.ru*, February 4, 2011.

143. Before the 1917 Revolution, local priests were the only authorities given the power to document birth, death and marriage in the rural parts of the deeply religious Russian Empire.

144. In Russia, Simonov's short poem "Wait for Me," addressed to Serova from the war front, is universally admired:

> Wait for me, and I'll come back!
> Wait with all you've got!
> Wait, when dreary yellow rains
> Tell you, you should not.

145. Anna Orlova, "Skandal vokrug seriala 'Zvezda epokhi,'" *Moskovsky Komsomolets*, April 26, 2005.

146. Alexander Shcherbakov and Vladimir Lukin, "Chernye pyatna na chistom nebe," *Izvestia*, October 11, 2007.

147. Dobryukha, "Khrushchev polzal za nim na kolenyakh." Despite all our efforts in 2013 the daily *Komsomolskaya Pravda* started a new weekly section, headed by Dobryukha, the widely discredited author. The new column was dedicated to the tales told by former KGB officers, and the first two installments began with Grandfather, of course, and all the bogus stories about Leonid's treason and Khrushchev crawling on his knees. See, Nikolai Nad (Dobryukha), "U predatelei ne bylo shansa vyzhit," *Komsomolskaya Pravda*, January 16, 2013 and "Poslednie dni Khruschcheva," *Komsomolskaya Pravda*, January 23, 2013.

148. Not all legal dramas remain unresolved in Putin's Russia. In cases, directly supported by the Kremlin, mentioning famous people *does require* the heirs's consent. In April 2007 director Andrei Panin released a comedy *Gagarin's Grandson*. The movie's main character, a black orphaned boy, tells everyone that he is the grandson of Yury Gagarin, the first man in space, "Gagarin was jet setting all over the world... In Cameroon he met my grandmother, she could not resist, and he did not resist either." At the end of the movie the child admits he lied. Nevertheless, Gagarin's daughters, Galina and Elena, friends of Putin, were incensed by what they considered a defamation of the good name of

their father, who died in 1968 during a training flight. In September 2007, two women filed a court case against the feature, which "presents information that doesn't correspond with reality." The court immediately ruled in the Gagarins' favor. The showing of the film was frozen indefinitely and the director, Panin, had to apologize. See, "Kinematografisty publichno izvinilis za 'Vnuka Gagarina,'" *Lenta.ru*, October 23, 2007.

149. For the Russians a doze of absurdity is a way of life, especially with court cases that are now being used, and abused, by anyone and everyone. Since Putin came to power Yakov Dzhugashvili's son Eugeny has got a good chance to dispute Stalin's involvement in *Holodomor*, the Great Purges, and World War II deaths. In the last ten years he has sued the archives, governments and media outlets for libel and defamation of his grandfather's memory.

In 2009 liberal newspaper *Novaya Gazeta* (New Paper) published an article about Stalin's responsibility for mass murders. (See, Anatoly Yablokov, "Vinovnym naznachen Beria," *Novaya Gazeta*, April 22, 2009.) Dzhugashvili demanded that the paper retract references to Stalin personally signing death warrants, as well as a compensation of ten million rubles ($350,000) for damage to his honor. The judge quickly ruled against Stalin's descendant, although my mother contends that his loss is not a liberal victory. A legal exoneration of Stalin would be a PR nightmare for the country. Since there are endless documents proving that Stalin did sign death warrants—his firm signature, "Yea, I. Stalin," in a customary thick blue pencil is unmistakable—the conspicuous court investigation would have resulted in a scandal. The documents would prove that he initiated genocide against his own nation, thus damaging Putin's political stance as a strong leader in the Stalin mold.

150. "Born in the U.S.A. The truth about Obama's birth certificate," *FactCheck.org*, August 21, 2008. In 2011 when the president made public his long-form Honolulu birth certificate the numbers finally went down to ten percent. See, *The Washington Post* Poll, April 28-May 1, 2011.

151. See, Andron Konchalovsky, "Uzhasnis sam sebe," *Kommersant Vlast*, February 27, 2012.

152. *Zhizdra News*, December 30, 2007; http://www.zhizdra.ru/news/new2007.htm

153. See, Sergei Khrushchev, *Khrushchev* (Moscow: Vagrius, 2001). Also cited from a Belorussian military newspaper *Vo Slavu Rodiny* (August 28, 1999) by Pavlov in "Leonid Khrushchev" and in A.M. Kachanov, "Geroi," *Duel*, July 27, 1999.

154. The website entry reads: "Leonid, the son of N.S. Khrushchev, died in an air battle north of Zhizdra. Thirty years later the former flight leader the Guard Senior lieutenant Zamorin disclosed the circumstances of his death in a letter to the Minister of Defense D.F. Ustinov. In a fight with two FockeWulfs one of them went under the lead plane. Covering Zamorin, Khrushchev himself caught fire. Officially the version was spread that L.N. Khrushchev was MIA, because the commanders of the Regiment didn't want to be responsible for the death of the Politburo member's son." See, "Date in History Military Calendar: 11 March 1943" on the Russian Ministry of Defense website.

155. Nikolai Poroskov, who interviewed Marshal Pstygo in 2004, now says he was "guilty of adding to the myth creation" about Leonid. Poroskov changed his mind after talking to Kirilin, who said that "when Khrushchev became the head of state, he turned everything upside down to find his son's plane...Why did Stalin award Khrushchev's son with the Order of the Great Patriotic War? Leonid was not a very disciplined person—a well-known fact, but he was a brave

lad...Besides, imagine an operation to kidnap a captured Soviet pilot...Such operations in the history of intelligence can be counted on your fingers...[T]o steal a man from the German SS! Impossible! I believe that story of Leonid Khrushchev's betrayal—a fabrication." These quotes are from Nikolai Poroskov, "Geroi i mify," *Vremya Novostei*, May 22, 2009.

156. Pavel Sudoplatov, *Spetsoperatsii: Lubyanka i Kreml, 1930-1950* (Moscow: Olma-Press, 2003), 260-261. Given Sudoplatov's very firm statement, it is inexplicable how the treason accusations can continue.

There are many other holes in that myth. A major one: The man who allegedly reported Leonid's betrayal to Stalin was Alexander Shcherbakov Sr. Stalin ordered the Soviet Army to steal Leonid back from the Nazis, and then supposedly called a special Politburo meeting during which Shcherbakov proposed that the *troika* military tribunal should decide Leonid's death. Beria, Molotov and Mikoyan unanimously voted in the affirmative. See, Sukhodeev, *Epokha Stalina.* Yet, Shcherbakov Jr. as well as Stepan Mikoyan, two sons of the party officials who allegedly witnessed Leonid's "conviction," have vehemently denied the tribunal occurrence or their fathers's involvement, branding the rumor "a grotesque lie."

157. See, V.A. Chernobrov, *Entsiklopedia zagadochnykh mest Kaluzhskoi oblasti* (Kosmopoisk, 2008).

158. Cited on the internet site *Gostevaya kniga Zhizdry,* July 15, 2011.

159. B.E. Pestov, "Pogib? Propal bez vesti? Zhiv?.." *Voenno-istorichesky Zhurnal,* No 4, 1990, 80.

160. Putin is indeed often vocal about Russia standing up to what he thinks is Western hypocrisy: "In the era of colonialism, colonialist countries talked about their so-called civilizing role. Today, [some countries] use slogans

of spreading democracy for the same purpose, and that is to gain unilateral advantages and ensure their own interests." Claire Bigg, "Russia: Putin Delivers Annual State-Of-The-Nation Address," RFERL, April 26, 2007.

161. For decades Stalin blamed the massacre on the Nazis, but in the 1950s during the Thaw Khrushchev offered full disclosure to Poland's communist leader Wladislaw Gomulka. "It would put an end to the whole terrible affair once and for all," the premier said. Gomulka rejected the idea, fearing "a chain reaction" that might discredit Polish communists. Khrushchev backed off—he was fine with dishonoring Stalin, but didn't want to hurt communism. See, Anna M. Cienciala, Natalia S. Lebedeva, and Wojciech Materski, eds. *Katyn: A Crime Without Punishment* Yale University Press, 2008, 240.

When the USSR dissolved, the Katyn order reemerged from the Kremlin archives. In 1992 Yeltsin, admitting full Soviet responsibility for almost 22,000 deaths, gave then Polish President Lech Walesa a copy of the March 5, 1940 murder decree, signed by Beria, Stalin, Molotov and Anastas Mikoyan, among others. Under Putin, the current Russian security agency, the FSB, backpedaled again, and the truth about Katyn returned to its Soviet-era secretive status. By 2010, however, denying Stalin's responsibility for Katyn was like denying evolution, and for the 70th anniversary of the massacre, Russia finally admitted what had happened. Putin invited Polish officials to honor the dead. But a new tragedy unfolded—a botched landing near Smolensk on April 10 killed Poland's President Lech Kaczynski, along with other 95 Polish dignitaries. This accident conjured up memories of the area as cursed, a Bermuda Triangle of sorts. Alexander Kwasniewski, Kaczynski's predecessor called the region "a damned place." See, Nicholas Kulish,

"Polish President Dies in Jet Crash in Russia," *The New York Times*, April 10, 2010.

162. J.V. Stalin, "Radio Broadcast," *Marxists Internet Archive.org*, July 3, 1941.

163. Vasily Lebedev-Kumach, "Svyashchennaya voina" (The Holy War), published for the country-wide circulation in *Pravda* and *Izvestia* June 24, 1941, two days after the war began. Music, written in the next few days following the poem's publication, is by composer A.V. Alexandrov. See, Aleksei Barinov, "Bard Stalinskoi epokhi," *Argumenty i Fakty*, August 8, 2003.

164. This and the following quote are from Tim McDaniel, *The Agony of the Russian Idea* (Princeton University Press, 1996), 22, 12.

165. Alexander Tvardovsky, "Ya ubit podo Rzhevom" in Alexander Tvardovsky, *Rossiya—Rodina moya* (Moscow: Khudozhestvennaya Literatura, 1967), 47.

166. Three thousand Hungarians died during the conflict and more than 200,000 fled to the West. Years later, in 1962, Khrushchev crushed another outburst of dissent, this one in Novocherkassk, a city 650 miles north of Moscow. The Soviet army massacred dozens of local factory workers. The state convicted others of disobedience, and sentenced seven people to death.

167. Instances such as this were highly exaggerated to meet the demands of the US's Cold War propaganda. In 1956, speaking at the Polish Embassy in Moscow, Khrushchev said to foreign diplomats, *My vas zakopaem* (we will dig you in), a reference to a line in Karl Marx's *The Communist Manifesto* about the proletariat as the bourgeoisie's own grave-digger. Incorrectly translated as "We will bury you," the statement sent chills throughout the Western world.

I am also compelled to comment on the infamous "shoe banging" incident. At that October 1960 session of the UN, Khrushchev constantly interrupted the American-allied speakers, slammed his fists on the desk and whistled. He was getting back at US President Dwight Eisenhower, who refused to acknowledge that back in May, Francis Gary Powers's U-2 reconnaissance plane was shot down over Soviet territory. Eisenhower's behavior was particularly cutting as the Soviets captured Powers. Still, Khrushchev actually never banged the shoe. There was no footage of it, even if all cameras were trained on Hurricane Nikita, and there was just one news report that described how Khrushchev "waved his shoe today and banged it on his desk." (Benjamin Welles, "Khrushchev Bangs His Shoe on Desk," *The New York Times*, October 13, 1960.) No other publication mentioned the banging. For more on the controversy see, William Taubman, "Did He Bang it?: Nikita Khrushchev And the Shoe," *The New York Times*, July 26, 2003.

Members of my family remember the shoe incident differently. Uncle Sergei recounted the event as such: "The shoe, new and tight, fell off when Father entered the Assembly. A person behind him stepped on it. Reluctant to trouble the crowd, Father didn't pick it up. Later the staffer put the shoe, wrapped in a napkin, on his desk. Father occasionally picked it up and tapped a bit. This is different from the banging everyone describes." But my mother said that Grandfather's wristwatch fell off, he reached under the desk to pick it up, and on a spur of the moment decided to teach the unfriendly audience a lesson: "Father waved his beige summer sandal. Heckling the UN crowd wasn't 'dramatic enough,' so the shoe became a tool of drawing attention to their disagreements." "Just having it out on the desk had them all scrambled," Khrushchev once told her, laughing. "Soon after, the Austrian delegation sent me a pair of massive red and white ski boots, wittily wishing me luck in even more successfully making my points."

A shoe on the UN desk was shocking enough. Yet some members of the press took things one step further, and thereby helped keep America's Red Scare alive. On October 13, *The Wall Street Journal* wrote, "Khrushchev removed his shoe as if to throw it." ("What's News.") Two weeks later the paper described the premier "hammering [it] on the rostrum." William Henry Chamberlin, "The Issue of U.S. Prestige," *The Wall Street Journal*, November 1, 1960.

168. This contradictory amalgamation was best captured by Ernst Neizvestny, a dissident sculptor who in 1962 sparred with the premier over artistic freedom at the Manezh. In a tribute to Khrushchev's humanity Neizvestny famously designed his gravestone. After much haggling with the Kremlin in 1974 Khrushchev's grave at Moscow's Novodevichie cemetery was topped with the monument, which held Grandfather's shining bronze head in between two jagged blocks—marble, white, and granite, black—the Soviet leader between the reformer and the reactionary.

169. Svetlana Alliluyeva, *Twenty Letters to a Friend* (Harper & Row, 1967), 74-75. See also, Abram Tertz, *A Voice from the Chorus* (New York: Farrar, Straus, and Giroux, 1976), 326-327.

170. At ten-years-old Tolya ran away from a local orphanage and turned up in Kuibyshev looking for his mother. But Grandmother Nina, who never warmed up to this child from Lyuba's first marriage, was unmoved. She gave Tolya clothes and money and sent him back. For years he bounced around the dreary group homes, escaping several times. Eventually Tolya joined a technical military school and became an engineer. In Kiev shortly before his death—he passed away in 2000 at age 67 from alcohol-induced heart failure—I asked him what he remembered of the past. "I remember," Tolya said crossly, "that I hate the Khrushchevs." He never forgave them for making him an orphan. They could have

adopted him as they had my mother. But there are many reasons why they didn't take in the young Tolya, even if according to Aunt Rada, many in Kuibyshev were critical of Grandmother's decision. Nina was a true communist, and in her mind, orphanages weren't horrible places for a child in the Soviet Union, as all the party's institutions were excellent. Nina had also warned Lyuba not to leave children during the war. By 1943 Leonid and Lyuba seemed to have drifted apart, and Nina didn't want the extra responsibility of caring for yet another, difficult, child, who wasn't even family. Over the years though Grandmother, perhaps feeling guilty, never failed to ask if I had visited Kiev and whether I found Lyuba and her son in good spirits.

171. "Politicheskie vzglyady rossiyan," *Levada-Center.ru*, July 29, 2013.

172. "A Man Like Putin," PBS.org (n.d.); http://www.pbs.org/soundtracks/stories/putin/

173. Nina L. Khrushcheva, "Russia's New Inspector General," *International Herald Tribune*, August 10, 2007.

174. In 2007 a new Russian official school teaching guide defended Stalin's rationale for killing millions. Although the manual admitted that Stalin engaged in "political repression," it also declared him the "most successful leader" because he transformed the USSR into an industrialized counterweight to America's military and economic might. "The result of Stalin's purges was a new class of managers able to solve the task of modernization during shortage of resources, loyal to the executive power and faultless from the point of view of discipline," the book said, lauding Stalin as a good "guardian" of his people. See, A.V. Filipov, *Noveishaya Istoriya Rossii 1945-2006: Kniga dlya uchitelya* (Moscow: Prosveshchenie, 2007), 87-90.

175. Magnitsky died in Moscow's prison in 2009 after having been refused medical treatment. The lawyer's death caused

an international outcry with Europe and United States slapping sanctions against dozens of Russian officials said to have been involved. The Russian parliament hit back with its own list of foreign politicians who were forbidden Russia entry for their human rights violations in Guantanamo, Cuba, following September 11 attacks of 2001.

176. Anna Arutunyan, "Thousands protest sentence for Putin critic," *USA Today*, July 18, 2013.

177. For more on Putin's holdings see a fascinating article by Eugenia Albats, "Chisto konkretnyi kandidat," *The New Times*, February 27, 2012. Also see, Emily Davies, "Vladimir Putin's spokesman earns double the President's salary," *Daily Mail*, April 13, 2013.

178. Under Putin police force has become brutal, in some parts of the country merging with criminal gangs; his controlled judiciary provides no relief to an ordinary man; and the country's military installations, oilrigs, mining shafts, hospitals and retirement homes blow up and collapse due to the state neglect. See, Vladimir Isachenkov, "Russian sub had nukes during December fire," AP, February 13, 2012; "Putin's Russia 'now a mafia state,'" BBC, February 29, 2012.

179. "Stalina podderzhivayut 50 % Rossiyan," May 22, 2013, *NIKA-Media.ru*. The poll also shows that Leonid Brezhnev is now the most popular leader with 56 percent approval, and people's nostalgia for the USSR is as strong as ever— over 50 percent of Russians regret Soviet disintegration. See, Zorkaya, *Obshchestvennoe mnenie*, 242.

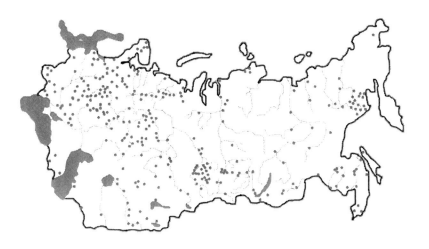

The gulag system of detention camps (dotted) across the Soviet
Union (from the Gulag Museum at Perm-36, 2010).

CPSIA information can be obtained at www.ICGtesting.com
Printed in the USA
LVOW13s1316080814

398199LV00010B/76/P